COMPLETE
DEHYDRATOR
COOKBOOK

COMPLETE DEHYDRATOR COOKBOOK

HOW TO DEHYDRATE FRUIT, VEGETABLES, MEAT & MORE

CAROLE CANCLER

CALLISTO PUBLISHING

Copyright © 2020 by Callisto Publishing LLC

Cover and internal design © 2020 by Callisto Publishing LLC

Photography © Darren Muir except Ivan Negin/Shutterstock, p. vii; Helene Dujardin, food styling by Anna Hampton, pp. 102, 126, 168. Author photo courtesy of © Cheryl Valle/ SurfCityImages.com.

Art Director: Lindsey Dekker

Art Producer: Michael Hardgrove

Editor: Pam Kingsley

Production Editor: Jenna Dutton

Production Manager: Martin Worthington

Published by Callisto Publishing LLC C/O Sourcebooks LLC

P.O. Box 4410, Naperville, Illinois 60567-4410

(630) 961-3900

callistopublishing.com

Printed and bound in China.

1010 27

*To ancient peoples who discovered
that foods could be dried by the sun, wind,
or fire and stored for long periods*

CONTENTS

INTRODUCTION

As the granddaughter of immigrant farmers and daughter of a modern mid-century mother, I learned from a young age about being thrifty in the kitchen. I learned how to can fruit, pickle vegetables, bake yeasted breads, and freeze all sorts of foods and prepared dishes.

As a food scientist and chef, I became fascinated with the oldest and most basic food preservation methods: fermenting and drying. These methods were discovered, not invented. Unlike modern inventions using refrigeration and canning equipment, fermenting and drying occur in nature without any human intervention.

Drying is likely the oldest form of food preservation. Ancient Egyptians dried fruits and vegetables in the desert sun. Vikings dried fish aboard ships by staking in the wind. Chinese dried plums in the hot, tropical climate and then stored them in salt. Many Indigenous cultures, from the Americas to Africa and across Asia, dried meats and fish over fire.

As a lifelong advocate of canning, I quickly adopted dehydration into my food preservation repertoire. Drying food is extremely easy to do, whether you are preserving seasonal produce, making snack foods, storing provisions for an emergency, or want a few convenience meals. Dried foods are lightweight and take up little space, making them efficient for storage and travel.

Even if you have modest cooking skills, drying food is easy to learn. An electric food dehydrator is inexpensive and certainly more reliable than traditional methods using sun, wind, or fire. And drying is adaptable to many types of foods.

- Berries, fruits, and vegetables make great chewy snacks and crispy chips.
- Meat and fish jerkies are often dried for snacking. But dried meats and fish can also be used in cooked dishes from soups to chilis and tacos to fried rice.

- Vegetables can be dried separately and packaged together for a homemade soup mix that is quick to prepare.
- Many other prepared meals can be dried, such as meat and vegetable stews, stir-fries, and curries.

People use dried foods for many different reasons.

- Gardeners want to preserve their bounty at the end of the growing season. Drying is a simple and inexpensive addition to pickling, canning, and freezing.
- Backpackers and campers want foods that are light to carry and easy to prepare. High-protein jerkies, trail mix, and energy bars keep them going during the day. Ready-to-heat meals provide a nourishing yet simple end to the day.
- Parents or anyone who wants to prepare clean foods without excess salt or additives can make kid-friendly finger foods, allergen-free snacks, and convenience foods.
- Preppers and those living "off the grid" want to store a variety of foods in different ways to ensure an adequate supply whenever it might be needed.
- Raw foodists want to make low-temperature plant-based foods and snacks, including fruit and vegetable chips, crackers, non-traditional breads, and protein bars.

The following chapters will guide you to the techniques and recipes for making all these dried foods.

CHAPTER 1

Dehydrating 101

Drying is one of the easiest ways to preserve most types of foods, including meats, fish, vegetables, herbs, fruits, nuts, and seeds. Dried foods can be kept at room temperature. Properly stored, they are safe to eat for weeks, months, or even years.

Types of food not suitable for home drying generally include high-fat foods, such as avocados, olives, and cheese. Eggs can give you mixed results. Though salad greens won't come back to life, dried vegetable salads are possible, and powdered dried vegetables and fruits can be used for beverages, soups, and sauces.

Historically, people dried foods outdoors using available techniques: warm shade, direct sun, indirect sun (solar), fire pit ovens, or conventional gas or electric ovens. These traditional methods have limitations. Most are difficult to control, resulting in a substandard product. Several methods are dependent on the weather. Ovens are costly due to fuel or energy use. Today, the electric dehydrator is an economical solution.

EQUIPMENT

An electric food-dehydrating appliance resolves issues presented by traditional food-drying methods. A dehydrator is easy to use and control, has few weather dependencies, and can consistently produce a quality product, even for those who are new to the practice.

DEHYDRATOR

An electric food dehydrator provides precise temperature control and consistent airflow. It is simple to operate, and even beginners can produce quality dried foods the first time. All dehydrators have a series of stacking or sliding trays or racks that hold the food to be dried.

Temperature Control

A temperature range of 85° to 185°F will allow you to dry all types of foods, from delicate herbs to meat jerkies and everything in between. Besides temperature, other features will affect the efficiency of your dehydrator, including the dehydrator's wattage, fan speed, airflow, and the number of drying trays.

Inexpensive models typically have limited temperature ranges, vertical airflow, single-wall construction, and smaller drying-tray capacity. Basic models are an excellent choice for first-time users, those who want to dry foods occasionally, or those who want to dry small amounts. Since they are compact, these basic appliances are a good choice for condo and apartment dwellers or RV enthusiasts.

More deluxe models can cost five times as much but offer features such as greater temperature range; higher wattage and fan speed; more efficient horizontal airflow for fast, even drying; energy-efficient double-wall construction; and larger drying-tray capacity.

A temperature control with a maximum of 160°F or less will limit your ability to dry meats and fish. If you are drying meat or fish below 185°F and want to make ready-to-eat snack foods that are consumed directly without cooking, you need to consider a precooking or curing step.

Dehydrator Trays

Depending on the manufacturer and model, drying trays can be made from stainless steel or plastic and have an open grid to allow for airflow. Grids of ½ to 1 inch can accommodate many foods, such as fruit halves, vegetable slices, and meat strips. For smaller foods like blueberries, chopped fruits and vegetables, or shredded potatoes, a fine mesh screen (¼ inch or smaller) needs to be placed on top of the grid to prevent the food from falling through. Some dehydrator models come standard with fine mesh screens designed to fit the drying tray while others offer them as an accessory.

IF YOUR DEHYDRATOR DOES NOT HAVE A TEMPERATURE CONTROL

Check the manufacturer specifications for the preset temperature, or verify with a thermometer, such as a digital thermometer with a probe.

Units without a temperature control are often designed for a specific purpose, such as jerky. The recommended drying temperature for herbs and flowers is 90° to 100°F, raw nuts and seeds after soaking is 95° to 115°F, fruits and vegetables is 125° to 135°F, and meats is 155° to 165°F or higher.

Throughout this book, I use "drying tray" to mean either the open-grid tray or a tray with a mesh screen as needed to accommodate smaller pieces.

If your dehydrator model does not offer fine mesh screens as an accessory, you can line the grid with cheesecloth, dehydrator mesh sheets (search for these online or ask for them at retailers selling dehydrator accessories), or a solid liner.

For pureed foods such as fruit leathers or mashed potatoes, a solid liner must be placed on the drying tray. When a solid liner is required in my recipes, the instructions will say to use a "lined drying tray."

Some manufacturers include solid liners to fit their drying trays or sell them separately as accessories. Solid liners are often sold as "fruit roll-up liners" for making fruit leathers, which is a common use. But solid liners are also used to dry bean or vegetable purees, tomato sauce, cracker batters, and more. As a substitute, you can use parchment paper, or Teflon or silicone baking mats that you cut to fit your drying trays.

When using your dehydrator, insert all the drying trays, even if they contain no food. If your dehydrator has vertical airflow (from the top or bottom instead of the side), rotate the drying trays every few hours to achieve uniform drying. Check the food more frequently as it reaches a fully dry stage.

KNIVES AND OTHER CUTTING TOOLS

Before putting food into the dehydrator, you need to cut it into uniform slices or pieces or puree it to produce fruit leathers and vegetable powders. The following tools will enable you to accomplish these tasks:

- A good 8- or 10-inch chef's knife can perform most cutting, slicing, and chopping tasks on all types of foods.

- A small paring knife is useful for finer tasks, such as hulling strawberries, coring tomatoes or apples, and trimming visible fat from meat.
- A vegetable peeler is useful for removing peels on potatoes, carrots, and other produce.
- A serrated tomato or vegetable utility or paring knife is useful for precise cutting of citrus fruits and tomatoes.
- A mandoline or V-blade adjustable slicer is an invaluable tool that even novice cooks can use to cut all types of fruits and vegetables into uniform slices, julienne sticks, or shreds.
- A food mill (hand tool) or food processor (electric appliance) is ideal for crushing fruits and vegetables into purees that can be dried to make leathers and powders.

OTHER FOOD-PREPARATION TOOLS

In addition to tools for trimming, slicing, chopping, and pureeing foods, the following tools are useful for various types of foods and preparations:

- Cutting boards, a colander, large bowls, trays or rimmed baking sheets, parchment paper or silicone baking mats or liners, and cloth or paper towels are helpful for washing, preparing, and transferring foods to the dehydrator.
- Fine mesh strainers or chinois sieves are useful to remove skins and seeds from foods such as blackberries, raspberries, and tomatoes, as well as to strain baby foods, clean herb seeds, and perform other tasks.
- Disposable gloves help protect hands when preparing meats or fish, large volumes of fresh produce, or irritating foods such as hot chiles.
- A steamer, large stockpot with vegetable basket, and/or wok with a steaming rack are useful tools if you plan to use steam-blanching methods.
- A stand or stick blender can also be used to puree fruits and vegetables, but it usually requires added water or cooking of the food, so it is less than ideal when preparing raw purees for drying.
- Depending on the amount and types of foods you expect to prepare, there are other tools that can make some tasks easier, such as an apple corer-peeler, banana slicer, bean slicer, cherry pitter, corn-kernel stripper, grater, grapefruit spoon, marinade injector, meat grinder, meat tenderizer, pea sheller, pineapple slicer, pomegranate seeder, and vegetable brush.

BEST PRACTICES FOR SAFE DEHYDRATING

- Clean and sanitize the work area and food-preparation tools.
- Wash hands when starting or switching tasks, such as preparing produce and then setting up the dehydrator.
- If you have cuts or sores on your hands, wear gloves or use utensils to handle food.
- Choose foods in perfect condition; drying does not improve quality.
- Keep foods cold until prepared or placed in the dehydrator.
- Choose lean cuts of meat, such as loin, flank, and round; fat turns rancid quickly.
- Freeze pork before drying to kill the *Trichinella spiralis* parasite, which may be present.
- If meat is frozen, thaw it in the refrigerator before preparing.
- Aged or ground meats naturally contain higher levels of bacteria and so require pretreatment or cooking when making jerky (see page 6).
- Carefully field-dress wild game and precook wild game to destroy any pathogens.
- Do not reuse meat marinades.
- Read more about Drying Meat Safely (page 66).
- Do not dehydrate produce with soft spots or bruises that can harbor bacteria.
- Before cutting any produce, thoroughly wash the outside under running water.
- Preheat the dehydrator for at least 10 minutes before loading food onto drying trays.
- To maximize airflow, place all drying trays in the dehydrator, even if they contain no food.
- Do not overload drying trays.
- Space dense, moist foods apart on drying trays to facilitate airflow.
- Condition foods after drying to check for excess moisture before storing.
- Seal dried foods in clean, sterile, airtight containers.
- Store dried foods in cool, dark places.
- Package food in small batches to avoid reopening and introducing moisture.
- Check dried foods monthly for signs of moisture and re-dry if needed.
- If mold is discovered in any container, discard all food in the container.

PRETREATMENTS

There are several pretreatment methods (they are outlined below and on the following pages), and some provide multiple benefits. Which method you choose is a matter of personal preference. Here are the benefits pretreatment before dehydrating can provide:

· Prevent browning in light-colored fruits and vegetables

· Deactivate spoilage enzymes for better-quality dried vegetables

· Inhibit harmful microbes to improve food safety

· Ensure even drying to improve storage life

STEAM BLANCHING

Two blanching methods, steam and water, are used to achieve different benefits. Steam blanching places food on a rack *over* (not in) boiling water. Cover the pot tightly and begin timing immediately. Blanch time depends on the type of food, the size of the pieces, and the intended preparation. It is used for two reasons:

· to prevent browning in susceptible fruits and vegetables such as apples, pears, peaches, apricots, bananas, artichokes, eggplants, and potatoes

· to inactivate spoilage enzymes in all dried vegetables to improve quality and storage life

Test for sufficient blanching by cutting through or biting into a piece. It should be tender-crisp (tender near the outside and firm or crunchy in the center). The blanch times given in my recipes are only guidelines; you are the final judge as to whether it hits the tender-crisp mark.

After blanching, drain, pat dry, and put in the dehydrator immediately.

WATER BLANCHING

Water blanching immerses fruit *briefly* in boiling water to create microscopic cracks that are invisible to the eye. It is used only for firm-skinned fruit, such as blueberries, cranberries, cherries, figs, grapes, and plums. This process, known as "checking" or "crazing," opens the pores of the fruit skin to help the fruit dry evenly and completely.

After blanching, drain, pat dry, and put in the dehydrator immediately.

ACIDULATING

Acids can prevent browning in fruits and vegetables by deactivating the enzymes that cause oxidation.

Prepare the produce and soak for 5 minutes in one of the following solutions, listed from the most to least effective. After soaking, drain, pat dry, and put in the dehydrator immediately.

- Ascorbic acid or vitamin C tablets without any additives. Dissolve 3,000 milligrams (crush six 500-milligram tablets) in 1 gallon of water.
- Freshly squeezed or bottled 100-percent fruit juice with no added sugar, such as apple, cranberry, white grape, lemon, lime, orange, and pineapple
- Commercial antioxidants. They are easy to use but may contain additives that create surreal colors. Use according to package directions.
- Citric acid powder. Dissolve 1 teaspoon (5 grams) of powder in 1 quart of water.

SUGAR SYRUPS

Sugar slows browning in fruit, though not as well as acid dips. However, an added benefit is that fruit simmered in a sugar syrup prior to dehydration ends up being plump and decadently sweet. Whether you use syrup is a matter of preference.

Simmer fruit gently for 1 to 2 minutes in one of the following solutions. Turn off the heat and let stand for 10 to 30 minutes, or until cool enough to handle. After simmering, drain, pat dry, and immediately put in the dehydrator.

- For a medium, heavy, or very heavy syrup, dissolve ⅓ cup, ½ cup, or ⅔ cup of sugar respectively in ¾ cup water. The syrup strength is a matter of preference, but sour fruits are candidates for the heaviest (sweetest) syrups.
- For honey syrup, replace half the sugar with honey. For example, for a heavy honey syrup, use ¼ cup of sugar, ¼ cup of honey, and ¾ cup of water.

SALT SOLUTIONS

Salt inhibits microbial growth in fruit, vegetables, and meat.

- For fruits or vegetables, dissolve 2 to 4 tablespoons of table or kosher salt in 1 gallon of water. Soak for 5 minutes.

- For meats, dissolve ½ to ⅔ cup of canning/pickling or table salt or ¾ to 1 cup of kosher salt in 1 quart of water. Soak in the refrigerator for 4 to 24 hours (the length of time depends on brine strength, thickness of meat strips, and how salty you want the meat to be). Add flavorings to the brine for a marinade, if desired. See Classic Beef Jerky (page 69) for a recipe using a seasoned salt solution to flavor meat.

After soaking, drain, pat dry, and put in the dehydrator immediately.

SODIUM NITRITE

Sodium nitrite inhibits microbial growth when drying meat. Use only pink curing salt or curing mix "#1"—a "fast" curing salt mixture containing sodium nitrite formulated for home use—and follow package instructions precisely. Be aware that pink salt is poisonous if ingested directly, even in small amounts. For more information on using it, see How to Use Curing Salt (page 67).

WHERE TO BUY PRETREATMENT PRODUCTS

- Ascorbic acid (also known as vitamin C) is available at drug stores or wherever vitamins are sold. Be sure to buy plain tablets, not time-released, and without bioflavonoids, flavoring, or other ingredients.

- Citric acid powder should be food-grade. It's usually easy to find at natural-food stores or retailers selling nutritional supplements or candy-making supplies.

- Commercial antioxidants, such as Fruit-Fresh, are readily available where canning supplies are sold.

- The sodium nitrite you want to use when drying meat is sold as cure #1, pink salt (but NOT Himalayan pink salt, something entirely different), Insta Cure No. 1 (formerly Prague Powder #1), Heller's Modern Cure, DC or DQ Curing Salt, or tinted curing mix (TCM). You can buy curing mixes online and in stores that sell sausage-making and meat-curing supplies.

HOW DRY IS DRY ENOUGH

The extent of drying required depends on the type of food, on its intended use, and somewhat on preference. Too dry is generally better than not dry enough.

Below is a list of general guidelines for different types of foods or uses to help you know when foods are adequately dry. Find more information for drying specific types of produce in chapter 2.

- If you want to eat fruit and meat as a snack, dry these foods until leathery and flexible.
  - "Leathery" means it should peel easily from the drying tray and not be sticky.
  - "Flexible" means it should bend without breaking but show no visible moisture when cut and squeezed, and separate readily if pressed together.
- Some high-sugar fruits, such as figs and cherries, may feel slightly sticky.
- Fruit purees dried to a flexible leather should be firm, with no soft or sticky spots, and peel easily in one piece from the drying tray while still warm.
- Vegetables dried for snack chips should rattle and be crisp.
- Chopped or sliced vegetables for use in recipes should dry until they rattle.
- Dry all herbs until brittle for best flavor retention.
- If you want to reduce rehydration time for cooked foods, dry until pliable, but storage time will be shortened.
- If you want to store dried foods longer, dry until they are brittle and break apart easily.
- Fruit and vegetable purees that you intend to grind into a powder after drying should be dehydrated until they are brittle and break apart easily.
- Meat and fish jerkies for snacking should be dried until they are evenly colored, smooth, firm, and pliable.
- Especially for pliable foods, you must confirm that enough moisture has been removed to prevent mold growth. See How to Condition Dried Foods (page 13).
- If you intend to use oxygen absorbers or to vacuum-package dried meats or vegetables, dry until they rattle to avoid botulin toxin formation during storage.
- Case hardening is something you want to avoid. It occurs when the surface of the food forms a tough, dry skin, yet the interior remains moist and resists further drying. It can happen when the drying temperature is too high, ambient humidity is low, airflow is restricted, or a combination of these factors.

FACTORS THAT CAN AFFECT DEHYDRATION TIMES

Drying time can fluctuate widely—by hours and sometimes days. It is influenced by several factors, including the type of food, preparation methods, amount and spacing of food in the dehydrator, and weather. Dehydrator features also affect drying time, including wattage, fan size and speed, direction of airflow, and number of drying trays.

- **Texture of the food.** Dense meat and fruit hang on to moisture, while vegetables with airy structure dry faster.
- **Size of the food.** Thin tomato slices and halved plum tomatoes will dry at very different rates.
- **Pretreatments.** Blanching, marinating, and other pretreatments that add moisture increase drying time.
- **Relative humidity (RH).** Drying time is shorter in the desert (less than 20 percent RH) or temperate climates (40 percent to 60 percent RH). It can increase fivefold or more above 60 percent RH.
- **Dehydrator temperature.** Lower dehydrator temperatures dry food more slowly than higher temperatures.
- **Ambient temperature.** Air temperature below 70°F can increase drying time, though to a lesser degree than humidity when drying indoors using a dehydrator.

Keep a record of the foods you dry to help you estimate dehydration times where you live. For each type of food you dry, record the size and thickness of the pieces, whether any pretreatment was used, the temperature and humidity on the day the food was dried, the length of drying time required, and the texture of the finished product (such as firm and chewy or crisp and crunchy). If you have a food scale, the weight of the food after being prepped for dehydration (trimmed, peeled, etc.) and its final weight after drying can also be useful information.

SAFE STORAGE

Dried foods are shelf-stable products that can be stored at room temperature. To maximize storage life, package foods in airtight containers and store in a cool, dark place. To extend storage life, add desiccants, vacuum seal, and/or refrigerate or freeze the packages.

Factors that decrease storage time include incomplete drying, porous packaging, reopening packages, light, and high temperature or humidity.

HOW LONG WILL IT KEEP?

Store dried foods in airtight containers in a dark, dry location at a constant temperature between 40° and 70°F.

Lower temperatures increase storage life. Each 10-degree rise cuts storage time in half. For example, dried food that lasts one month at 70°F will keep three months at 60°F, six months at 50°F, and one year at 40°F.

The following general storage times apply at room temperature (70°F or less):

- Crisp, brittle fruits, vegetables, and herbs may keep up to 1 year.
- Leathery, pliable fruits and vegetables will keep 1 to 3 months.
- Dried nuts, seeds, and grains will keep 1 to 3 months.
- Dried meat and fish jerkies will keep 1 to 3 weeks.
- Mixtures of foods, such a dried soup mix, will keep only as long as the product with the shortest storage life.

Storage time can be increased by using pretreatments, vacuum sealing, desiccants, or refrigerating or freezing. Also, examine packages monthly to check for evidence of moisture and return to dehydrator if needed.

JARS/CONTAINERS VS. STORAGE BAGS

Store dried foods in airtight containers such as glass canning jars, food-safe metal containers, or zip-top freezer-grade bags.

Rigid containers are recommended if you live where there is the possibility of critter interference, such as insects or rodents. Containers must be clean and should be sterilized. Here is how to sterilize different types of containers:

- To sterilize glass canning (heat-safe) jars or metal containers and lids in boiling water, set them in a large pot, cover with water, bring to a boil, and boil for 10 minutes. Remove from the water with tongs, invert onto a clean rack, and let air-dry.

- To sterilize rigid plastic containers in boiling water, bring a large pot of water to a boil, add the containers and lids, and boil for 5 minutes. Remove from the water with tongs, invert onto a clean rack, and let air-dry.

- To sterilize glass, plastic, or metal containers with bleach, combine 2 teaspoons of unscented bleach and 1 gallon of water in a clean basin. Submerge the containers and let soak for 2 minutes. Remove from the bleach solution, invert onto a clean rack, and let air-dry.

- Zip-top freezer-grade plastic bags previously used for storing dehydrated fruits or vegetables may be washed, sterilized, and reused. Wash them by hand or in a dishwasher using hot soapy water; do not use abrasive cleaners. Sterilize with bleach following the instructions above.

- New, unused zip-top bags do not need to be sterilized.

If using glass or metal containers, choose a size that holds only enough food to be used at one time to avoid reopening containers or leaving extra space, which can introduce moisture and cause mold growth. Otherwise, use zip-top plastic bags that allow you to push out excess air.

You can further inhibit moisture in containers by taping over container enclosures and/or using a food-safe desiccant inside the container.

VACUUM SEALING

You can increase the storage time of your dried foods by three to five times or more with vacuum sealing. Vacuum sealing requires the use of another electric appliance that removes air from the container, creating an airtight seal. Like food dehydrators, there are a variety of models, from inexpensive handheld sealers to full-featured tabletop models costing much more. Which one you choose is a matter of preference.

Foods can be vacuum-sealed in containers with specially designed lids that fit wide-mouth canning jars or in specially designed one-time-use plastic bags.

HOW TO CONDITION DRIED FOODS

To guard against mold growth, you need to check for excess moisture before you store the food, a process known as conditioning.

Since individual pieces of food in any given batch will dry at different rates, some pieces will be left with more moisture than others. If any pieces still contain too much moisture, they can grow mold and contaminate the entire batch.

To condition dried foods, place the batch in a tightly closed container at room temperature. See-through glass or plastic containers are preferable. Stir or shake the contents every day for a week. If you open the container to stir the contents, be sure to close it again tightly.

During conditioning, the moisture will equalize—that is, excess moisture will transfer to drier pieces, until it is evenly distributed throughout the batch. If moisture forms on the inside of the container, the batch is not sufficiently dry and you need to return it to the dehydrator.

KEEPING IT DRY: DESICCANTS AND OXYGEN ABSORBERS

If your goal is to store dried foods for long periods, consider using a desiccant. Desiccants are substances that can absorb moisture, oxygen, or both. You've likely seen small desiccant packets in many products you buy, from shoes to electronics to beef jerky.

Food-safe moisture-absorbing desiccant packets are made with clay, silica gel, or calcium chloride. Your choice depends on cost, storage temperature and humidity, and personal preference. Review manufacturers' recommendations to choose the most effective desiccant for your situation.

- Bentonite clay (calcium aluminosilicate) is naturally occurring and nonhazardous.
- Silica or silicon dioxide (SiO_2) is a nontoxic synthetic compound.
- Calcium chloride ($CaCl_2$) can be naturally or synthetically manufactured. Handling or ingesting $CaCl_2$ directly can irritate the skin and pose other health hazards.

While these desiccants are safe for home use, the packets can be a choking hazard for small children. Calcium chloride packets pose additional hazards if accidentally opened.

Foods that can act as moisture desiccants include salt, rice, and cornmeal. However, storing dried foods in these products isn't practical, economical, or reliable.

Oxygen absorbers are small packets containing an iron powder. When used in a closed container, they create a nitrogen-rich environment that prevents the growth of most spoilage and pathogenic organisms, mold, and insects. They are especially useful for long-term storage of very dry foods.

Note that you cannot pair moisture-absorbing desiccants with oxygen-absorbing desiccants because the latter require moisture in order to work properly.

When storing dried meats or vegetables in reduced-oxygen packaging, you run the risk of botulism poisoning if the food contains too much moisture. Therefore, when vacuum-sealing dried meats or vegetables, which can potentially form botulinum toxin, it is recommended that you use moisture-absorbing desiccants instead of oxygen absorbers.

HOW TO REHYDRATE

To rehydrate dried foods, you soak them in water until plump and tender. The amount of water depends on the intended use. As a rule, use half the volume of water to food for dry preparations such as a salad or stir-fry mix. Use equal parts water to food for saucy dishes like stew. And use twice the amount of water for soup. Always start with a lesser amount; you can always add more water if needed.

Like drying time, rehydration time can vary and depends on the type of food, the size of the pieces, the extent of dryness, and the rehydration method used (cold, hot, or combination soak).

Here are some of the different ways you can soak and rehydrate foods. For more information about the ratio of water to food and other details, see Rehydration 101 (page 132):

- **Cold soak** is useful for cold dishes, such as salads or fruits. Soak food in cold water for 20 to 90 minutes or overnight. If the food will be soaking longer than 2 hours, refrigerate it, for safety's sake.

- **Hot soak** is the fastest method and can be used for most foods. Pour boiling liquid over the dried food, cover, and let stand 10 to 20 minutes. If a longer soak is needed, a combination soak usually works better.

- **Combination soak** is useful for very dry foods and meals such as soups or stews to be consumed while hot. It also saves fuel when camping or backpacking. Soak the food in cold liquid for 10 to 15 minutes, then bring it to a boil, reduce the heat, cover, and simmer for 10 to 15 minutes.

FRESH AND DRIED FRUIT AND VEGETABLE EQUIVALENTS

The following dried and fresh vegetable amounts are roughly equivalent and can be used as a guide when using or substituting dried fruits, vegetables, and powders in recipes.

- 1 to 2 tablespoons powder
- 4 to 6 tablespoons dried chopped
- 4 to 6 tablespoons fresh pureed
- 1 cup chopped fresh
- 1 cup loosely packed chopped greens (such as spinach, kale, parsley)
- 1 medium to large fruit or vegetable (such as an apple or onion)
- 2 to 3 medium celery stalks, chopped
- 3 to 4 medium carrots, chopped

Dehydrating Produce

It is most important to select ideally ripe fruits and vegetables in perfect condition for dehydrating. Underripe fruits will not become sweet and vegetables will be bland. Bruised or blemished produce can harbor microbes that could cause the food to spoil in storage.

You must remove enough moisture to prevent mold growth. However, foods may be dried until pliable or crisp depending on intended use. Pliable, chewy foods take less time to rehydrate but storage life is shortened. Crisp, brittle foods can be stored for longer but also take more time to rehydrate.

Several factors affect drying time. Thicker pieces, high sugar content, and high ambient humidity increase drying time; start at the higher temperature for the first two hours under these conditions. If humidity is low, always use the lower temperature for best quality. Check the food at intervals, rotate the drying trays, and remove pieces that are sufficiently dry.

TROUBLESHOOTING YOUR DEHYDRATED FOOD

PROBLEM	LIKELY REASON	HOW TO FIX IT
Food has been in the dehydrator 24 hours and still isn't dry.	Some foods take a long time to dry.	Be patient with foods that may take a long time to dry, such as tomato halves and prunes.
	Drying times given for various foods are only a guideline. Your results may vary widely.	To minimize drying time, cut foods into thinner or smaller pieces, press with towels to remove excess moisture before drying, dry at correct temperature for the type of food, and dry foods on warm, breezy days and/or in air-conditioned rooms.
	Ambient humidity is high (above 70 percent), room temperature is cool (below 65°F), and/or food contained excess moisture (such as from blanching).	If the food is not case hardened, place it between towels and press to remove excess moisture, then return to dehydrator. Raise the temperature of the dehydrator (to the maximum for the type of food). Raise the temperature of the room if possible and/or add a room fan to increase air circulation.
Food is leathery, but the interior is still too moist and/or conditioning indicates moisture in food.	Food has case hardened.	Slit or cut the pieces in half and continue drying. If the food is still not dry after several hours, refrigerate and use within 3 days or freeze for up to 1 month. Or put in a food processor with enough liquid to blend into a paste, dehydrate the paste, and grind into a powder. To prevent case hardening, cut food into uniform pieces and use lower drying temperature to promote gradual drying.
Some fruits are difficult to dry and/or become moldy quickly during storage, such as cherries, blueberries, grapes, and plums.	These fruits and berries have tough, waxy skins that resist drying.	Fruits with tough skins must be pierced or "checked" before drying, to allow moisture to escape. Do this by physically slitting or poking the skin with a knife or fork. Or open the pores of the skin by briefly water-blanching (a process called checking or crazing).

PROBLEM	LIKELY REASON	HOW TO FIX IT
Some of my fruits and vegetables turned brown when dried.	Many light-colored fruits and vegetables contain enzymes that cause them to oxidize or turn brown when exposed to air, including apples, pears, bananas, peaches, apricots, eggplants, and potatoes.	Pretreat fruits and vegetables susceptible to browning before putting in the dehydrator.
My dried vegetables have lost a lot of color.	The vegetables were not blanched before drying or were exposed to light or heat during storage.	While blanching isn't necessary, it does protect color and flavor in dried vegetables by deactivating enzymes. All dried foods should be stored in a cool, dark, dry location.
Dried foods look fine but taste bad.	Different types of foods were dried together, for example, bananas and apples, or meats and fish.	Dry foods separately to avoid mixing flavors and aromas, unless they are to be used together (for example, carrots and onions).
	Food contained oil or fat that has gone rancid.	When making jerky or meat stews, use lean cuts and trim meat of any visible fat. Minimize use of oil or fat when cooking a dish that you intend to dehydrate.
Containers of dried foods contain mold.	Food was not conditioned before storage and contained too much moisture. Or moisture was introduced in the package by a bad seal or by opening the container and not resealing properly.	Moldy food is not safe to eat and must be discarded. Condition all foods before storing to verify that foods are adequately dried. Check stored foods monthly for moisture inside the container and re-dry if mold growth is not already present.
Dried foods contain bugs (insects, moths, etc.).	Food has been improperly packaged or stored.	Discard the infested food. Examine other packages for possible infestation. Clean the pantry shelves thoroughly before returning stored foods. To avoid the problem in the future, package dried foods in airtight containers and store in a cool (40° to 60°F), dry, dark location. Dried foods often last only until the next growing season (when the weather warms up and humidity increases), unless extra measures are taken, such as refrigerating, freezing, vacuum-sealing, or using desiccants.

FRUITS AND NUTS

APPLES

Apples are pome fruits like pears, with a hard core containing several small seeds. Thousands of varieties exist, but only about 100 are available commercially. Orchards and farm stands often feature more obscure heirlooms. Apples are described by their color (green, yellow, and red), texture (crisp to soft), and flavor (tangy to sweet). Use dried apples for snack chips, trail mixes, energy bars, smoothies, fruit teas, baked goods, hot or cold cereals, salads, pies or cobblers, applesauce, and leathers.

Preparation: Wash the apples and peel them if desired; unpeeled apples take longer to dry. Use a corer to remove the core, or cut into halves or quarters to trim the core with a paring knife. Cut into rings, wedges, or chunks ⅛ to ¼ inch thick. If not cored and sliced into rings, be sure to remove seeds, which can make you sick if you eat enough of them. Thicker pieces take longer to dry. Pretreat for browning; see Steam Blanching and Acidulating (pages 6–7). To steam-blanch, steam a shallow layer (1 to 2 inches) of apples over boiling water for 3 to 5 minutes, depending on the size of the pieces and the texture of the apples. After pretreatment, pat dry and arrange on the drying trays in a single layer without overlapping.

Drying Temp & Time: 125° to 135°F for 6 to 16 hours, thin slices until crisp or thicker pieces until pliable but not sticky, with no visible moisture if cut.

APRICOTS

Apricots and their hybrids plumcots and apriums are drupes, fruits with pits or stones. Pits can range in size from 1 to 2 inches. Choose "freestone" varieties with easy-to-remove pits, rather than "cling" types. Use dried apricots for trail mixes, energy bars, fruit teas, baked goods, hot or cold cereals, salads, fruit sauces, and leathers.

Preparation: Wash the apricots gently to avoid bruising. Cut them in half along the indentation and remove the pits. Do not peel, as apricots can bruise easily. If desired, cut into quarters or smaller pieces. Pretreat for browning; see Steam Blanching, Acidulating, and Sugar Syrups (pages 6–7). To steam-blanch, steam a single layer of apricots over boiling water for 3 to 5 minutes, depending on the size of the pieces. Arrange cut-side up on the drying trays in a single layer without overlapping.

Drying Temp & Time: Dry halves at 125° to 135°F for 16 to 20 hours, until pliable but not sticky, with no moisture evident during conditioning. To reduce overall drying time, you may first dry the halves at 145° to 155°F for 2 hours, then reduce to 125° to 135°F to avoid case hardening.

BANANAS AND PLANTAINS

Bananas and plantains are starchy fruits that get sweeter as they ripen. Bananas are usually eaten raw, and plantains are usually cooked, but these are not strict rules. Use them dried for snack chips, trail mixes, energy bars, smoothies, baked goods, hot or cold cereals, and leathers. Use plantains like you would potatoes. For leathers, combine with other fruits, such as apples, oranges, pineapple, or berries.

Preparation: Peel ripe bananas or plantains. Put in the freezer for 10 minutes to firm before slicing. Cut into ⅛- to ¼-inch-thick slices, across, lengthwise, or diagonally as preferred. Pretreat for browning; see Acidulating (page 7). Arrange on the drying trays in a single layer without overlapping.

Drying Temp & Time: 125° to 135°F for 6 to 12 hours, until pliable or crisp but not sticky, with no visible moisture if cut.

BLUEBERRIES

Blueberries are firm fruits, like their relatives cranberries, that grow well in cool climates. Requiring very little preparation, they are one of the easiest foods to dry. Due to their small size, you need a fine mesh screen or liner on the drying trays. Use blueberries for trail mixes, energy bars, smoothies, fruit teas, baked goods, hot or cold cereals, salads, pies or cobblers, sweet or savory sauces, and leathers.

Preparation: Wash the blueberries and pick out any stems or leaves. To pretreat, see Water Blanching (page 6). Dip into boiling water for 30 seconds to craze the skins with very fine cracks that facilitate drying. If you skip this step, drying time can double, and some berries may not dry completely. Drain and transfer to the dehydrator. Arrange on the drying trays in a single, even layer.

Dehydration Temp & Time: 125° to 135°F for 10 to 20 hours, until leathery but not sticky, with no moisture evident during conditioning.

FLAVORED TEA AND TISANE MIXES

Any of these blends are good hot or iced, and the recipes are easily doubled. Each of the following recipes (except Horchata) makes about 1 cup of tea mix, enough for 8 servings or a pitcher of iced tea. *To make a cup of tea:* Steep 2 tablespoons of mix in 8 ounces of water for 5 minutes. Strain and sweeten to taste with sugar or honey.

FRUIT-INFUSED TEA

½ cup black or green tea leaves

2 tablespoons dried chopped ostrawberries

2 tablespoons dried chopped blackberries

2 tablespoons dried chopped pineapple

1 tablespoon chopped dried lemon zest

1 tablespoon dried mint leaves or chamomile buds

BERRY-ROSE TEA

½ cup white or green tea leaves

¼ cup crushed dried rose petals

2 tablespoons dried minced apples

1 tablespoon dried minced berries (strawberry, blueberry, raspberry, etc.)

1 tablespoon chopped dried orange zest

LEMON-GINGER TEA

½ cup chopped dried lemon slices

½ cup chopped dried ginger slices

PEACHY LAVENDER PUNCH

¾ cup dried chopped peaches

3 tablespoons chopped dried lemon zest

1 tablespoon dried lavender buds

APRICOT-FENNEL-MINT TEA

½ cup dried chopped apricots

¼ cup dried chopped fennel bulb

2 tablespoons chopped dried lemon zest

2 tablespoons dried mint leaves

WATERMELON-COCONUT REFRESHER

¾ cup dried chopped watermelon

3 tablespoons dried shredded coconut

1 tablespoon chopped dried lime zest

CUCUMBER-MELON ZINGER

½ cup dried chopped cucumber

¼ cup dried chopped honeydew melon

1 tablespoon chopped dried lime zest

1 tablespoon dried chopped jalapeño pepper

ZESTY PEAR-MINT TEA

¾ cup dried chopped pears

2 tablespoons dried mint leaves

2 tablespoons dried chopped ginger

FRUITY FLORAL-GINGER TEA

½ cup dried chopped hibiscus fruit
(calyx) or rose hips

¼ cup dried chopped fruit, such as kiwi,
mango, strawberries, or pineapple

3 tablespoons dried chopped ginger

1 tablespoon chopped dried lime zest

REFRESHING CHAMOMILE-LAVENDER TEA

¾ cup dried chamomile buds

3 tablespoons dried mint leaves

1 tablespoon dried lavender buds

ARTICHOKE-HERB INFUSION

½ cup dried chopped artichoke hearts

¼ cup dried minced apples

2 tablespoons dried chopped ginger

1 tablespoon chopped dried lemon zest

1 tablespoon dried basil or rosemary

HORCHATA WITH MELON

*To prepare, stir ¼ cup of mix into
1 cup of hot or cold water (do not
strain), and enjoy!*

1¼ cups finely ground dried coconut or
cooked rice

½ cup dried minced cantaloupe or
other melon

¼ cup finely ground dried pumpkin
seeds or almonds

1 teaspoon ground cinnamon

CHERRIES

Cherries are a drupe, a fruit with a pit or stone. There are two main types: sweet and sour (also called pie cherries). Sweet varieties are usually enjoyed raw, and sour cherries are usually baked in pies, but these are not strict rules. Use dried cherries for trail mixes, energy bars, smoothies, fruit teas, baked goods, hot or cold cereals, pies or cobblers, sweet or savory sauces, and leathers.

Preparation: Wash and stem the cherries. If drying whole cherries, pretreat their tough skins by piercing with a knife or water-blanching for 30 seconds to craze the skins with very fine cracks that facilitate even drying. Pit whole cherries for the most flexibility in use and faster drying. Remove the pits with a cherry pitter; most varieties have pits that cling to the fruit and are difficult to remove by hand. Pretreat yellow cherries for browning; see Steam Blanching, Acidulation, and Sugar Syrups (pages 6–7).

Drying Temp & Time: Dry whole cherries at 125° to 135°F for 12 to 16 hours, until leathery but not sticky, with no moisture evident during conditioning. To reduce overall drying time, you may first dry the cherries at 145° to 155°F for 2 hours, then reduce to 125° to 135°F to avoid case hardening.

CITRUS

Citrus are agrumes, or sour fruits, though their flavors range from sweet to bitter. Common types include oranges, lemons, limes, grapefruits, and tangerines. Variations include blood oranges, Meyer lemons, pomelos, tangerines, mandarins, clementines, kumquat, yuzu, and many others. If drying the zest or peel, select organic fruits. Use dried citrus for snack chips, smoothies, fruit teas, sweet or savory sauces, and leathers.

Preparation: Wash the fruits and cut peeled or unpeeled whole fruits crosswise into ⅛- to ¼-inch-thick slices. Remove any seeds before drying. To dry the zest, remove the peel without any of the white pith, using a zesting tool or a paring knife, and then cut into thin strips. Wheels or peels (zest with pith) can be candied before drying by simmering in sugar syrup until the pith is translucent, about 1 hour. Arrange slices on the drying trays in a single layer without overlapping. Arrange zest or peels in a single, even layer.

Drying Temp & Time: 125° to 135°F for 3 to 6 hours for plain or candied zest or peel and 8 to 16 hours for citrus slices, until pliable or crisp, with no visible moisture if cut. Candied citrus will remain soft and chewy due to the high sugar content.

COCONUTS

The coconut is a drupe and not a nut, but it bears no resemblance to either nuts or other drupes such as cherries, peaches, and plums. Use dried shaved or grated coconut meat for snack chips, trail mixes, energy bars, smoothies and lassis, fruit teas, baked goods, and hot or cold cereals and to coat battered and fried foods.

Preparation: To loosen coconut meat from the shell, heat a whole, unshelled coconut in a 350°F oven for 20 minutes. Allow to cool. Using a screwdriver or ice pick, poke a hole in the softest of the three indentations. Shake the coconut to extract the water. Wrap the drained coconut in a towel and tap firmly around the hole until it breaks in two. Using a coconut tool, large soup spoon, or table knife, pry the white coconut meat from the hard shell. The thin brown skin is edible; remove if desired, using a vegetable peeler. Thinly slice, shave, grate, or shred the coconut meat. Arrange on the drying trays in a single, even layer.

Drying Temp & Time: 125° to 135°F for 2 to 8 hours, until pliable or crisp, with no visible moisture if cut. Stir occasionally to facilitate even drying.

CRANBERRIES

Cranberries are firm fruits like their relatives blueberries and require very little preparation. Due to their small size, you need a fine mesh screen or liner on the drying trays. Use dried cranberries for trail mixes, energy bars, fruit teas, baked goods, hot or cold cereals, salads, pies or cobblers, and sweet or savory sauces. To make leathers, combine with sweet fruits, such as apples, oranges, pears, strawberries, bananas, or pineapple.

Preparation: Wash the cranberries and pick out any leaves. To pretreat, see Water Blanching (page 6). Dip into boiling water for 30 seconds to craze the skins with very fine cracks, which will facilitate drying. If you skip this step, drying time can double, and some cranberries may not dry completely. Drain and transfer to the dehydrator. Arrange on the drying trays in a single, even layer.

Drying Temp & Time: 125° to 135°F for 8 to 14 hours, until leathery but not sticky, with no moisture evident during conditioning.

DATES

Dates grow on a variety of flowering palm trees. Commonly available types ripen from yellow to brown, becoming slightly shriveled. During storage, white sugar crystals may form on the surface of the fruit. Use dates for trail mixes, energy bars, fruit teas, baked goods, hot or cold cereals, and sweet or savory sauces, to add interesting texture to leathers made with other fruits, and in savory pilafs, curries, or stews.

Preparation: Wash dates. Remove pits by one of the following methods: Slit the side and pull out the pit with your fingers, push a chopstick into the stem end and through the fruit until the pit comes out the opposite side, or grasp the date opposite the stem end and squeeze gently but firmly to expose the pit at the stem end and pull it out. Cut dates into halves, quarters, or pieces. Arrange on the drying trays in a single layer without overlapping.

Drying Temp & Time: 125° to 135°F for 16 to 24 hours, until firm and chewy but not sticky, with no moisture evident during conditioning. *For date sugar:* Grind dried pitted dates into small pieces and dry again at 125° to 135°F for 8 to 12 hours, until rock hard. Grind into a powder in a spice or coffee grinder or high-speed blender.

FIGS

Fresh figs vary in color from golden to green and brown to purple, some with mottled skins. The interiors also range from pale to deep red, and the flavors from mild to sweet. Try drying different varieties to find the ones you prefer. Use dried figs for trail mixes, energy bars, fruit teas, baked goods, hot or cold cereals, and sweet or savory sauces, to add interesting texture to leathers made with other fruits, and in savory pilafs, curries, or stews.

Preparation: Wash the figs; handle carefully to avoid bruising. To pretreat, see Water Blanching (page 6). Dip into boiling water for 30 seconds to craze the skins with very fine cracks, which will facilitate moisture loss. You may leave small (1-inch) figs whole, but cut a small slit on opposite sides of the fruit to promote drying. Otherwise, trim the stem and cut the figs into halves, quarters, or pieces. Arrange on the drying trays in a single layer without overlapping.

Drying Temp & Time: 125° to 135°F for 8 to 24 hours, until firm and chewy but not sticky, with no moisture evident during conditioning.

GRAPES

Grapes can be golden to green (called white grapes) or red to dark purple (called black grapes). Wine grapes are not usually dried, since they have thicker skins and always contain seeds. Dried grapes are called by their French name, "raisin." Use raisins for trail mixes, energy bars, fruit teas, baked goods, hot or cold cereals, salads, and sweet or savory sauces, to add interesting texture to leathers made with other fruits, and in savory pilafs, curries, or stews. To make leathers, cook to a puree-like jam to remove moisture and/or combine with other fruits such as pears or berries.

Preparation: Wash and stem the grapes. To pretreat, see Water Blanching (page 6). Dip into boiling water for 30 seconds to craze the skins with very fine cracks, which will facilitate moisture loss. For seeded grapes, cut in half and remove the seeds before drying. Arrange (cut-side up for halved grapes) on the drying trays in a single, even layer.

Drying Temp & Time: 125° to 135°F, halves for 6 to 16 hours or whole for 24 to 48 hours, until leathery but not sticky, with no moisture evident during conditioning.

KIWIFRUIT

Egg-size kiwifruit have fuzzy brown skins, bright-green interiors, soft edible black seeds, and luscious sweet fruit described as strawberry-pineapple flavored. Choose soft, ripe fruit for drying. Use dried kiwi for snack chips, trail mixes, energy bars, smoothies, fruit teas, baked goods, hot or cold cereals, pies or cobblers, sweet or savory sauces, and leathers.

Preparation: Wash the kiwifruit. Wear gloves if working with large quantities of kiwi, as they contain a papain, an enzyme that can irritate the skin. The peel is edible; rub to remove the peach-like fuzz and then rinse the fruit under running water. If you prefer to remove the peel, cut off both ends and use a paring knife to trim the peel; or insert a large spoon between the fruit and peel and rotate the fruit to separate the flesh and peel. Slice or dice to ¼ inch thick. To denature the papain, steam-blanch the cut fruit for 20 to 30 seconds or syrup-blanch in medium to heavy syrup. Arrange on the drying trays in a single layer without overlapping.

Drying Temp & Time: 125° to 135°F for 6 to 12 hours, until pliable but not sticky, with no visible moisture if cut. Syrup-blanched fruit will remain soft and chewy due to the high sugar content.

MANGOS

The tropical mango is related to the cashew and pistachio. It is a drupe fruit with a large, flat central stone. Different varieties are available throughout the year. Color is not an indicator of ripeness. A ripe mango will give slightly. Use mangos for trail mixes, energy bars, smoothies, fruit teas, baked goods, hot or cold cereals, pies or cobblers, sauces, and leathers. Mango puree makes excellent fruit leather and pairs nicely with strawberry, orange, and pineapple.

Preparation: Wash the mangos and stand them stem-end up; slice a small piece from the opposite end to stabilize the fruit. Cut lengthwise down around the stone, about ¼ inch on either side of the center. Or use a mango splitter tool. Without cutting through the skin, cut ¼-inch-thick slices or cubes in the fruit, then remove the pieces from the peel by scooping with a spoon. Arrange on the drying trays in a single layer without overlapping.

Drying Temp & Time: 125° to 135°F for 6 to 12 hours, until pliable but not sticky, with no visible moisture if cut.

MELONS

Melons are sweet fruits related to cucumbers and zucchini. Their flesh comes in a range of colors. Popular varieties include cantaloupe (orange), honeydew (green), watermelon (red), and casaba (pale/green). Marco Polo allegedly described dried melon as "sweet as honey." Ambrosial, really. Use dried melon for snacks, smoothies, and fruit teas. See also Pumpkin, Melon, and Papaya Seeds (page 57).

Preparation: Wash the melon, cut in half, and scoop out the seeds. Cut into thick (1 to 2 inch) slices to more easily then cut the fruit from the rind. Slice thin (⅛ inch) or thick (¼ inch). Pat dry to remove excess moisture. Arrange on the drying trays in a single layer without overlapping. If desired, sprinkle lightly with salt.

Drying Temp & Time: 125° to 135°F for 4 to 20 hours, thin pieces until crisp and thick pieces until pliable but not sticky, with no visible moisture if cut.

NUTS

True nuts are a dry fruit with one seed, like the hazelnut. What we call nuts are mostly something else, such as a drupe fruit, seed, or legume. These include almonds, Brazil nuts, cashews, pine nuts, pistachios, walnuts, peanuts, and pecans. But they all have a hard shell and something delicious inside that we call a nut. Use dried nuts for trail mixes, energy bars, baked goods, hot or cold cereals, salads, pilafs, curries, and stir-fries. Use ground nuts to thicken soups and stews.

Preparation: Soak raw nuts to improve digestibility and to make nuts crunchy when dried. For each 1 cup of nuts, soak in 1 quart of water (plus 1 teaspoon of salt for flavor if desired) in the refrigerator for 8 to 24 hours, then drain. For use in baked goods, you may wish to blanch the nuts to remove the skins of almonds, hazelnuts, and peanuts. For 1 cup of nuts, water-blanch in 2 cups of boiling water for 1 to 3 minutes, until the skin slips easily from a test nut. For hazelnuts, add 3 tablespoons baking soda to the boiling water before adding the nuts to easily remove these tough skins. After blanching, transfer nuts to a bowl of ice water. Squeeze each nut to pop it from its skin. Arrange on the drying trays in a single, even layer.

Drying Temp & Time: 95° to 115°F for 12 to 24 hours, until crunchy, with no moisture evident during conditioning. Alternatively, you may toast nuts in the oven (see page 30).

PAPAYAS

Papayas are tropical fruits with sweet orange flesh and edible seeds, both of which can be dried. The rind turns yellow as the papayas ripen. Use dried papaya fruit for trail mixes, energy bars, smoothies, fruit teas, baked goods, hot or cold cereals, pies or cobblers, sauces, and leathers. See also Pumpkin, Melon, and Papaya Seeds (page 57).

Preparation: Wash the papaya and cut in half lengthwise. Scoop out the seeds; you can use them, fresh or dried (see page 30), in recipes calling for mustard seeds or black pepper. Cut the papaya into quarters or wedges to more easily trim the skin from the fruit using a paring knife. Slice or dice into ¼-inch-thick pieces. Arrange on the drying trays in a single layer without overlapping.

Drying Temp & Time: 125° to 135°F for 6 to 12 hours, until pliable but not sticky, with no visible moisture if cut.

HOW TO TOAST NUTS, SEEDS, AND SPICES

Some of the recipes in this book call for toasting nuts, seeds, and/or spices. You can toast these items in the oven or on the stovetop. Unless you have a small amount, oven-toasting is best for nuts and seeds, since it gives more consistent results and is less prone to burning. Skillet-toasting works well for spices and small amounts of nuts or seeds.

Nuts, seeds, and spices burn quickly, so be sure to watch them carefully; don't multitask or get distracted while toasting them. For best results, leave them whole and toast one type at a time. Smaller nuts, seeds, or spices toast more quickly than larger ones.

To toast nuts or seeds in the oven: Preheat the oven to 350°F. Line a baking sheet with parchment paper if desired to promote even browning. Arrange the nuts on the baking sheet in a single, even layer. Bake 5 to 15 minutes, stirring once after the first 4 to 5 minutes to redistribute for even browning. Then check and stir every 2 to 3 minutes until fragrant and golden.

To toast nuts, seeds, or spices in a skillet: Preheat a plain skillet (without nonstick coating) over medium heat until hot, 1 to 2 minutes. Add the nuts, seeds, or spices in a single, even layer. Let cook for 1 minute, then toss or stir. Continue to toast until fragrant and golden, 1 to 5 minutes for spices or seeds and 5 to 10 minutes for nuts, tossing or stirring every 30 to 60 seconds.

Immediately after toasting, transfer to a heatproof dish to stop the cooking. When cool, package in an airtight container and store at room temperature for up to 2 weeks or freeze for up to 3 months.

You can also toast in the microwave, but I find it produces inconsistent results and can burn more quickly than other methods. If you want to try it, microwave on high for 1 to 2 minutes, then continue to microwave and stir every 30 to 60 seconds until golden.

PEACHES AND NECTARINES

Peaches and nectarines are drupes, fruits with stones or pits. Peaches have fuzzy skins and yellow or white flesh. Nectarines are a fuzz-free variety of peach. For drying, choose "freestone" varieties with easy-to-remove pits, rather than "cling" types. Use dried peaches and nectarines for snacks, trail mixes, energy bars, smoothies, fruit teas, baked goods, hot or cold cereals, salads, pies or cobblers, sweet or savory sauces, and leathers.

Preparation: Wash the fruit. If desired, water-blanch peaches for 30 to 60 seconds to peel the fuzzy skins. Nectarines are not usually peeled. Cut the fruit in half to remove the pits. Cut into slices, wedges, or chunks from ⅛ to ¼ inch thick. Thicker pieces take longer to dry. Pretreat for browning; see Steam Blanching, Acidulation, and Sugar Syrups (pages 6–7). To steam-blanch, steam in a shallow layer (1 to 2 inches) over boiling water for 3 to 5 minutes, depending on the size of the pieces. Pat dry. Arrange on the drying trays in a single layer without overlapping.

Drying Temp & Time: 125° to 135°F for 6 to 12 hours, until pliable but not sticky, with no visible moisture if cut.

PEARS AND QUINCES

Pears and quinces are pome fruits. When ripe, they might be yellow, green, brown, red, or speckled. The flesh can be dry or juicy, and the flavors bright, floral, or sweet. Tear-shaped European pears are soft when ripe, while round Asian Nashi pears remain crisp. Tough, astringent quinces are usually poached in syrup to bring out their sweetness and soft pink hue. Use pears for snacks, smoothies, fruit teas, baked goods, and salads. Use pears or quinces for pies or cobblers and leathers.

Preparation: Wash the fruit and peel if desired; unpeeled fruit takes longer to dry. Cut into halves or quarters to remove the core. Cut into slices, wedges, or chunks from ⅛ to ¼ inch thick. Thicker pieces take longer to dry. Pretreat for browning; see Steam Blanching, Acidulating, and Sugar Syrups (pages 6–7). To steam-blanch, steam in a shallow layer (1 to 2 inches) over boiling water for 3 to 5 minutes, depending on the size of the pieces and the texture of the fruit. Pat dry. Arrange on the drying trays in a single layer without overlapping.

Drying Temp & Time: 125° to 135°F for 6 to 16 hours, thin slices until crisp or thicker pieces until pliable but not sticky, with no visible moisture if cut. Syrup-blanched fruit will remain soft and chewy due to the high sugar content.

PINEAPPLES

The pineapple is a tropical fruit native to South America. There are a few dozen types with yellow or white flesh. Some are available fresh only where they grow, and others only canned. You will find mostly fresh yellow pineapples. Use dried pineapple for snacks and baked goods, smoothies, fruit teas, pies or cobblers, and leathers and to adorn savory dishes such as burgers and roasted or grilled meats.

Preparation: Scrub the rind and rinse well before cutting the pineapple. Cut a thick slice to remove the leafy crown at the top and a thin slice at the bottom. Stand the pineapple on one end and shave off the rind in strips going around the fruit. Trim any remaining "eyes." Cut the pineapple into quarters, cut off the core, and then cut into slices or chunks up to ¼ inch thick. If you want rings, use a pineapple corer on the whole fruit and then slice. Pat dry. Arrange on the drying trays in a single layer without overlapping.

Dehydration Temp & Time: 125° to 135°F for 6 to 16 hours, thin slices until crisp or thicker pieces until pliable but not sticky, with no visible moisture if cut.

PLUMS

Plums are drupes, fruits with stones or pits. There are also plum-apricot hybrids, plumcots and pluots. Different varieties may have green, yellow, red, purple, black, or mottled skins and green, yellow, or red flesh. For drying, choose "freestone" varieties with easy-to-remove pits, rather than "cling" types. Like raisins, dried plums are called by their French name, "prune." Use them for snacks, trail mixes, energy bars, smoothies, fruit teas, baked goods, sweet or savory sauces, and leathers.

Preparation: Wash the plums. To pretreat, see Water Blanching (page 6). Dip into boiling water for 30 seconds to craze the skins with very fine cracks to facilitate even drying. Cut in half and remove the pits. If desired, cut into quarters, slices, or chunks. Arrange on the drying trays in a single layer without overlapping. When making leather, puree with the skins, taste, and sweeten as desired; some varieties are tart.

Drying Temp & Time: Dry halves at 125° to 135°F for 12 to 16 hours, until leathery but not sticky, with no moisture evident during conditioning. To reduce overall drying time, you may first dry the plums at 145° to 155°F for 2 hours, then reduce to 125° to 135°F to avoid case hardening.

RASPBERRIES AND BLACKBERRIES

Technically, raspberries and blackberries aren't berries, but rather many tiny fruits clustered tightly together called an "aggregate fruit." You'll find a variety of colors, including gold, red, and purple. There are also loganberries, boysenberries, and others formed by crossing different types of both fruits. There are seedless varieties that some people prefer for drying. Use berries for trail mixes, energy bars, smoothies, fruit teas, baked goods, hot or cold cereals, pies or cobblers, and leathers.

Preparation: If preferred, select seedless berries for drying. Wash soft berries by dipping them briefly in a basin of cold water. Drain on towels to remove excess moisture. Leave the berries whole for drying. Arrange on the drying trays in a single, even layer.

Drying Temp & Time: 125° to 135°F for 6 to 12 hours, until leathery but not sticky, with no moisture evident during conditioning.

RHUBARB

Rhubarb is a vegetable masquerading as a fruit, since it is usually prepared for desserts. Common rhubarb is red; however, pink, green, and speckled varieties exist. Connoisseurs of rhubarb believe that pink and green rhubarb are often sweeter, with more robust flavor than red varieties. Use rhubarb for fruit teas, baked goods, pies or cobblers, sweet or savory sauces, and leathers. To sweeten rhubarb for snacks and cereals, blanch in sugar syrup before drying.

Preparation: Wash the rhubarb; trim and discard any leaves, which contain high levels of irritating oxalic acids. Cut stalks crosswise into ¼- to ½-inch-thick slices. Pretreat for browning; see Steam Blanching and Sugar Syrups (pages 6–7). To steam-blanch, steam in a shallow layer (1 to 2 inches) over boiling water about 2 minutes. Pat dry. For snacking, cut into long diagonal slices or slice thin lengthwise into ribbons and cut into 2-inch chips. Blanch chips in heavy or very heavy syrup. Arrange on the drying trays in a single layer without overlapping. *For rhubarb leather:* Simmer 1 pound of rhubarb with 2 tablespoons of water and 2 tablespoons of sugar or honey until softened; cool and puree. If desired, puree the rhubarb with sweet fruits such as strawberries, sweet cherries, pears, and oranges.

Drying Temp & Time: 125° to 135°F, for 4 to 10 hours for raw or steam-blanched pieces until pliable, with no visible moisture if cut, or until brittle. For 10 to 12 hours, for syrup-blanched pieces until pliable but not sticky. For 4 to 8 hours for leather. Syrup-blanched rhubarb will remain soft and chewy due to the high sugar content.

STRAWBERRIES

Strawberries are sweet, soft, bright-red fruits. Technically, they aren't berries but rather an aggregate fruit, like raspberries and blackberries. Use strawberries for trail mixes, energy bars, smoothies, fruit teas, baked goods, hot or cold cereals, pies or cobblers, sauces, and leathers.

Preparation: Wash the strawberries before hulling. To "hull" a strawberry means to remove the hull, or calyx (the green leafy portion). Insert the point of a paring knife at an angle next to the hull, and then twist the knife in a circular motion while pulling. This removes the hull along with any white core. A special strawberry-hulling tool is also available. Leave small (½-inch) berries whole for drying. Larger strawberries may be halved, quartered, or sliced. Arrange on the drying trays in a single layer without overlapping.

Drying Temp & Time: 125° to 135°F for 6 to 12 hours, until leathery but not sticky, with no moisture evident during conditioning.

WATERMELONS

Most common watermelons have red flesh with black seeds, but there are also white-, pink-, yellow, and orange-fleshed varieties with black, red, tan, or speckled seeds. The seeds and rind are edible, but "seedless" varieties are also available; they still have white, immature seeds. Used dried watermelon for snacks, smoothies, fruit teas, and sauces.

Preparation: Wash the watermelon and trim the ends; cut the watermelon lengthwise into quarters. (Depending on size, you may wish to cut the watermelon into 6 or 8 wedges instead of 4.) Cut along the rind to remove the flesh from rind. Cut each wedge crosswise into ⅛- to ¼-inch-thick slices. Alternatively, cut into ½-inch slices, and then into cubes. Pat dry to remove excess moisture. Arrange on the drying trays in a single layer without overlapping. If desired, sprinkle lightly with salt.

Drying Temp & Time: 125° to 135°F for 4 to 20 hours, thin pieces until crisp and thick until pliable but not sticky, with no visible moisture if cut.

VEGETABLES, HERBS, AND AROMATICS

ARTICHOKE HEARTS

Artichoke hearts are the immature flower buds of a thistle plant. The outer leaves of the thistle can be steamed fresh and used for dipping. Use artichoke hearts for herbal teas, salads, soups, fritters, pizza toppings, skillet pastas, gratins, and casseroles. You can also stuff the heart with meat fillings, vegetable hashes, or grain pilafs.

Preparation: Wash the artichokes and remove the dark outer leaves until you reach the soft, pale interior leaves—the artichoke heart. Unless you want to leave them whole for stuffing later, cut the hearts in half to facilitate removal of the fuzzy choke. Use a spoon to remove the inedible choke in the center of the heart—young artichokes may have little or no choke. Cut the artichoke halves into quarters or ⅛-inch-thick slices. Pretreat for browning; see Steam Blanching (page 6). To steam-blanch, steam in a shallow layer (1 to 2 inches) over boiling water 3 to 6 minutes. Pat dry. Arrange on the drying trays in a single layer without overlapping.

Drying Temp & Time: 125° to 135°F for 6 to 12 hours, until the pieces rattle.

ASPARAGUS

Asparagus stalks are young shoots. White asparagus are green stalks deprived of sunlight while growing. Purple asparagus is best served raw, since cooking or steaming turns it green again. Use dried asparagus in herbal teas, salads, pickles, soups, vegetable sides, pizza toppings, skillet pastas, pilafs, casseroles, curries, and stir-fries.

Preparation: Wash the asparagus. For larger stalks, peel the tough ends; otherwise, trim with a knife or bend until the stalk breaks. Leave stalks whole or cut into even lengths or bite-size pieces. Most vegetables benefit from blanching; see Steam Blanching (page 6). Steam-blanch in a shallow layer (1 to 2 inches) over boiling water about 2 to 4 minutes. Pat dry. Put the asparagus tips, peeled ends, and center stalk pieces on separate drying trays, since each dries at a very different rate. Arrange on the drying trays in a single layer without overlapping.

Drying Temp & Time: 125° to 135°F for 6 to 18 hours, until the pieces rattle.

BEANS, GREEN, AND PEA PODS

Green (and yellow) edible pods include snap beans, string beans, yellow wax beans, haricots verts, scarlet runner beans, Italian flat beans, snow peas, and sugar snap peas. Purple bean varieties are best served raw, since cooking or steaming turns them green. Use dried pods for snacks, salads, pickles, soups, stews, vegetable sides, skillet pastas, pilafs, casseroles, curries, and stir-fries.

Preparation: Wash the pods. Sugar snap peas should be left whole, as both the pea and the pod are eaten. For beans and snow peas, trim the stem ends and remove the strings if present. Leave whole, or cut into bite-size pieces or julienne strips (also known as French cut). Most vegetables benefit from blanching; see Steam Blanching (page 6). Steam-blanch in a shallow layer (1 to 2 inches) over boiling water about 1 to 4 minutes. Pat dry. Arrange on the drying trays in a single layer without overlapping.

Drying Temp & Time: 125° to 135°F, thin pieces for 2 to 6 hours and larger pieces or whole pods for 6 to 12 hours, until the pods rattle.

BEANS, MATURE

As bean pods mature on the vine, large seeds form inside the pod. Varieties include black, turtle, red, kidney, cannellini, white, navy, yellow, canary, butter, lima, garbanzo (chickpea), and many others. Use dried beans for salads, soups, chilis, stews, fritters, falafel, skillet pastas, pilafs, casseroles, and stir-fries and to replace meat in vegan dishes such as burgers and tacos. Use dried powders to make spreads or dips and to thicken soups and stews.

Preparation: Sort to remove debris and shriveled or broken beans. They need to be cooked prior to drying. To shorten cooking time, soak the beans. *For cold soak:* Cover with 2 inches of water and soak in the refrigerator for 8 to 24 hours. *For quick soak:* Boil, covered with water, for 2 minutes; turn off the heat and let stand in the cooking water for 1 hour. *To cook beans:* For best flavor and texture, cook the beans in their soaking water. If desired, cook the beans with salt, adding 1 teaspoon of salt (or to taste) per pound of beans. Bring soaked or unsoaked beans to a boil, reduce the heat, and simmer until just tender, 40 to 90 minutes (unsoaked beans and older beans take longer). Old beans may not rehydrate successfully and are best for puree. Use a strainer to transfer to towels and remove excess moisture. Arrange on the drying trays in a single, even layer. Alternatively, puree the beans with just enough water to form a thick paste and spread on lined drying trays in a thin layer.

Drying Temp & Time: 125° to 135°F for 6 to 12 hours, until the beans rattle or the puree is crumbly.

BEETS

Beets are bulbous root vegetables that may be yellow, red, purple, or multicolored; may be round or oval; and vary in size from 1 to 3 inches or more in diameter. Beets pair well with apples and pears, berries, citrus, nuts, chocolate, and herbs such as chives, coriander, dill, fennel, mustard, and tarragon. Use dried beets for snack chips, salads, pickles, stews, and vegetable sides. Use beet powder for smoothies, leathers, and baked goods, especially with chocolate.

Preparation: Scrub the beets well with a stiff brush under running water. If precooking beets, bake, boil, or steam unpeeled beets until tender, cool, and then peel if desired. For small to medium beets, cut into halves, quarters, or eighths. For medium to large beets, cut into thin (⅛-inch) slices for chips or ¼-inch dice, or shred. Arrange on the drying trays in a single layer without overlapping.

Drying Temp & Time: 125° to 135°F for 2 to 10 hours, until the pieces are leathery and thin chips are crisp. Raw beets will take longer to dry than cooked beets.

BROCCOLI AND CAULIFLOWER

Broccoli and cauliflower are cruciferous vegetables with large flowering heads. Peel the thick broccoli stem to reveal a tender edible core. Purple broccoli turns green when cooked, but gold, green, and purple cauliflower retain their color if roasted or lightly steamed. Use both for salads, soups, vegetable sides, skillet pastas, casseroles, and stir-fries. Cauliflower is popular in curries. The tender hybrid Romanesco broccoli doesn't hold up to drying. See also broccoli rabe and Chinese broccoli on page 40.

Preparation: To draw any worms out of the heads, soak for 20 to 60 minutes in a clean sink or basin of cold water with ¼ cup of salt and 2 tablespoons of distilled white vinegar. If necessary, weight down the vegetables with a plate to keep them submerged. Rinse thoroughly under running water. Cut the florets into bite-size pieces. If desired, shred the stems or peel and cut into strips or coins. Most vegetables benefit from blanching; see Steam Blanching (page 6). Steam-blanch in a shallow layer (1 to 2 inches) over boiling water about 1 to 4 minutes. Pat dry. Place the florets, shreds, and coins on separate drying trays, since they dry at different rates. Arrange in a single, loose layer with some space throughout to facilitate airflow.

Drying Temp & Time: 125° to 135°F for 4 to 10 hours, until the pieces rattle.

BROCCOLI RABE AND CHINESE BROCCOLI (GAI LAN)

Rabe and gai lan are leafy green vegetables related to turnips and broccoli. They have small or flowering heads, slender stems, and large leaves. Rabe goes by other names, including raab and rapini. Use dried rabe for soups, vegetable sides, skillet pastas, casseroles, and stir-fries.

Preparation: Cut off and discard 1 inch from stem ends. Rinse thoroughly under running water. Cut the leaves from the stems, reserving them, separate the head, and cut the stems into 1-inch pieces. Most vegetables benefit from blanching; see Steam Blanching (page 6). Steam-blanch in a shallow layer (1 to 2 inches) over boiling water 2 to 4 minutes. Pat dry. Place the leaves and stems on separate drying trays, since they dry at different rates. Arrange on the drying trays in a single layer without overlapping.

Drying Temp & Time: 125° to 135°F, leaves for 4 to 8 hours, until crumbly, and stems 6 to 18 hours, until the pieces rattle.

BRUSSELS SPROUTS

Brussels sprouts are cruciferous vegetables that look like miniature cabbage heads. Shredded sprouts can be used in place of cabbage in vegetable slaws. Roasting brings out their sweetness in savory preparations. Use Brussels sprouts for snack chips or salads, and use roasted quarters or slices to add to soups, stews, vegetable side dishes, fritters, and skillet pastas or to substitute for cabbage in any recipe.

Preparation: Wash the Brussels sprouts and remove any bruised outer leaves. Cut the sprouts into halves, quarters, or ⅛- to ¼-inch-thick slices. Most vegetables benefit from blanching; see Steam Blanching (page 6). Steam-blanch in a shallow layer (1 to 2 inches) over boiling water about 1 to 4 minutes. Pat dry. Alternatively, roast plain or seasoned sprouts cut-side down at 425°F for 20 to 30 minutes, until browned. Arrange on the drying trays in a single layer without overlapping.

Drying Temp & Time: 125° to 135°F for 6 to 8 hours, until the pieces rattle.

CABBAGE

Cabbage is a cruciferous vegetable related to mustard, kale, broccoli, and Brussels sprouts. It grows in many forms: green or white, red, savoy, and napa or Chinese cabbage, dark-green leafy bok choy, and pale-green compact baby bok choy. Use them interchangeably in recipes. Use dried cabbage for salads and slaws, soups, stews, casseroles, curries, and stir-fries.

Preparation: Wash the cabbage heads and peel away the 2 or 3 outermost leaves. Cut the head in quarters and cut out the core. Grate or slice each quarter into ¼-inch shreds. Most vegetables benefit from blanching; see Steam Blanching (page 6). Steam-blanch in a shallow layer (1 to 2 inches) over boiling water about 1 to 2 minutes. Pat dry. Arrange on the drying trays in a single, loose layer.

Drying Temp & Time: 125° to 135°F for 8 to 10 hours, until the shreds are crisp.

CARROTS

The carrot is a tapered root vegetable related to parsley. Commonly orange, carrots can also be white, yellow, red, or purple. Darker colors tend to have more robust flavor. Carrots with solid color all the way through will retain their color when steamed or roasted. Use carrots for snack chips, salads, soups, stews, vegetable sides, fritters, hashes, pilafs, baked goods, energy bars, and leathers. Use carrot powder (page 42) for juices, soups, and smoothies.

Preparation: Cut off the green tops if present. Wash the carrots and peel if desired. If not peeling the carrots, scrub with a stiff brush under running water. If desired, to concentrate flavor, first roast the carrots at 425°F until browned, 15 to 20 minutes. Cut raw or roasted carrots into sticks, slices, or shreds. For sticks, cut across into 2-inch sections, cut each section lengthwise into ¼-inch-thick slabs, and then cut the slabs into sticks of equal width. For slices, cut crosswise into diagonal slices or coins, ¼ inch thick for most uses or ⅛ inch thick to make snack chips. Shred the carrots for use in salads and baked goods. Most vegetables benefit from blanching; see Steam Blanching (page 6). Steam-blanch in a shallow layer (1 to 2 inches) over boiling water about 1 to 4 minutes. Pat dry. Arrange sticks or slices on the drying trays in a single layer without overlapping and shreds in a single, loose layer.

Drying Temp & Time: 125° to 135°F for 6 to 12 hours, until brittle or leathery, with no moisture evident during conditioning.

FRUIT/VEGGIE/AROMATIC POWDERS

Any crisp dried fruit, vegetable, or herb can be reduced to powder. Listed on the following pages are tips and suggestions for preparing, storing, and using powders. To make a powder, grind with a mortar and pestle, a coffee grinder reserved for spices, or a spice grinder or mill.

TIPS FOR GRINDING POWDERS

- Grinding dried purees is easier than grinding dried pieces, but either method will work.
- Condition dried pieces before grinding to avoid clumping.
- To make grinding easier, freeze the dried fruit, since its natural sugars make it gummy.
- Add ½ to 1 teaspoon of arrowroot powder or cornstarch for every 1 cup of fruit to reduce stickiness when grinding.

TIPS FOR STORING POWDERS

Condition dried pieces before grinding to avoid mold growth in storage. Fruit and vegetable powders soak up moisture readily during storage, turning them into solid bricks. If powders become solid, just scrape off what you need. To avoid clumping in storage:

- Use zip-top freezer bags and press out the air.
- Add a few beans, grains of raw rice, or soda crackers to the storage container.
- Add an oxygen absorber to the storage container.
- Vacuum-seal in jars or bags.

GUIDELINES FOR RECONSTITUTING POWDERS

- Whisk 1 part powder with ½ to 1 part water to make a paste.
- Whisk 1 part powder with 3 to 6 parts water to make sauce or baby food.
- Whisk 1 part powder with 6 to 8 parts water to make juice or soup.

SUGGESTIONS FOR USING POWDERS

- To make tomato paste, use 2 parts tomato powder to 1 part water; to make tomato sauce, 1 part tomato powder to 6 parts water.

- To make the equivalent of one 15-ounce can of tomato sauce, whisk ⅓ cup of tomato powder with 2 cups of water.

- Use vegetable powders to color and season salad dressings, sauces, grilled foods, baked goods, pickles, smoothies, and popcorn.

- Roast vegetables (such as peppers) before drying to make powders with a smoky flavor (for example, smoked paprika peppers or jalapeños for chipotle).

- Use root vegetable, bean, and other legume powders to thicken soups, stews, and sauces or to bind meatballs and burgers, or reconstitute for dips and spreads.

- Use aromatic vegetable powders sparingly, including onions, garlic, ginger, and citrus.

- Use fruit powders to color and flavor hot or iced tea, smoothies, and desserts such as ice cream, cheesecake, and frosting.

- Add 1 to 2 teaspoons of certain raw fruit powders (Asian pear, fig, ginger, kiwi, mango, papaya, and pineapple) to marinades and rubs to tenderize meats, especially thin cuts like steak. Don't overdo it, or the meat will get mushy.

- Use fruit and vegetable powders (especially beet, carrot, coconut, and date) to reduce or replace the cane sugar in recipes.

MAKING AROMATIC SALTS

You can also use these powders to make homemade flavored salts:

- For celery salt, mix 1 part celery powder with 1 part salt. Commercial celery salt is made with celery seed, so you will find powdered celery stalks have a very different flavor.

- For onion salt, mix 1 part onion powder with 1 part salt.

- For garlic salt, mix 1 part garlic powder with 4 parts salt.

CELERY AND CELERIAC

Common pascal celery varieties grow as a group of stalks, called petioles, with leafy tops. Today, pale, sweet stalks are the most desired. Other celery varieties include leaf celery, with thin, bitter stalks, and the large, bulbous celeriac root. Use stalk celery for salads, sandwiches, soups, stews, casseroles, and stir-fries. Use leaf celery as you would parsley. Prepare and use celeriac as you would parsnips (see page 55).

Preparation: Separate the stalks, wash, and trim the ends and tops. Cut the stalks crosswise into ¼- to ½-inch-thick slices. Most vegetables benefit from blanching; see Steam Blanching (page 6). Steam-blanch in a shallow layer (1 to 2 inches) over boiling water about 1 to 2 minutes. Pat dry. Arrange on the drying trays in a single layer without overlapping.

Drying Temp & Time: 125° to 135°F for 4 to 10 hours, until brittle.

COLLARDS, KALE, AND OTHER HARDY GREENS

Collards and kale can be grouped with related brassicas, including mustard and turnip greens. Tough stems, like those found in collards and kale, are often removed, but they don't need to be for long-simmered dishes. Use dried greens for snack chips, salads, soups, stews, skillet pastas, casseroles, and stir-fries or as a substitute for parsley in any recipe. Use green powder in juice and smoothies.

Preparation: Trim tough stems; fold each leaf in half and tear or cut away the stem. Swish the leaves in a large sink or basin of cold water and let stand 5 minutes. Lift from the water and drain in a colander. If there is sand in the basin, repeat the process until the leaves are completely clean. Cut the leaves into bite-size pieces. Place the wet greens in a large skillet, cover, turn the heat to medium-high, and steam 2 to 3 minutes, just until they begin to wilt. Drain in a colander and press firmly with the back of a spoon to remove excess water. Fluff the greens. Arrange on the drying trays in a single, even layer.

Drying Temp & Time: 115° to 125°F for 4 to 8 hours, until brittle and crumbly.

CORN

Corn, or maize, is the seed of a species of grass. Different varieties of corn are grown for eating fresh (sweet corn), cornmeal, and popcorn. Sweet corn can be pureed to make dried corn chips. Used dried corn for salads, soups, stews, fritters, casseroles, and stir-fries. Ground dried corn can be used for grits and in recipes calling for cornmeal.

Preparation: Remove the husks and silks from fresh corn. Corn should be cooked before drying. Boil corn in water for 7 to 9 minutes. To cut the kernels off the cob, you can stand the cob upright and cut down vertically or lay the cob on a work surface and cut horizontally. Either way, cut a wide strip of kernels off the cob, rotate the cob, and continue until all the kernels are removed. Arrange on the drying trays in a single layer without overlapping. *For corn chips:* Puree the kernels with salt and onion powder to taste and spread in a thin layer on lined drying trays.

Drying Temp & Time: Dry kernels at 125° to 135°F for 6 to 10 hours, until they rattle. Dry puree at 145° to 155°F for 8 to 12 hours, until crisp; after drying for 2 hours, score the puree into strips or triangle shapes, then break into chips when dry.

CUCUMBERS

Any type of cucumber can be dried: slicing or salad cucumbers, pickling, or seedless, also called burpless. Cucumber varieties include Armenian, English, lemon, and Persian. If you garden and end up with a bumper crop, drying is a nice alternative preservation method to pickling and relish. Use dried cucumber slices for snack chips, beverages, salads, and sandwiches. Use cucumber powder in beverages, sauces, marinades, rubs, pickles, and dips.

Preparation: Wash the cucumbers and, if desired, score or peel them. Cut crosswise or on the diagonal into ⅛-inch-thick slices. Arrange on the drying trays in a single layer without overlapping. If desired, sprinkle lightly with salt or the seasoning blend of your choice.

Drying Temp & Time: 125° to 135°F for 4 to 8 hours, until leathery or crisp, with no moisture evident during conditioning.

EDIBLE FLOWERS

Common edible flowers include borage, calendula, chamomile, chive, dandelion, lavender, lemon verbena, mint, marigold, nasturtium, pansy, rose, sorrel, and viola. Use flower buds and petals for herbal tea and salad garnish. Use the buds (unopened blossoms), blossoms (newly opened buds), and petals (pulled from the blossoms) to garnish salads or cakes, add to a stir-fry, or flavor foods such as herbal tea, ice cream, vinegar, soft cheeses, and butter.

Preparation: Gather flowers or buds in late morning after the dew has dried. Be certain they have not been treated with chemicals. Do not use desiccant powders because they are not formulated for culinary use. Wash buds or flowers very gently by swishing in a large basin of clean water. If you see insects, sprinkle a little table salt over the flowers. Let stand for up to 5 minutes, swish again, and drain in a colander. Shake or pat gently with towels to remove excess water, taking care not to bruise them. Arrange on the drying trays in a single layer without overlapping.

Drying Temp & Time: 90° to 100°F for 2 to 8 hours for small flower or petals or 1 to 2 days for bigger, thicker buds or flowers, until no moisture is evident during conditioning.

EGGPLANTS

Eggplants, also known as aubergines, come in a wide variety of sizes, from two-inch spheres to banana-size to large tear-shaped globes. Colors include white, green, lavender, dark purple, and two-toned. Use eggplants for pickles, soups, stews, gratins, and curries. Seasoned crisp strips make great snacks. Stuff dried shells or and layer or roll slices with meat filling or pilaf. Classic eggplant dishes include ratatouille, caponata, parmigiana, moussaka, and baba ghanoush.

Preparation: Wash the eggplants and peel if desired, especially for making dips or spreads. Cut into ¼-inch-thick slices or strips or ½-inch cubes. Scoop the pulp from small eggplants, leaving a ¼-inch-thick wall to make dried shells for stuffing; reserve the pulp for another use. Pretreat for browning; see Steam Blanching and Acidulating (pages 6–7). Steam-blanch slices in a single layer or diced eggplant in a shallow layer (1 to 2 inches) over boiling water about 1 to 2 minutes. Pat dry. Alternatively, grill the eggplant slices to capture a roasted flavor. Arrange on the drying trays in a single layer without overlapping. If desired, sprinkle thin slices lightly with seasoning salt or brush sparingly with vinaigrette and dry until crisp for snacking.

Drying Temp & Time: 125° to 135°F for 10 to 20 hours, until leathery or crisp, with no moisture evident during conditioning. Shells usually collapse when dried but can be rehydrated for filling and baking.

FENNEL BULBS

Fennel is enjoyed for its anise aroma and taste. While feathery fennel leaves and seeds are used for seasoning, the thick, light-green stalks and white bulb can be used as a vegetable. Use fennel in herbal teas, salads and slaws, soups, stews, and skillet pastas. Fennel complements pork, chicken, seafood, apples, and citrus.

Preparation: Cut off the leaves, or fronds. Separate the stalks and bulb, then wash. Trim the bulb root end and any bruised or brown parts. Cut the stalks crosswise into ¼- to ½-inch-thick slices. Cut the bulb lengthwise into ⅛- to ¼-inch strips; if desired, cut the strips into dice. Thinner pieces are best for salads, thicker pieces for cooked dishes where the flavor is softened. Most vegetables benefit from blanching; see Steam Blanching (page 6). Steam-blanch in a shallow layer (1 to 2 inches) over boiling water about 1 to 2 minutes. Pat dry. Arrange on the drying trays in a single layer without overlapping.

Drying Temp & Time: 125° to 135°F for 4 to 10 hours, until the pieces rattle.

GARLIC

Garlic is an aromatic bulb in the onion family. Spring shoots of the garlic plant, called garlic scapes, can also be used fresh or dried like herb leaves. Dry chopped garlic and grind to a powder if desired.

Preparation: Separate the garlic cloves from the bulb, trim the root end, and peel the cloves. Cut the cloves in half and remove any green shoots if present. Dry the halves or chop the garlic. Arrange garlic halves on the drying trays in a single layer without overlapping. Arrange chopped garlic in a single, even layer.

Drying Temp & Time: 125° to 135°F for 4 to 12 hours, until the pieces rattle.

GINGER AND TURMERIC ROOT

Ginger root adds characteristic piquancy to many Asian, Caribbean, and Indian dishes. Turmeric is ginger's milder, earthy cousin with a brilliant golden color. Use dried ginger and turmeric slices to flavor beverages and stocks. Use them chopped or ground in soups, stews, curries, stir-fries, trail mixes, energy bars, smoothies, fruit teas, baked goods, hot or cold cereals, pies or cobblers, applesauce, and leathers. The leaves of either plant may be dried as you would herb leaves.

Preparation: Young ginger has a thin, yellowish peel that does not need to be removed. Do peel turmeric and mature ginger with its papery, russet-colored skin. Tip: It's easier to scrape off the peel using a spoon than to peel it with a knife or vegetable peeler. Slice the roots across or lengthwise into ⅛-inch or thinner slices. If desired, cut the slices into sticks or chop. For desserts or snacks, pretreat the slices of either root with sugar syrup, salt solution, or a mix of the two if desired (page 7–8); drain well after pretreatment. Arrange slices on the drying trays in a single layer without overlapping. Arrange chopped ginger or turmeric on the drying trays in a single, even layer.

Drying Temp & Time: 125° to 135°F for 1 to 4 hours, until the pieces rattle.

AROMATIC EQUIVALENTS

- Dried chopped garlic: ½ teaspoon equals 1 garlic clove
- Dried minced garlic: ¼ teaspoon equals 1 garlic clove or 1½ teaspoons minced fresh garlic
- Garlic powder: ⅛ teaspoon equals 1 garlic clove
- Dried chopped onion: ¼ cup equals 1 cup chopped fresh onions
- Dried minced onion: 3 tablespoons equal 1 cup chopped fresh onions
- Onion powder: 1 tablespoon equals 1 cup chopped fresh onions
- Dried minced ginger: ¼ to ½ teaspoon equals a 1-inch piece of fresh ginger root or 1 tablespoon chopped or 1 teaspoon grated fresh ginger
- Ginger powder: $1/16$ to ⅛ teaspoon equals 1 tablespoon chopped fresh ginger
- Dried lemon zest: 1 teaspoon equals 1 tablespoon grated fresh lemon
- Dried herbs: 1 teaspoon equals 1 tablespoon chopped fresh herbs
- Dried mushrooms: 2½ ounces equal 1 pound fresh mushrooms
- Mushroom powder: 1 tablespoon equals 4 ounces (¼ pound) fresh mushrooms

HERB LEAVES

For the best flavor, harvest herbs from plants that have not flowered on a cloudy day in late morning after dew has dried. Culinary herbs should not be treated with chemical sprays. For best flavor, never fertilize herb plants. Dry whole stems for sturdy herbs such as mint, marjoram, oregano, rosemary, sage, savory, tarragon, and thyme. Snip and dry tender leaves from basil, celery, chives, dill, fennel, lemon balm, lemon verbena, and parsley. Use herbs for herbal teas and for seasoning all kinds of dishes.

Preparation: Handle carefully to avoid bruising tender leaves. Wash the stems or leaves gently by swishing in a large basin of clean water. If you see insects, sprinkle the herbs lightly with table salt. Let stand for up to 5 minutes, swish again, and drain in a colander. Shake or pat gently with towels to remove excess water. To dry stem herbs in bundles without a dehydrator, tie 10 to 12 stems with cotton twine and hang upside down in a shaded area (such as a porch or shed) with good air circulation for 3 to 4 days; to protect flavor, do not dry herbs in full sun. In a dehydrator, arrange stems or leaves on the drying trays in a single, even layer.

Drying Temp & Time: 95° to 105°F for 1 to 4 hours. Dry until brittle and crumbly. Remove leaves from stems for storage.

HERB SEEDS

Popular herb seeds to grow for culinary use include anise, caraway, coriander (cilantro), chamomile, cumin, dill, fennel, mustard, and sesame (benne). Harvest at the end of the growing season when seedpods or heads are fully mature and have changed color (usually from green to brown or gray) but before the rainy season begins. Use herb seeds to season many sweet and savory dishes.

Preparation: To dry without a dehydrator, hang seed head or bract upside down in a shaded area (such as a porch or shed) with good air circulation for 3 to 4 days. Some people like to tie a fine mesh bag or brown paper bag over the heads to catch any falling seeds. In a dehydrator, arrange pods on the drying trays in a single layer without overlapping.

Drying Temp & Time: 95° to 105°F for 2 to 6 hours, until no moisture is evident during conditioning. Before storing, shake the seeds from the pod or seed head into a fine mesh strainer and pick out any leaves, stems, or other debris. *For herb seed salts:* Grind 1 part seeds with 4 parts salt.

SEASONING BLENDS

Here are some basic seasoning blends you can make from ingredients in your dried pantry. Store-bought dried herbs and spices can be substituted if desired. These mixtures are coarse blends of herbs, spices, and aromatics. They can be ground to a powder, preferably right before using to retain their potency. Store them in an airtight container in a cool, dark place.

ITALIAN HERB SEASONING BLEND

Yield: about 7 tablespoons
For marinara, vegetable soups, meat stews, and garlic butter.

2 tablespoons crushed dried oregano leaves
2 tablespoons crushed dried basil leaves
1 tablespoon crushed dried parsley leaves
1 tablespoon onion powder
1½ teaspoons garlic powder
1 teaspoon crushed dried hot red chiles or ground black pepper

POULTRY HERB SEASONING BLEND

Yield: 3½ tablespoons
For chicken, turkey, stuffing, pot pie, and vegetarian dishes.

4 teaspoons crushed dried sage leaves
2 teaspoons crushed dried thyme leaves
2 teaspoons crushed dried marjoram leaves
1 teaspoon crushed dried rosemary leaves
1 teaspoon ground white or black pepper
½ teaspoon ground nutmeg

LEMON-PEPPER SEASONING

Yield: about 2 tablespoons
For chicken, fish, vegetables, salad dressing, and popcorn.

1 tablespoon minced dried lemon zest
1½ teaspoons ground white or black pepper
¾ teaspoon dried chopped onion
¾ teaspoon crushed dried fennel, coriander, or celery seed, or combination
½ teaspoon crushed dried bay or parsley leaves
¼ teaspoon crushed dried thyme leaves

BERBERE ETHIOPIAN SPICE BLEND

Yield: about 5½ tablespoons
For lamb, pork, poultry, bean dishes meatballs, and burgers.

¼ cup dried finely chopped or minced sweet red chiles or bell peppers
1 teaspoon dried chopped ginger
1 teaspoon dried chopped onion
1 teaspoon dried coriander seeds
½ teaspoon crushed dried hot chiles
½ teaspoon crushed dried cumin seeds
½ teaspoon crushed dried anise seeds
¼ teaspoon ground allspice
¼ teaspoon ground cinnamon
¼ teaspoon ground cloves

MADRAS CURRY SPICE MIX

Yield: 6 tablespoons
This British-style curry powder works well with any meat or legume curry.
1 tablespoon dried chopped turmeric
    root (or 1 teaspoon powder)
1 tablespoon dried chopped ginger (or
    1 teaspoon powder)
1 tablespoon dried coriander seeds
1 tablespoon dried cumin seeds
2 teaspoons ground black pepper
1 teaspoon dried mustard seeds
1 teaspoon dried fenugreek seeds
1 dried bay leaf, crushed
¼ to 1 teaspoon crushed dried hot chiles,
    or to taste

COCONUT CURRY SPICES (GODA MASALA)

Yield: about 7 tablespoons
Good in lamb, chicken, fish, and vegetarian dishes.
¼ cup dried chopped or
    shredded coconut
2 tablespoons dried white sesame seeds
2 tablespoons dried coriander seeds
1 teaspoon dried cumin seeds
½ teaspoon dried fennel seeds
½ teaspoon ground black pepper
¼ teaspoon ground cinnamon
¼ teaspoon ground cloves
¼ teaspoon crushed dried hot chiles,
    or to taste

TACO AND CHILI SEASONING BLEND

Yield: about ½ cup
Great in Latin American dishes or any stew, soup, or bean dish, and sprinkled on popcorn.
¼ cup dried finely chopped mild red
    chiles (ancho/poblano, guajillo,
    mulato, New Mexico, pasilla/negro,
    paprika)
2 tablespoons crushed cumin seeds
1 tablespoon salt
1 teaspoon crushed dried hot red chiles
    (arbol, cascabel, cayenne, habanero,
    scotch bonnet), or to taste
1 teaspoon crushed dried oregano leaves
1 teaspoon garlic powder
1 teaspoon ground black pepper

RANCH DRESSING SEASONING MIX

Yield: 5 tablespoons
For buttermilk salad dressing, as well as meat, poultry, fish, and popcorn.
2 tablespoons crushed dried
    parsley leaves
1 tablespoon crushed dried chives
2 teaspoons onion powder
2 teaspoons garlic powder
1 teaspoon crushed dried dill fronds
1 teaspoon salt
1 teaspoon ground black pepper

Continued...

Continued . . .

EGYPTIAN DUKKAH NUT AND SPICE SEASONING

Yield: about 9 tablespoons
Dukkah is best when prepared from freshly roasted nuts, seeds, and spices. The final mixture is usually coarsely ground. Try it sprinkled on meat, eggs, cheese, tofu, winter squash, mushrooms, and salads.

¼ cup dried or toasted hazelnuts or almonds, finely chopped

3 tablespoons dried or toasted sesame seeds

1 tablespoon crushed dried or toasted coriander seeds

1 teaspoon crushed dried or toasted cumin seeds

1 teaspoon crushed dried mint leaves

1 teaspoon kosher salt

½ teaspoon ground black pepper

¼ teaspoon crushed dried hot chiles, or to taste

GEORGIAN SPICE BLEND (KHMELI-SUNELI)

Yield: about 9 tablespoons
Use like curry powder with meats, beans, eggplant, mushrooms, and salads. The ingredients can vary with the preferences of the creator. Depending on the specific variety, calendula petals can be slightly bitter to earthy or mildly sweet to citrusy.

2 tablespoons ground dried petals of calendula or pot marigold (not to be confused with common or ornamental marigold)

2 tablespoons crushed dried marjoram or savory leaves

2 tablespoons crushed dried mint or tarragon leaves

1 tablespoon ground coriander seeds

1 tablespoon crushed dried dill fronds

2 teaspoons salt

1 teaspoon ground fenugreek seeds

1 teaspoon ground black pepper

JAPANESE HOT PEPPER BLEND (SHICHIMI TOGARASHI)

Yield: about 5 tablespoons
For noodles, rice, eggs, marinades, rubs, and salad dressing, and sprinkled on popcorn.

½ sheet nori, coarsely shredded or ground, or 1 teaspoon coarse kosher salt

2 tablespoons crushed dried hot chiles, or to taste

1 tablespoon dried finely chopped or minced orange or tangerine zest

1 tablespoon white or black sesame seeds, or a combination

1 teaspoon poppy seeds or 1 teaspoon dried chopped or grated lemon zest

1 teaspoon coarsely ground Sichuan, sansho, white, or black peppercorns

LEEKS

Leeks look like giant scallions and have a mild, delicate onion flavor. If you find the center of the leek is round and hard, the leek is old and better used for soup or stew rather than dried. Use dried leeks in any dish you would use onions in, but particularly those with potatoes, rice, peas, spinach, mushrooms, artichokes, ham, chicken, and mild fish.

Preparation: Trim off the roots and dark-green tops and cut the leeks in half lengthwise. Cut the white and tender, light-green parts into ¼-inch-thick slices. Swish the slices in a large sink or basin of cold water and let stand 5 minutes. Lift the leeks from the water and drain in a colander. If there is sand in the basin, repeat the process until the leeks are completely clean. Drain and pat dry. Arrange on the drying trays in a single, even layer.

Drying Temp & Time: 125° to 135°F for 6 to 10 hours, until the pieces rattle.

MUSHROOMS

There are thousands of mushroom varieties. Commercially available ones that dry successfully are white button, brown cremini, portobello, chanterelle, shiitake, and porcini. Delicate varieties like oyster may break down into pieces during the drying process. Use dried mushrooms for soups, stews, skillet pastas, pilafs, gratins, casseroles, curries, and stir-fries.

Preparation: If whole mushrooms have closed gills, swish briefly in a large basin of clean water, and drain in a colander. If there is debris in the basin, repeat the process until the mushrooms are completely clean, then drain and pat dry. Alternatively, brush or wipe debris from the caps. Remove the stems of woody varieties, such as shiitake. Otherwise, trim or remove stems as desired. Quarter small mushrooms and cut larger ones into ¼-inch-thick slices. Long portobello slices can be cut shorter as desired. If you prefer to dehydrate cooked mushrooms, steam-blanch in a shallow layer (1 to 2 inches) over boiling water about 1 to 3 minutes. Pat dry. Alternatively, you may brown the mushrooms in a hot skillet over medium-high heat without oil (do not crowd the pan—cook in batches if necessary) until they release their liquid and turn brown; stir occasionally to prevent burning. Arrange on the drying trays in a single layer without overlapping.

Drying Temp & Time: 95° to 115°F for 2 hours, then increase the temperature to 125° to 135°F and dry for 2 to 6 hours, until the pieces rattle.

OKRA

Okra, a relative of hibiscus, is common in Creole, African, Indian, and Caribbean cuisines. It is best known as an ingredient in gumbo, acting as both a vegetable and a thickener. For many, it's a love-hate thing. To dry okra, be sure to choose bright-green, firm, dry pods no longer than 3 to 4 inches. Use dried okra for snacks, pickles, soups, chowders, gumbos, pepper pots, stews, casseroles, curries, and stir-fries.

Preparation: Wash the okra pods and leave whole, cut in half, or trim the top and cut into ¼- to ½-inch-thick slices. Place on drying trays in a single, loose layer with some space throughout to facilitate airflow. *For spicy dried okra snacks:* Wash the pods and pat dry. Leave whole or cut in half. Toss with a drizzle of oil (3 to 4 teaspoons per pound), salt and pepper, or the seasonings of your choice (1 to 2 tablespoons per pound), such as lemon pepper, or curry powder. Arrange on the drying trays in a single layer without overlapping.

Drying Temp & Time: 125° to 135°F for 4 to 6 hours for thin slices and 18 to 24 hours for whole pods, until they rattle, with no moisture evident during conditioning.

ONIONS AND SHALLOTS

Globe or bulb onions are white, brown, or red and range from sweet to tear-inducing pungent. Smaller, lavender-hued shallots are often described as mild, garlicky onions.

Preparation: Trim off the top and root ends and cut the onion in half, then peel the skin and any layer that is not firm and dry. Cut the bulb crosswise or lengthwise as desired into ⅛- to ½-inch-thick slices. If desired, cut across slices into dice. Thinner pieces are best for salads, thicker pieces for cooked dishes. To reduce onion odor (which is significant) during drying, see Steam Blanching (page 6). Steam-blanch in a shallow layer (1 to 2 inches) over boiling water about 1 to 6 minutes. Pat dry. Arrange on the drying trays in a single layer without overlapping.

Drying Temp & Time: 135° to 145°F for 6 to 12 hours, until the pieces rattle.

PARSNIPS

Parsnips look like ivory-colored carrots, to which they are related. However, they turn brown when exposed to air, so plan to pretreat them. Raw parsnips have a zesty bite like radishes but become sweet when roasted. Prepare them in many of the same ways as carrots and potatoes. Use dried parsnips for snack chips, soups, stews, vegetable sides, and hashes.

Preparation: Cut off the green tops if present. Wash the parsnips and peel if desired. If not peeling the parsnips, scrub with a stiff brush under running water. If desired, roast at 425°F until browned, 15 to 20 minutes. Cut raw or roasted parsnips into sticks or slices or shreds. If the parsnips contain a woody core, they're very mature and not the best choice for dehydrating. For sticks, cut across in 2-inch sections, cut each section lengthwise into ¼-inch slabs, and then cut the slabs into sticks of equal width. For slices, cut crosswise into diagonal slices or coins, ¼ inch thick for most uses or ⅛ inch thick for snack chips. Use shredded parsnips for salads and baked goods. Pretreat for browning; see Steam Blanching (page 6). Steam-blanch in a shallow layer (1 to 2 inches) over boiling water about 1 to 4 minutes. Pat dry. Arrange sticks or slices on the drying trays in a single layer without overlapping and shredded parsnips in a single, even layer.

Drying Temp & Time: 125° to 135°F for 6 to 12 hours, until the pieces are leathery or rattle with no moisture evident during conditioning.

PEAS AND LENTILS

Green peas, green and yellow split peas, black-eyed peas, and lentils are legumes that are used in the same way as mature dried beans. However, they cook more quickly and do not need to be presoaked. Use dried legumes for salads, soups, chowders, chilis, stews, fritters, and falafel and to replace meat in vegan dishes such as burgers and tacos. Use dried powders to make spreads or dips or to thicken soups and stews.

Preparation: Sort to remove debris and any shriveled or broken pieces. Rinse and cover with water. If desired, for each pound of legumes add 1 teaspoon of salt (or to taste) to the water before cooking. Bring to a boil, reduce heat, and simmer for 15 to 20 minutes, until barely tender. Use a strainer to transfer legumes to towel-lined trays to remove excess water. Arrange on the drying trays in a single, even layer. Some varieties, such as red lentils, completely break down during cooking; dry them like you would other purees; spread on a lined drying tray in a thin layer.

Drying Temp & Time: 125° to 135°F for 6 to 12 hours, until the pieces rattle, with no moisture evident during conditioning. Dry purees until brittle and crumbly.

PEPPERS, HOT

Any type of hot pepper can be dried. Thin-walled chiles (such as cayenne and habanero) dry faster than thick ones (jalapeño and serrano). Hot peppers give off pungent fumes while drying, so you may want to move your dehydrator to a well-ventilated room away from the main living area. Use them to add heat to pickles, soups, chilis, stews, skillet pastas, pilafs, and stir-fries.

Preparation: Wear gloves when handling chiles, since the active ingredient, capsaicin, can linger on your hands for days. Wash the chiles and, if drying whole, pierce on opposite sides to facilitate drying. Otherwise, cut ¼ inch off the top of the pepper. Leave whole or cut in half lengthwise and use a spoon to scrape out the white ribs and seeds. Cut the chiles into ¼-inch strips or dice. For making a pure chile powder, many people include the ribs and seeds (that is where the heat is concentrated) and roughly chop the peppers for faster drying. Arrange on the drying trays in a single layer without overlapping.

Drying Temp & Time: 125° to 135°F for 4 to 12 hours, until the peppers rattle. Leave whole or grind into a powder or pulse to make red pepper flakes.

PEPPERS, SWEET

Any type of sweet pepper can be dried, including bell, frying, Marconi, pimento, shishito, green, red, and yellow. Thin-walled peppers (such as Anaheim and pepperoncini) dry faster than thick ones (banana and poblano). Dry halves to stuff and bake. Use sweet peppers for snacks, salads, sandwiches, soups, chilis, stews, vegetable sides, fritters, hashes, pizza toppings, skillet pastas, pilafs, casseroles, and stir-fries. Use ground peppers in salad dressings, marinades, dips, rubs, and seasoning blends.

Preparation: Wash the peppers and cut them in half, snap off the stem, and scrape out the white ribs and seeds. Tip: It's easier to scrape the inside of peppers with a spoon than with a paring knife. If desired, cut peppers into quarters, ¼-inch strips, or dice. Arrange on the drying trays in a single layer without overlapping.

Drying Temp & Time: 125° to 135°F for 4 to 12 hours, until the peppers rattle.

POTATOES

There are thousands of potato varieties. They can be grouped into three types: starchy, waxy (low starch), and "all-purpose" (medium starch). Russet potatoes are starchy, new potatoes and fingerlings are waxy, and Yukon Golds are all-purpose. Use waxy or all-purpose potatoes when you want them to hold their shape in salads, soups, stews, hashes, gratins, and curries. Use starchy or all-purpose potatoes for potato chips or for potato flakes to thicken soups and stews and soften baked goods.

Preparation: Scrub the potatoes with a brush under running water and peel if desired. Hold peeled potatoes in cold water after peeling and before cooking to prevent browning. Cook the potatoes before drying, or they can turn gray or black in storage. Cook potatoes al dente, until slightly firm, in one of the following ways:

- Boil whole potatoes for 7 to 9 minutes, drain, and refrigerate overnight. Slice, dice, or shred the cold potatoes for drying.

- Steam-blanch peeled or unpeeled thin or thick slices or cubes for 1 to 6 minutes, drain, and pat dry.

- Roast slices or cubes, seasoned if desired, at 425°F for 20 to 30 minutes.

Arrange sliced or diced potatoes on the drying trays in a single layer without overlapping and shreds in a single, even layer.

Drying Temp & Time: 125° to 135°F for 6 to 12 hours, until the pieces rattle.

PUMPKIN, MELON, AND PAPAYA SEEDS

The seeds inside pumpkins and other winter squashes and inside canteloupes and other melons are edible and can be dried. Use them instead of nuts for snacks, baked goods, cereals, and salads. Grind to powder for use in the Mexican beverage horchata or as a thickener for soups or stews. Use whole or ground papaya seeds to add zest to salad dressings, marinades, rubs, or anywhere you would normally use mustard seeds or black pepper.

Preparation: Scoop the seeds from the cavity of halved fruits. Rub the seeds with your hands in a large bowl of water to remove the soft fibers and any juice. Discard any seeds that float. Rinse and repeat until the seeds are clean. For crispy dried seeds, simmer them in twice the volume of water for 10 minutes. For example, simmer 1 cup of seeds in 2 cups of water. Drain. Arrange on the drying trays in a single, even layer.

Drying Temp & Time: 115° to 120°F for 1 to 2 hours for pumpkin and melon seeds and 2 to 4 hours for papaya seeds, until the seeds rattle, with no moisture evident during conditioning.

RADISHES AND DAIKONS

Radishes are root vegetables related to mustard and turnips, which explains their characteristic peppery flavor. Varieties of radish include small round or oval bulbs, elongated, carrot-like icicle radishes, and large daikons or lobaks. Radishes come in many colors: white, pink, red, purple, green, and black. Use them for snack chips or pickles and in salads and sandwiches.

Preparation: Trim any leaves but leave some stem to use as a handle when slicing. Wash the radishes and trim the root, then cut into ⅛-inch-thick slices for chips. Or trim the top and bottom and cut into thin wedges. If desired, toss with herbs or other seasonings before drying. Arrange on the drying trays in a single layer without overlapping.

Drying Temp & Time: 125° to 135°F for 4 to 6 hours, until the pieces rattle.

RUTABAGAS AND TURNIPS

Rutabagas and turnips are bulbous root vegetables in the cabbage family. Rutabagas are usually pale yellow with a purple blush and nutty, faintly sweet flavor. Turnips can be white or pale yellow with a green or purple blush and a sweet, peppery flavor when young, becoming bitter and hot as they mature. Both are good fried or mashed like potatoes. Use both for snack chips, salads, soups, stews, hashes, gratins, and spice cakes.

Preparation: Scrub with a vegetable brush under running water. Peel and cut into ⅛-inch-thick slices for snack chips or shred or cut into ¼-inch-thick wedges, slices, sticks, or dice. Most vegetables benefit from blanching; see Steam Blanching (page 6). Steam-blanch in a shallow layer (1 to 2 inches) over boiling water about 1 to 4 minutes. Pat dry. Alternatively, roast rutabagas or turnips at 425°F until browned, 15 to 20 min. Arrange cut pieces on the drying trays in a single layer without overlapping and shreds in a single, even layer.

Drying Temp & Time: 125° to 135°F for 2 to 10 hours, until the pieces rattle.

SCALLIONS (GREEN ONIONS)

Scallions and green onions are the same onion, usually grown from a bunching onion variety that does not form bulbs. However, early spring bulb onions may be harvested and used as scallions. Even as their bulbs become progressively larger, spring onions may be used interchangeably with scallions. Use scallions in salads, soups, stews, fritters, hashes, skillet pastas, pilafs, casseroles, curries, and stir-fries.

Preparation: Wash and pat dry. Trim the roots and at least 1 inch from the tops. Each part of the scallion dries at a different rate, so first cut the white part off. Then trim the dark-green tops from the light-green middle. Slice into uniform pieces, 1 to 2 inches, to flavor broths and thinner slices to add to recipes. Arrange on the drying trays in a single, even layer.

Drying Temp & Time: 95° to 105°F for 6 to 10 hours, until the pieces rattle. You can use a higher temperature, up to 125° to 135°F; however, some people find low and slow results in better flavor retention with these delicate onions.

SPINACH, SWISS CHARD, AND OTHER TENDER GREENS

Greens with tender stems that do not need to be removed include spinach, Swiss chard, dandelion greens, arugula, watercress, and beet greens. Use dried greens in soups, stews, skillet pastas, casseroles, and stir-fries or substitute for parsley in any recipe. Use green powder for juice, soup, and smoothies.

Preparation: Separate the leaves from the stems and swish in a large sink or basin of cold water, let stand for 5 minutes, lift the leaves from the water, and drain in a colander. If there is sand in the basin, repeat the process until the leaves are completely clean. Cut the leaves into 1-inch pieces. Place the wet greens in a large skillet, cover, turn the heat to medium-high, and steam just until they begin to wilt, 1 to 2 minutes. Drain in a colander and press firmly with the back of a spoon to remove excess water. Arrange on the drying trays in a thin, even layer.

Drying Temp & Time: 125° to 135°F for 4 to 8 hours, until brittle and crumbly.

SQUASHES, SUMMER

There are many varieties of summer squash, and some produce bland dried product, so dry different kinds to find the ones you prefer. Light-green ribbed Italian Costata Romanesco zucchini and golden zucchini are known to be good for drying. Use summer squash for snack chips and in salads, sandwiches, soups, stews, fritters, gratins, stir-fries, and baked goods.

Preparation: Wash the squash. Blanching is not recommended. Trim the ends and grate into large shreds or cut across or on the diagonal into ⅛- to ¼-inch-thick slices. Or scoop out halves, leaving a ⅛- to ¼-inch-thick shell, and dry these "boats" for stuffing and baking. Arrange on the drying trays in a single layer without overlapping. If desired, season slices or shreds lightly with salt and pepper or the seasonings of your choice.

Drying Temp & Time: 125° to 135°F for 6 to 12 hours, until leathery or crisp, with no moisture evident during conditioning.

SQUASHES, WINTER AND PUMPKIN

There are many varieties of winter squash, including butternut, carnival, kabocha, spaghetti, and sugar pumpkin, to name a few. Varieties with young, tender rinds, such as acorn and delicata, do not need to be peeled. There are many ways to prepare squash in both savory and sweet recipes. Use squash for soups, stews, hashes, casseroles, curries, baked goods, leathers, smoothies, and desserts such as pie and cheesecake.

Preparation: Wash the squash. Large squash can be difficult to prepare. One of the easiest methods is to bake the whole squash before cutting or peeling. Pierce the rind with a sharp knife on 4 sides. Place the squash in a shallow baking pan, add 1 inch of water, and bake at 350°F for 30 minutes, until the squash is tender but not completely cooked. If you overcook the squash, simply mash and dry the puree. Cut the squash in half and scoop out the soft pulp and seeds; the seeds can be cleaned and dried separately (see page 30). Cut the squash into ½-inch-thick slices, then peel the skin from the flesh. Or cut into 1-inch-thick slices, peel, and cut the slices into cubes. Arrange pieces on the drying trays in a single layer without overlapping. Spread puree on lined drying trays in a thin, even layer, no more than ¼ inch thick.

Drying Temp & Time: 125° to 135°F for 10 to 14 hours, until the pieces rattle or the pureed squash is crumbly. After 4 to 6 hours, when the pureed squash is firm enough to hold together, turn it over to speed up drying.

SWEET POTATOES AND YAMS

Sweet potatoes (*Ipomoea batatas*) are often mislabeled yams (*Dioscorea batatas*), which are uncommon in the United States. Sweet potato flesh may be white, yellow, orange, red, or purple, with skins from tan to deep red. Although unrelated to potatoes, they can be prepared in many of the same ways, but especially in curries and baked goods.

Preparation: Scrub with a brush under running water; peel if desired. Cut into wedges, slices, or cubes. Most vegetables benefit from blanching; see Steam Blanching (page 6). Steam-blanch in a shallow layer (1 to 2 inches) over boiling water about 1 to 6 minutes. Pat dry. Alternatively, prepare mashed sweet potatoes for drying. Boil peeled and quartered potatoes in salted water until very tender, about 15 minutes, then mash. Arrange cut pieces on the drying trays in a single layer without overlapping. Spread mashed potatoes in a thin, even layer no more than ¼ inch thick.

Drying Temp & Time: 125° to 135°F for 6 to 12 hours, until the pieces rattle or the mashed potatoes are crumbly. After 4 to 6 hours, when the mashed potatoes are firm but still moist, turn them over to speed up drying.

TOMATILLOS

Tomatillos or husk tomatoes are cousins to potatoes, tomatoes, and eggplant. They are distinguished by an inedible husk. Use when underripe, green, and firm for tangy, citrusy flavor; pick them just after the husk splits. Ripe fruit turns yellow or purple, soft, and bland. Use tomatillos for soups, stews, sauces, and vegetable sides. They are the key ingredient in salsa verde. Use tomatillo powder to thicken soups and stews.

Preparation: Peel off the papery husk and discard. Soak the tomatillos in warm water to soften the sticky residue that coats them, then rinse under water until it's removed. It's not necessary to remove tomatillo cores if they are small. Halve, quarter, slice, or dice into ⅛- to ⅜-inch-thin slices for drying crisp and thicker ones for pliable pieces. Or puree and simmer until thickened before drying. Arrange pieces on the drying trays in a single layer without overlapping. If desired, sprinkle lightly with salt or other seasonings of your choice. Spread puree on lined drying trays in an even layer no more than ¼ inch thick.

Drying Temp & Time: 125° to 135°F for 4 to 10 hours, until pieces or slices are pliable or brittle, thin slices are crisp, and puree is crumbly.

TOMATOES, RIPE

There are thousands of tomato varieties in all sizes, shapes, and colors (yellow, orange, brown, purple, or green). Any tomato can be dried; juicier ones simply take longer. There are three basic types: salad or slicing, sauce or plum, and cherry or grape.

Preparation: Wash and remove the core with a paring knife or tomato "shark" tool; coring is not necessary with small tomatoes like cherry, grape, or "patio." Optionally, roast tomatoes before drying and/or blanch to peel, cut in half, and remove the seeds. Halve or quarter small tomatoes up to 3 inches in diameter. Quarter or cut large tomatoes into ⅛- to ⅜-inch-thick slices, thin for crisp slices and thicker for pliable pieces. Arrange cut pieces on the drying trays in a single layer without overlapping. If desired, sprinkle lightly with salt, herbs, or other seasonings of choice. After several hours, peel the shriveled but still moist tomatoes from the drying tray, and turn over to facilitate further drying. (If they don't peel easily, they need more drying time.) Or puree tomatoes and simmer until thickened before drying. Spread the puree on lined drying trays in a thin, even layer, no more than ¼ inch thick.

Drying Temp & Time: 125° to 135°F for 4 to 20 hours, until pieces or slices are pliable or crisp, and puree is leathery or crumbly.

TOMATOES, UNRIPE (GREEN)

A few tomato varieties, especially heirlooms, are green when fully ripe. Ripe green tomatoes will yield to pressure and be juicy and sweet. However, unripe green tomatoes will feel very firm and solid and will have dry flesh and a tart, acidic flavor. Use unripe tomatoes as you would ripe ones in soups and stews. Unripe tomatoes are also great for fried green tomatoes, pickles, fritters, and desserts such as pie.

Preparation: Wash the tomatoes. Remove the core if large. Optionally, roast green tomatoes before drying. Do not peel or remove seeds. Halve, quarter, slice, or dice into ⅛- to ⅜-inch-thick pieces. Or puree tomatoes and simmer until thickened before drying. Arrange cut pieces on the drying trays in a single layer without overlapping. If desired, sprinkle lightly with salt, herbs, or other seasonings of your choice. Spread puree on lined drying trays in a thin, even layer, no more than ¼ inch thick.

Drying Temp & Time: 125° to 135°F for 4 to 20 hours, until pieces or slices are pliable or crisp, and puree is leathery or crumbly.

CHAPTER 3

Meat and Fish Jerky

Before refrigerators came into common use early in the 20th century, drying was one of the many methods used by cultures around the world to preserve meats and seafood. Romans air-dried salted meat. Native Americans dried meat and fish over smoky fires. Africans dried meat under the desert sun. Jerky is a type of seasoned meat, either sun-dried or smoked.

Prevailing stories attribute the term *jerky* to an Incan dried meat known as *ch'arki* or *charqui*. Once a survival food, today jerky is enjoyed for snacks and is easy to make using an oven or food dehydrator.

Almost any type of meat or fish can be dried if properly prepared. The following 25 recipes demonstrate many ways to make jerky and dried meats, for snacks or to store in the pantry for use in recipes and meals.

Like other dried foods, drying time for jerky can fluctuate widely in response to a number of factors, such as the size and thickness of the meat strips, marinades with high sugar content, using the lower temperature setting, or less than ideal drying conditions like high humidity. For more information see Factors That Can Affect Dehydration Times (page 10).

DRYING MEAT SAFELY

Most of the recipes in this chapter call for drying raw meat at 165° to 185°F, as recommended by the U.S. Department of Agriculture (USDA) in order to achieve a safe internal temperature. However, many jerky aficionados prefer the texture of meat dried at lower temperatures. To safely dry meat without using a high-heat method, you have several other options:

- Precook the meat before drying to an internal temperature of 160°F for beef and pork and 165°F for poultry. For best results, a moist-heat method is recommended. Boil the meat strips in marinade for 5 minutes; any other liquid may be used, such as water, broth, wine, or beer. Check the temperature of several strips by wrapping each one around an instant-read thermometer. Remove the meat from the cooking liquid, drain, and pat dry. It is important to thoroughly dry the meat so that it gets to a safe temperature as quickly as possible. Immediately proceed to dry the meat at a lower temperature of 140° to 160°F until the strips crack when bent but do not break.

- Use pink curing salt #1 containing sodium nitrite (see How to Use Curing Salt, page 67), which helps inhibit bacterial growth when drying at lower temperatures. After curing, dry the meat at 140° to 160°F until the strips crack when bent but do not break.

- Pasteurize the meat immediately after drying if you did not confirm the jerky reached a safe internal temperature within the first two hours of drying, or the meat is dried at a temperature lower than 165°F *and* a precooking or curing step was not used. To pasteurize, preheat the oven to 275°F, place the dried meat on a baking sheet in a single layer without overlapping, and bake for 10 minutes.

- Whatever method you choose, after drying, cool and package the jerky as directed in step 5 and the storage instructions of Classic Beef Jerky (page 69).

- Refrigerate jerky that is not well dried or not dried to a safe temperature. Treat it like fresh food: keep it cold, consume within 3 days or freeze for longer storage, and discard if left at room temperature for more than 2 hours.

HOW TO USE CURING SALT

Sodium nitrate, aka saltpeter, is rarely used today as a meat preservative. The curing salts we list, all versions of "#1," contain sodium nitrite, and no nitrate. Curing salts "#2" do contain sodium nitrate, but "#2" is used only for dry cured meats, which is a whole other specialty process that has nothing to do with jerky or drying meat or the contents of this book.

Curing salt or sodium nitrite is also known as InstaCure, Prague Powder, and pink curing salt. For details on where you can buy it, see page 8. There are different formulations of curing salt depending on the type of curing you want to do (ham, bacon, corned beef, jerky, etc.). For cooked jerky, use pink curing salt #1, a "fast" cure containing 6.25 percent sodium nitrite.

Pink curing salt is poisonous if ingested directly. That's why it's dyed pink, to distinguish it from table salt. Do not confuse pink curing salt with Himalayan pink salt, which is merely a table salt containing minerals that give the salt its characteristic glow.

Here are the effective, safe amounts in which to add pink curing salt #1 containing sodium nitrite to jerky recipes:

- 1 teaspoon of pink curing salt #1 per 5 pounds of meat in dry rubs, marinades, or ground meat mixtures
- 2 tablespoons of pink curing salt #1 per 1 quart of water for brines

Should you wish to add nitrite to any of the recipes in this chapter, many use 1¼ pounds of meat or fish, requiring ¼ teaspoon of pink curing salt in spice rubs and dry mixtures or 1 quart of brine. Other recipes use twice these amounts, or 2½ pounds of meat or fish, requiring ½ teaspoon of pink curing salt for mixtures or 2 quarts of brine. For the cure to penetrate the meat fully, do not cut strips thicker than ¼ inch; any width or length is okay.

Nitrite or curing salt is not required when making jerky. However, curing salt is recommended or desirable for some preparations:

- when making ground meat and game meat jerkies, which have higher levels of bacteria
- when drying meat at lower temperatures so that the jerky will not achieve a safe internal temperature within two hours
- when you desire the color and flavor changes produced by nitrite

TIPS FOR SAFE JERKY STORAGE

Here are some guidelines for storing jerky or any dried meat or fish. How long your jerky will last depends on many factors: preparation, extent of drying, clean and airtight packaging, and storage location.

Jerky can be stored at room temperature (68°F) in a dark, dry location for 1 to 2 weeks, in the refrigerator for 1 to 2 months, or in the freezer for up to 6 months. Refrigeration can lead to mold growth. Add a moisture desiccant to the package to help prevent mold growth, especially if the jerky was not thoroughly dried or the packaging seeps air.

For longer storage, vacuum-seal the package. Vacuum sealing can extend storage life at room temperature up to 2 months, in the refrigerator up to 6 months, or in the freezer up to 2 years. If desired, add an oxygen absorber to vacuum-sealed packages, which works best for hermetically sealed packages at room temperature.

Do not use desiccants and oxygen absorbers together in the same package. Desiccants absorb the small amount of moisture that oxygen absorbers need to work properly. See page 13 for more on desiccants and oxygen absorbers.

CLASSIC BEEF JERKY

Prep Time (including marination): 2 to 10 hours | **Drying Temp & Time:** 165° to 185°F for 4 to 6 hours | **Yield:** 14 to 20 (1-ounce) servings

Here is a great recipe if you're making jerky for the first time. It's a classic beef jerky with simple pepper and smoke flavors. There are many variations to hone your skills and find the jerky style you prefer. Try different types of meat or cut the meat in different thicknesses, both across and with the grain. Marinate the meat strips for shorter and longer times. Study the various ways to make safe jerky (see page 13) and decide which method you prefer. Note that drying time can vary widely depending on temperature, meat thickness, how close together the pieces are placed on the drying trays, ambient humidity, dehydrator features, and other factors.

¼ cup table salt or ½ cup
    kosher salt

¼ cup granulated or
    brown sugar

3 tablespoons liquid smoke

½ teaspoon ground
    black pepper

1 quart cold water

2½ pounds beef round steak
    or roast, sirloin, flank, or
    lean brisket

1. In a large bowl or container, stir the salt, sugar, liquid smoke to taste, and pepper into the water until the salt and sugar are completely dissolved. Cover and refrigerate until ready to use. May be prepared up to 3 days in advance.

2. Trim the meat of all visible fat, or your jerky will go rancid very quickly. Freeze the meat for 30 to 90 minutes to firm it up for easier slicing (or have a butcher slice it for you). For tender jerky, cut against the grain (strips come apart if pulled). For chewy jerky, cut with the grain (strips stretch when pulled). For chewy-tender jerky, use a meat tenderizer mallet to pound slabs cut with the grain. Cut the meat into even slabs between ⅛ and ⅜ inch thick. If desired, cut across slabs into short squares or chip-size pieces or lengthwise into long strips of any width.

3. Immerse the beef strips in the marinade, cover, and refrigerate for 1 to 8 hours.

4. Preheat a food dehydrator to 165° to 185°F. Remove the meat from the marinade, drain, and pat dry. It is important to thoroughly dry the meat so that it gets to a safe temperature as quickly as possible. Arrange the meat on the drying trays without touching. Within the first 2 hours of drying, confirm the meat has reached a safe internal temperature of 160°F. Test the temperature of at least one piece on every tray by wrapping it around an instant-read thermometer. If the meat

continued

is under 160°F, consider a pasteurization step (see Drying Meat Safely, page 66) after drying is complete. Continue to dry the meat until the pieces crack when bent but do not break, usually another 2 to 4 hours but possibly longer for thick pieces, if using a marinade with a high sugar content, if using the lower drying temperature, or in less-than-ideal conditions such as high humidity.

5. Turn off the dehydrator and expose the trays to the air. Remove any visible oil beads by patting the meat with towels. Cool until no longer warm, about 30 minutes.

STORAGE: 1 to 2 weeks at room temperature (68°F) in a dark, dry location in an airtight container, 1 to 2 months refrigerated, or 6 months frozen.

HOT CHILE PEPPER BEEF JERKY

Prep Time (including marination): 2 to 9 hours | Drying Temp & Time: 165° to 185°F for 4 to 6 hours | Yield: 4 to 8 ounces

This beef jerky packs heat by replacing black pepper with hot chile pepper, then balances that heat with some sweetness. Feel free to increase or decrease the pepper, sugar, or salt to suit your taste. If you dry and grind your own hot pepper, the heat and flavor possibilities are considerably expanded. You might consider the bright character of a jalapeño or Fresno, fruity habaneros, or mind-numbing ghost chiles. Smoking any of these chiles further changes their flavor profile.

1¼ pounds lean beef such as round, sirloin, or flank steak

1 tablespoon granulated or brown sugar

1 to 2 tablespoons crushed or ground hot chiles (cayenne, jalapeño, habanero, etc.), divided

1 teaspoon kosher salt

1. Trim and cut the meat into squares or strips as described in step 2 of Classic Beef Jerky (page 69). In a large bowl or container, combine the sugar, 1 tablespoon of the hot chiles, and salt. Add the beef, toss until evenly coated, cover, and refrigerate for 1 to 8 hours.

2. Preheat a food dehydrator to 165° to 185°F. Remove the meat from the marinade, drain, and pat dry. If desired, sprinkle the meat on both sides with the remaining 1 tablespoon of hot chiles. Arrange the pieces on the drying trays without touching. Within the first 2 hours of drying, confirm the meat has reached a safe internal temperature of 160°F. Test the temperature of at least one piece on every tray by wrapping it around an instant-read thermometer. If the meat is under 160°F, consider a pasteurization step (see Drying Meat Safely, page 66) after drying is complete. Continue to dry the meat until the pieces crack when bent but do not break, another 2 to 4 hours.

3. Turn off the dehydrator and expose the trays to the air. Remove any visible oil beads by patting the meat with towels. Cool until no longer warm, about 30 minutes.

STORAGE: 1 to 2 weeks at room temperature (68°F) in a dark, dry location in an airtight container, 1 to 2 months refrigerated, or 6 months frozen.

HOMEMADE BRAISED PASTRAMI-SPICED JERKY

Prep/Cook Time (including marination): 4½ to 5 days | Drying Temp & Time: 130° to 140°F for 4 to 6 hours | Yield: 14 to 20 (1-ounce) servings

Pastrami is essentially corned beef with a spice coating. To make corned beef, you cure beef brisket using salt and spices. There is no corn involved. Corning is an old English term that refers to pellets of salt, once called corns. Curing salt containing sodium nitrite gives the meat its characteristic pink color and flavor. Otherwise it would just be roast beef. To become pastrami, the corned beef is given a coating of spices and then smoked. Without a smoker, oven-braising the meat with a small amount of beer or cider and some liquid smoke produces delicious meat with minimal effort. Because the meat is precooked, it is dried at a much lower temperature.

FOR THE SEASONED BRINE:

½ cup kosher salt

½ cup packed brown sugar

¼ cup pink curing salt #1

1 teaspoon black peppercorns

1 teaspoon mustard seed

1 teaspoon coriander seed

1 teaspoon red pepper flakes

2 quarts water

2½ pounds fat-trimmed beef brisket, preferably from the flat end, or flank steak

5 garlic cloves, cut in half

3 dried ginger slices

1 bay leaf

FOR THE RUB AND BRAISING:

2 tablespoons cracked black peppercorns

2 tablespoons cracked coriander seeds

1 to 2 tablespoons liquid smoke (optional)

About 12 ounces beer (hard cider, apple juice, or water may also be used)

1. **FOR THE SEASONED BRINE,** in a large bowl or container, stir the salt, brown sugar, pink curing salt, peppercorns, mustard seed, coriander seed, and red pepper flakes into the water until the salt and sugar dissolve. Add the beef brisket, garlic, ginger, and bay leaf. Weight down the meat with a clean plate to keep it submerged. Cover and refrigerate for 3 days.

2. **FOR THE RUB AND BRAISING,** remove the brisket from the brine and rinse with water to remove any clinging spices. Shake off any excess water, but do not dry the meat. In a small bowl, combine the peppercorns and coriander seeds; rub the spices evenly on all sides of the brisket. Refrigerate, uncovered, for 24 hours to let the spices penetrate the meat, as well as to let the cure equalize.

3. Preheat the oven to 300°F. Wrap the meat tightly in a piece of heavy-gauge aluminum foil. Place the foil packet in a large heavy casserole dish or roasting pan. Stir the liquid smoke (if using) into the beer. Pour the beer around the foil packet to a depth of about ¼ inch. Cover the dish and bake until the meat shrinks by almost half, is deeply colored, and is tender when pierced with a knife, or the internal meat temperature reaches 200°F, 2 to 2½ hours.

4. Preheat a food dehydrator to 130° to 140°F. When the pastrami is cool enough to handle, cut into even slabs ⅛ to ⅜ inch thick. If desired, cut across slabs into chip-size pieces, making sure each piece has some of the spice coating on

the side. Place the pastrami slices on drying trays without touching. Dry until the meat cracks when bent but does not break, 4 to 6 hours.

5. Turn off the dehydrator and expose the trays to the air. Remove any visible oil beads by patting the meat with towels. Cool until no longer warm, about 30 minutes.

STORAGE: 1 to 2 weeks at room temperature (68°F) in a dark, dry location in an airtight container, 1 to 2 months refrigerated, or 6 months frozen.

TERIYAKI BEEF JERKY

Prep Time (including marination): 2 to 9 hours | Drying Temp & Time: 130° to 140°F for 4 to 6 hours | Yield: 14 to 20 (1-ounce) servings

This Japanese teriyaki grilling sauce recipe includes the classic sweet, salty, and sour ingredients of brown sugar, soy sauce, and wine or vinegar. Seasoned with scallions, garlic, ginger, and pepper, the marinade will permeate your jerky deliciously. It works equally well for beef or chicken. For a Hawaiian-style huli-huli marinade, add the pineapple and tomato powders. Teriyaki marinade is a good choice when precooking the meat before drying; the sweet marinade forms a glaze on the dried jerky. Because the meat is precooked, it is dried at a much lower temperature.

2½ pounds lean beef such as round, sirloin, or flank steak

¼ cup soy sauce

¼ cup packed brown sugar

¼ cup sake, rice vinegar, or white wine

1 tablespoon pineapple powder , or 2 to 4 tablespoons pineapple juice (optional)

1 teaspoon tomato powder, or 1 tablespoon ketchup (optional)

1 teaspoon scallion powder

½ teaspoon ground black pepper

¼ teaspoon garlic powder

¼ teaspoon ginger powder

1. Trim the meat and cut into slabs or strips as described in step 2 of Classic Beef Jerky (page 69). In a large bowl or container, combine the soy sauce, brown sugar, sake, pineapple and tomato powders (if using), scallion powder, pepper, garlic powder, and ginger powder. Add the beef and toss until evenly coated. To enhance the flavor, cover and refrigerate for 1 to 8 hours.

2. Preheat a food dehydrator to 130° to 140°F. In a large covered skillet, over medium-high heat, boil the meat strips in the teriyaki marinade for 5 minutes, or to an internal temperature of 160°F. Check the temperature of several strips by wrapping each one around an instant-read thermometer.

3. Remove the meat strips from the marinade, drain, and pat dry. Place the strips on drying trays without touching. Dry the meat until the strips crack when bent but do not break, 4 to 6 hours.

4. Turn off the dehydrator and expose the trays to the air. Remove any visible oil beads by patting the meat with towels. Cool until no longer warm, about 30 minutes.

STORAGE: 1 to 2 weeks at room temperature (68°F) in a dark, dry location in an airtight container, 1 to 2 months refrigerated, or 6 months frozen.

THAI-STYLE DRIED BEEF (NEAU DAD DEAW)

Prep Time (including marination): 2 to 9 hours | Drying Temp & Time: 165° to 185°F for 4 to 6 hours | Yield: 14 to 20 (1-ounce) servings

Neau dad deaw is a sweet and garlicky peppered beef. The traditional preparation is to cut the meat into either thin squares or thick fingers (strips 4 inches long, ½ inch wide, and ¼ inch thick), then partially sun-dry the meat, leaving it flexible and moist. The dried meat is then deep-fried for 2 to 3 minutes, until crispy, and served with sticky rice, fresh vegetables, and dipping sauce. Of course, I recommend fully drying the meat for snacks or recipes. Rehydrating the meat makes it ready for stir-fries, salads, and wraps.

⅔ cup table salt or
    1⅓ cups kosher salt

⅓ cup fish sauce (or soy
    sauce or a combination)

2 tablespoons palm sugar,
    brown sugar, or honey

1 tablespoon dried minced
    shallot (white part of
    leek or scallion may be
    substituted)

2 teaspoons crushed dried
    cilantro stems (optional)

2 teaspoons garlic powder

2 teaspoons ground
    white pepper

1 teaspoon ginger powder

2½ pounds lean beef or
    pork such as round
    or loin

1. In a large bowl or container, combine the salt, fish sauce, sugar, shallot, cilantro (if using), garlic powder, pepper, and ginger powder. Cover and refrigerate until ready to use. May be prepared up to 3 days in advance.

2. Trim and cut the meat into squares or strips as described in step 2 of Classic Beef Jerky (page 69). Add the beef to the marinade, toss until evenly coated, cover, and refrigerate for 1 to 8 hours.

3. Preheat a food dehydrator to 165° to 185°F. Remove the meat from the marinade and drain well, but do not pat dry. Arrange the pieces on the drying trays without touching. Within the first 2 hours of drying, confirm the meat has reached a safe internal temperature of 160°F. Test the temperature of at least one piece on every tray by wrapping it around an instant-read thermometer. If the meat is under 160°F, consider a pasteurization step (see Drying Meat Safely, page 66) after drying is complete. Continue to dry the meat until the pieces crack when bent but do not break, another 2 to 4 hours.

4. Turn off the dehydrator and expose the trays to the air. Remove any visible oil beads by patting the meat with towels. Cool until no longer warm, about 30 minutes.

STORAGE: 1 to 2 weeks at room temperature (68°F) in a dark, dry location in an airtight container, 1 to 2 months refrigerated, or 6 months frozen.

BULGOGI-STYLE KOREAN DRIED BEEF

Prep Time (including marination): 2 to 3 hours | Drying Temp & Time: 165° to 185°F for 4 to 6 hours | Yield: 14 to 20 (1-ounce) servings

Classic Korean *bulgogi* ("fire meat") is made with thinly shaved meat that has been marinated in a sweet and savory sauce of soy sauce, pear, and sesame. A dark, fermented Japanese soy sauce will certainly work for bulgogi. But, if you can find the "regular" Korean soy sauce, *yang jo gan jang*, you might make someone's grandmother cry. See the note about preparing pork jerky in the headnote to the recipe for Maple Brown Sugar Pork Jerky (page 86).

¼ cup soy sauce

2 tablespoons brown sugar

2 tablespoons sesame seeds, toasted (page 30)

1 tablespoon pear powder (preferably Asian pear, or substitute apple powder)

1 tablespoon scallion powder (or substitute any other type of onion powder)

1 teaspoon ginger powder

½ teaspoon garlic powder

½ teaspoon ground black pepper

¼ teaspoon hot chile powder (optional)

2½ pounds beef or pork such as round or loin

1. In a large bowl or container, combine the soy sauce, brown sugar, sesame seeds, pear powder, scallion powder, ginger powder, garlic powder, black pepper, and chile powder (if using). Cover and refrigerate up to 3 days.

2. Trim and cut the meat into squares or strips as described in step 2 of Classic Beef Jerky (page 69). Bulgogi is traditionally cut into thin (⅛-inch-thick) squares. Add the meat to the marinade, toss until evenly coated, cover, and refrigerate for 1 to 2 hours; longer may be too strong for thinly sliced meat.

3. Preheat a food dehydrator to 165° to 185°F. Remove the meat strips from the marinade and drain well, but do not pat dry. Place the strips on drying trays without touching. Within the first 2 hours of drying, confirm the meat has reached a safe internal temperature of 160°F. Test the temperature of at least one meat strip on every tray by wrapping it around an instant-read thermometer. If the meat is under 160°F, consider a pasteurization step (see Drying Meat Safely, page 66) after drying is complete. Continue to dry meat until the strips crack when bent but do not break, another 2 to 4 hours.

4. Turn off the dehydrator and expose the trays to the air. Remove any visible oil beads by patting the meat with towels. Cool until no longer warm, about 30 minutes.

STORAGE: 1 to 2 weeks at room temperature (68°F) in a dark, dry location in an airtight container, 1 to 2 months refrigerated, or 6 months frozen.

BARBECUE-STYLE GROUND BEEF JERKY

Prep Time: 1 hour | Drying Temp & Time: 130° to 140°F for 4 to 6 hours | Yield: 7 to 10 (1-ounce) servings

Ground beef jerky is fast and easy to make. Perhaps the one drawback of the soft texture is that it's easy to eat a lot of it! Because it's ground meat, I recommend using curing salt (see How to Use Curing Salt, page 67). Ground meat jerkies need a precooking step due to higher bacterial counts inherent in all ground meat. These types of jerkies also resist pasteurization after drying. To counteract these limitations, grind the meat yourself or have it ground to order at a local butcher shop, keep it very cold while mixing, use curing salt, and precook before drying. For best results, use 90 to 96 percent lean meat (maximum 10 percent fat). Beef, pork, lamb, venison, and other game meats work well. Because the meat is precooked, it is dried at a much lower temperature.

1¼ pounds very lean ground beef

2½ teaspoons chili seasoning mix

1¼ teaspoons tomato powder

1¼ teaspoons kosher salt or ¾ teaspoon table salt

1¼ teaspoons brown sugar

¼ teaspoon pink curing salt #1

1 tablespoon cold Worcestershire sauce

1 tablespoon ice water, if needed for mixing

Several drops liquid smoke

1. Preheat a conventional oven to 300°F. Line two baking sheets with silicone baking mats or parchment paper.

2. Take extra care to keep ground meat extremely cold during handling. Ground meat has a greater surface area, resulting in inherently higher bacteria counts. In a large bowl, combine the chili seasoning mix, tomato powder, salt, brown sugar, curing salt, Worcestershire sauce, ice water, and liquid smoke. Add the meat and, using your hands or a fork, toss until well mixed. Flatten the mixture, place on the lined baking sheet, and cover with a piece of foil, plastic wrap, or parchment paper. Use a rolling pin to flatten the meat mixture to ¼ inch thick. Remove the foil, plastic, or parchment, and score the meat into strips 1 to 2 inches wide and any length. Alternatively, load the seasoned ground meat into a jerky gun, and shoot 4- to 5-inch strips onto the lined baking sheets.

3. Bake the meat strips until they reach an internal temperature of 160°F, 8 to 10 minutes.

continued

4. Preheat a food dehydrator to 130° to 140°F. Using an offset spatula, transfer the cooked meat strips to towels and pat dry. Arrange the strips on drying trays without touching. Dry the meat until it feels soft to the touch, is not hard on the outside, and bends without breaking in half, 4 to 6 hours.

5. Turn off the dehydrator and expose the trays to the air. Remove any visible oil beads by patting the meat with towels. Cool until no longer warm, about 30 minutes.

STORAGE: 1 to 2 weeks at room temperature (68°F) in a dark, dry location in an airtight container, 1 to 2 months refrigerated, or 6 months frozen.

AFRICAN-STYLE DRIED MEAT JERKY

Prep Time (including marination): 2 to 48 hours | Drying Temp & Time: 165° to 185°F for 4 to 6 hours | Yield: 14 to 20 (1-ounce) servings

Biltong and *guedid* are similar unsmoked spiced dried meats made in various regions of Africa. The primary differences are type of meat, thickness of the strips, and method of drying. *Biltong* is made in South Africa from long, thick strips of beef round marinated in spices and vinegar and then shade-dried until very firm using hot, circulating air. In the north, Moroccans marinate long, thin strips of calf, lamb, camel, and, more recently, turkey. *Guedid* is dried in the hot sun for 3 to 7 days until very dry and crisp. *Biltong* is enjoyed as snack food, while *guedid* is intended for cooking. It is rehydrated and used in soups, stews, and other dishes.

2 tablespoons table salt or ¼ cup kosher salt

2 to 4 tablespoons ground coriander seeds

1 to 2 tablespoons other spices (optional), such as ground cumin, anise, fennel, black pepper, or garlic

2 tablespoons white vinegar (optional)

1 to 2 tablespoons brown sugar (optional)

2½ pounds lean lamb leg, beef round, lean game meat, or turkey breast

1. In a large bowl or container, combine the salt, coriander to taste, other spices to taste (if using), vinegar (if using), and brown sugar (if using). Cover and refrigerate until ready to use. May be prepared up to 3 days in advance.

2. Trim and cut the meat into squares or strips as described in step 2 of Classic Beef Jerky (page 69). Add the meat to the marinade and toss until evenly coated, cover, and refrigerate for 2 to 48 hours.

3. Preheat a food dehydrator to 165° to 185°F. Remove the meat strips from the marinade and pat dry. Place the strips on the drying trays without touching. Within the first 2 hours of drying, confirm the meat has reached a safe internal temperature of 160°F. Test the temperature of at least one meat strip on every tray by wrapping it around an instant-read thermometer. If the meat is under 160°F, consider a pasteurization step (see Drying Meat Safely, page 66) after drying is complete. Continue to dry the meat until the strips crack when bent but do not break, another 2 to 4 hours.

4. Turn off the dehydrator and expose the trays to the air. Remove any visible oil beads by patting the meat with towels. Cool until no longer warm, about 30 minutes.

STORAGE: 1 to 2 weeks at room temperature (68°F) in a dark, dry location in an airtight container, 1 to 2 months refrigerated, or 6 months frozen.

NEPALESE-STYLE SMOKED DRIED MEAT (SUKUTI)

Prep Time (including marination): 1 to 2 days | Drying Temp & Time: 165° to 185°F for 4 to 6 hours | Yield: 14 to 20 (1-ounce) servings

Sukuti is a pepper-spiced smoked meat originating in the South Asian country of Nepal, where it is made from water buffalo. It is enjoyed as a snack but is also used to make a simple stir-fry dish with vegetables in a tomato sauce or rehydrated in curries. I've adapted the idea for an aggressively spiced meat jerky using ingredients from your dried pantry. The combination makes a great jerky for beef, buffalo, and flavorful meats such as lamb and wild game. Make it as hot as you like. If you don't have a smoker, you can simulate the flavor with liquid smoke.

1 tablespoon table salt or
  2 tablespoons kosher salt

1 tablespoon onion or
  shallot powder

1 tablespoon molasses
  or honey

1 tablespoon liquid smoke
  (optional)

1 to 3 teaspoons hot chile
  powder of your choice

1 teaspoon ground
  black pepper

½ teaspoon ground
  coriander

½ teaspoon ground cumin

½ teaspoon ginger powder

½ teaspoon turmeric powder

¼ teaspoon garlic powder

2½ pounds lean beef, lamb,
  buffalo, or game, such as
  round, sirloin, or flank

1. In a large bowl or container, combine the salt, onion powder, molasses, liquid smoke (if using), chile powder to taste, black pepper, coriander, cumin, ginger powder, turmeric powder, and garlic powder. Cover and refrigerate until ready to use. May be made 3 days in advance.

2. Trim and cut the meat into squares or strips as described in step 2 of Classic Beef Jerky (page 69). Add the meat to the marinade and toss until evenly coated, cover, and refrigerate for 8 to 24 hours.

3. Preheat a food dehydrator to 165° to 185°F. Remove the meat strips from the marinade and pat dry. Place the strips on the drying trays without touching. Within the first 2 hours of drying, confirm the meat has reached a safe internal temperature of 160°F. Test the temperature of at least one meat strip on every tray by wrapping it around an instant-read thermometer. If the meat is under 160°F, consider a pasteurization step (see Drying Meat Safely, page 66) after drying is complete. Continue to dry the meat until the strips crack when bent but do not break, another 2 to 4 hours.

4. Turn off the dehydrator and expose the trays to the air. Remove any visible oil beads by patting the meat with towels. Cool until no longer warm, about 30 minutes.

STORAGE: 1 to 2 weeks at room temperature (68°F) in a dark, dry location in an airtight container, 1 to 2 months refrigerated, or 6 months frozen.

MEXICAN DRIED BEEF (CARNE SECA)

Prep Time (including marination): 9 hours to 2 days | Drying Temp & Time: 165° to 185°F for
4 to 6 hours | Yield: 7 to 10 (1-ounce) servings

The unique characteristic of this *carne seca* that distinguishes it from other dried meats is the way the meat is sliced back and forth "accordion style" to form one long thin piece. *Carne seca* can be used as a jerky snack but is often shredded and rehydrated for tacos and burritos or prepared as *machaca,* mixed into scrambled eggs or a stir-fry with peppers and onions. For these uses, simply season the meat with salt before drying as the Incans did to make *charqui,* or use salt and lime juice. In the recipe below, you have a choice of other spices for full-flavored *carne seca* jerky snacks.

2 tablespoons sweet or smoked paprika, or a combination

1½ teaspoons table salt or 1 tablespoon kosher salt

1 teaspoon ground cumin

1 teaspoon crushed dried oregano leaves

1 teaspoon onion powder

½ teaspoon garlic powder

½ teaspoon hot chile powder

1 tablespoon fresh lime zest or 1 teaspoon chopped dried lime zest or ⅛ teaspoon lime zest powder (optional)

1¼ pounds beef round or brisket

2 tablespoons fresh lime juice (optional)

1. In a small bowl or container, combine the paprika, salt, cumin, oregano, onion powder, garlic powder, chile powder, and lime zest (if using).

2. Trim and cut the meat into squares or strips as described in step 2 of Classic Beef Jerky (page 69). Or, if you wish to try the "accordion" cut, make a thin ⅛ inch cut with the grain across the top of the block of meat, stopping ⅛ inch from end, turning the knife blade 180° and continuing the cut in the opposite direction, stopping again ⅛ inch from end. Turn again and continue cutting the meat in this back-and-forth manner until the entire block has been reduced to one long piece ⅛ inch thick. If needed, cut across the strip in lengths to fit your drying trays. If using the lime juice, rub it over the meat then rub with the spice mixture. Or, rub the spice mixture directly over the meat. Cover and refrigerate for 8 to 48 hours.

3. Preheat a food dehydrator to 165° to 185°F. Remove the meat from the marinade and pat dry. Place the meat on the drying trays without touching. Within the first 2 hours of drying, confirm the meat has reached a safe internal temperature of 160°F. Test the temperature of at least one meat strip on every tray by wrapping it around an instant-read thermometer. If the meat is under 160°F, consider a pasteurization step (see Drying Meat Safely,

continued

page 66) after drying is complete. Continue to dry the meat until the strips crack when bent but do not break, another 2 to 4 hours.

4. Turn off the dehydrator and expose the trays to the air. Remove any visible oil beads by patting the meat with towels. Cool until no longer warm, about 30 minutes.

STORAGE: 1 to 2 weeks at room temperature (68°F) in a dark, dry location in an airtight container, 1 to 2 months refrigerated, or 6 months frozen.

GYRO-STYLE BEEF AND LAMB JERKY

Prep Time: 1 hour | **Drying Temp & Time:** 130° to 140°F for 4 to 6 hours | **Yield:** 7 to 10 (1-ounce) servings

This ground meat jerky uses classic gyro. Because the meat is precooked, it is dried at a much lower temperature. It can be enjoyed as a jerky snack, but it can also be rehydrated for gyro sandwiches.

1 to 2 tablespoons cold red wine, wine vinegar, or ice water as needed to facilitate mixing

1½ teaspoons table salt or 1 tablespoon kosher salt

1½ teaspoons crushed dried oregano or marjoram leaves

1½ teaspoons onion powder

½ teaspoon garlic powder

½ teaspoon crushed dried rosemary or mint leaves

½ teaspoon ground cumin

½ teaspoon ground black pepper

¾ pound very lean (90 to 96 percent) ground beef

½ pound very lean (90 to 96 percent) ground lamb

1. Preheat a conventional oven to 300°F. Line 2 baking sheets with silicone baking mats or parchment paper.

2. Take extra care to keep the meat extremely cold during handling. Ground meat has a greater surface area, resulting in inherently higher bacteria counts. In a large bowl, combine the wine, salt, oregano, onion powder, garlic powder, rosemary, cumin, and pepper. Add the meat and, using your hands or a fork, toss until well mixed. Flatten the mixture, place on the lined baking sheet, and cover with a piece of foil, plastic wrap, or parchment paper. Use a rolling pin to flatten the meat mixture to ¼ inch thick. Remove the foil, plastic, or parchment, and score the meat into strips 1 to 2 inches wide and any length. Alternatively, load the seasoned ground meat into a jerky gun, and shoot 4- to 5-inch strips onto the lined baking sheets.

3. Bake the meat strips until they reach an internal temperature of 160°F, 8 to 10 minutes.

4. Preheat a food dehydrator to 130° to 140°F. Using an offset spatula, transfer the meat strips to towels and pat dry. Arrange the strips on the drying trays without touching. Dry until the meat feels soft to the touch, is not hard on the outside, and bends without breaking in half, 4 to 6 hours.

5. Turn off the dehydrator and expose the trays to the air. Remove any visible oil beads by patting the meat with towels. Cool until no longer warm, about 30 minutes.

STORAGE: 1 to 2 weeks at room temperature (68°F) in a dark, dry location in an airtight container, 1 to 2 months refrigerated, or 6 months frozen.

BOURBON-GLAZED VENISON OR ELK JERKY

Prep Time (including marination): 9 to 25 hours | Drying Temp & Time: 165° to 185°F for 4 to 6 hours | Yield: 7 to 10 (1-ounce) servings

Several of the preceding recipes would work very nicely with venison and elk: Classic Beef Jerky, Homemade Braised Pastrami-Spiced Jerky, Hot Chile Pepper Beef Jerky, Teriyaki Beef Jerky, and Barbecue-Style Ground Beef Jerky. These jerky marinades have strong flavors that enhance game meat. Another good preparation for venison is with fruit powder, which serves to tenderize the meat as well as impart great flavor. Finish the fruit-spiked jerky with a bourbon-honey glaze, and you've got yourself a winner. I recommend curing salt when preparing game meat jerky due to its higher inherent bacterial counts.

1¼ pounds venison or elk round, rump, or leg (see Tip)

2 tablespoons peach powder (apple, pineapple, and mango are also good)

2 tablespoons brown sugar

1 teaspoon table salt or 2 teaspoons kosher salt

½ teaspoon dry mustard

¼ teaspoon garlic powder

¼ teaspoon pink curing salt #1

1 tablespoon coarsely ground black pepper (optional)

¼ cup bourbon

¼ cup honey or maple syrup

1. In a large bowl or container, combine the fruit powder, sugar, salt, mustard powder, garlic powder, and curing salt. Trim the meat of all visible fat and cut into squares or strips as described in step 2 of Classic Beef Jerky (page 69). Venison jerky is best when the meat is cut thin. Add the meat and toss until evenly coated, cover, and refrigerate for 8 to 24 hours.

2. Preheat a food dehydrator to 165° to 185°F. Remove the meat strips from the marinade, drain, and pat dry. For spicy jerky, sprinkle the strips on both sides with the coarse black pepper to taste (if using) and press lightly into the meat. Place the strips on the drying trays without touching. In a small bowl, combine the bourbon and honey; brush half of the mixture over the meat strips. Within the first 2 hours of drying, confirm the meat has reached a safe internal temperature of 160°F. Test the temperature of at least one meat strip on every tray by wrapping it around an instant-read thermometer. If the meat is under 160°F, consider a pasteurization step (see Drying Meat Safely, page 66) after drying is complete. Turn the strips over and brush with the remaining bourbon-honey glaze. Continue to dry the meat until the strips crack when bent but do not break, another 2 to 4 hours.

3. Turn off the dehydrator and expose the trays to the air. Remove any visible oil beads by patting the meat with towels. Cool until no longer warm, about 30 minutes.

STORAGE: 1 to 2 weeks at room temperature (68°F) in a dark, dry location in an airtight container, 1 to 2 months refrigerated, or 6 months frozen.

TIP: It is recommended that you freeze wild game meat before using it to make jerky to kill the trichinella parasite if present. Cut portions that are 6 inches thick or less, wrap well, and freeze at 0°F or below for at least 30 days. Thaw in the refrigerator before slicing and preparing jerky.

MAPLE BROWN SUGAR PORK JERKY

Prep Time (including marination): 9 to 24 hours | Drying Temp & Time: 165° to 185°F for 4 to 6 hours | Yield: 7 to 10 (1-ounce) servings

This simple recipe is a real crowd pleaser. Be sure to trim all visible fat as well as any silverskin—the thin, shiny layer covering parts of the meat. It's very tough to chew, so you want to remove it, using a thin-blade boning knife. Slide the knife blade under a layer of silverskin for about 1 inch, to create a tail you can grasp. Hold this tail and use a gentle, back-and-forth sawing motion to cut just under the silverskin down the length of the meat until it is removed.

¼ cup maple syrup

¼ cup water

1 tablespoon brown sugar

1½ teaspoons table salt or 1 tablespoon kosher salt

1¼ pounds pork loin

1. In a large bowl or container, combine the maple syrup, water, brown sugar, and salt. Cover and refrigerate until ready to use. May be prepared up to 3 days in advance.

2. Remove the silverskin as described above. Trim and cut the meat into squares or strips as described in step 2 of Classic Beef Jerky (page 69). Add the meat to the marinade, toss to coat, cover, and refrigerate for 8 to 24 hours.

3. Preheat a food dehydrator to 165° to 185°F. Remove the meat from the marinade, drain, and pat dry. Place the strips on the drying the trays without touching. Within the first 2 hours of drying, confirm the meat has reached a safe internal temperature of 160°F. Test the temperature of at least one strip on every tray by wrapping it around an instant-read thermometer. If the meat is under 160°F, consider a pasteurization step (see Drying Meat Safely, page 66) after drying is complete. Continue to dry until the strips crack when bent but do not break, another 2 to 4 hours.

4. Turn off the dehydrator and expose the trays to the air. Remove any visible oil beads by patting the meat with towels. Cool until no longer warm, about 30 minutes.

STORAGE: 1 to 2 weeks at room temperature (68°F) in a dark, dry location in an airtight container, 1 to 2 months refrigerated, or 6 months frozen.

TIP: Although not required for pork raised commercially today, you may want to freeze the pork before using it to make jerky. See the tip about freezing meat on page 85.

SESAME-GLAZED CHAR SIU-STYLE PORK JERKY

Prep Time (including marination): 9 to 25 hours | **Drying Temp & Time:** 165° to 185°F for 4 to 6 hours | **Yield:** 7 to 10 (1-ounce) servings

Traditional *char siu* is skewered and roasted pork belly. Lean cuts of meat required for jerky also work well with, the flavors in *char siu* marinade. It's great as a snack or rehydrated to serve with rice and greens for a complete meal or as an ingredient in soup, fried rice, or stir fry. I use curing salt in this recipe to impart its characteristic color and flavor to the *char siu*.

¼ cup packed brown sugar

2 tablespoons rice or white wine

2 tablespoons hoisin sauce

2 tablespoons soy sauce

1½ teaspoons table salt or 1 tablespoon kosher salt

1 teaspoon tomato powder or 1 tablespoon ketchup

½ teaspoon ground fennel or anise seeds, or a combination

½ teaspoon ground white or black pepper

¼ teaspoon ginger powder

¼ teaspoon garlic powder

¼ teaspoon pink curing salt #1

1¼ pounds pork tenderloin (95 percent lean)

2 tablespoons dried sesame seeds

3 tablespoons honey thinned with 1 tablespoon water

1. In a large bowl or container, combine the brown sugar, wine, hoisin, soy sauce, salt, tomato powder, fennel, pepper, ginger powder, garlic powder, and curing salt. Cover and refrigerate up to 3 days in advance.

2. Remove the silver skin as described in the recipe for Maple Brown Sugar Pork Jerky (page 86). Trim and cut the meat into squares or strips as described in step 2 of Classic Beef Jerky (page 69). Toss the pork with the marinade, cover, and refrigerate for 8 to 24 hours.

3. Preheat a food dehydrator to 165° to 185°F. Remove the pork from the marinade, drain, and pat dry. Sprinkle the strips on both sides with the sesame seeds and press lightly into the meat. Place the strips on the drying trays without touching. Brush half of the honey mixture over the meat. Within the first 2 hours of drying, confirm the meat has reached a safe internal temperature of 160°F. Test the temperature of at least one strip on every tray by wrapping it around an instant-read thermometer. If the meat is under 160°F, consider a pasteurization step (see Drying Meat Safely, page 66) after drying is complete. Turn the strips over and brush with the remaining honey mixture. Continue to dry until the strips crack when bent but do not break, another 2 to 4 hours.

4. Turn off the dehydrator and expose the trays to the air. Remove any visible oil beads by patting the meat with towels. Cool until no longer warm, about 30 minutes.

STORAGE: 1 to 2 weeks at room temperature (68°F) in a dark, dry location in an airtight container, 1 to 2 months refrigerated, or 6 months frozen.

MALAYSIAN LUNAR NEW YEAR GROUND PORK JERKY (BAKKWA)

Prep Time (including marination): 5 hours | **Drying Temp & Time:** 130° to 140°F for 4 to 6 hours | **Yield:** 7 to 10 (1-ounce) servings

This sweet-salty pork snack is made in Singapore and Malaysia for the Lunar New Year. Although it is usually grilled or roasted, it also makes a great jerky. Because the meat is precooked, it is dried at a much lower temperature. When making ground meat jerkies, 90 percent lean (10 percent fat) is recommended. Because it's a ground meat jerky, I also recommend curing salt. Many connoisseurs of *bakkwa* prefer a slightly higher fat content (20 percent fat) to make a soft, chewy meat. Just know that higher fat will shorten the storage time. However, no one has been able to confirm this, since it's never around long enough.

FOR THE BAKKWA:

2 tablespoons brown sugar

2 tablespoons soy sauce

1 teaspoon red pepper flakes

1 teaspoon ground white or black pepper

1 teaspoon ground fennel or anise seeds, or a combination

½ teaspoon ginger powder

¼ teaspoon pink curing salt #1

1¼ pounds ground pork (80-percent lean), or rib chop or center cut chops

1 tablespoon ice water, rice wine, or sherry if needed

FOR THE HONEY GLAZE:

2 tablespoons honey

1 tablespoon hoisin sauce (oyster or fermented bean sauce may be substituted)

1 tablespoon soy sauce or fish sauce

1. Preheat a conventional oven to 250°F. Line two baking sheets with silicone baking mats or parchment paper.

2. **FOR THE BAKKWA,** take extra care to keep ground meat extremely cold during handling. Ground meat has a greater surface area, resulting in inherently higher bacteria counts. If you prefer to grind the pork yourself, cut, season and grind the pork chops as described in step 2 of Spicy Curry Ground Turkey Jerky (page 92). In a large bowl or container, combine the brown sugar, soy sauce, red pepper flakes, pepper, fennel or anise, ginger powder, and curing salt. Add the meat and mix wel. If the meat becomes sticky, add ice water as needed to facilitate mixing. Cover and refrigerate for 4 hours. Flatten the seasoned mixture, place on the lined baking sheet, and cover with a piece of foil, plastic wrap, or parchment paper. Use a rolling pin to flatten the meat mixture to ⅛ to ⅜ inch thick depending on whether you want crispy or chewy *bakkwa*. Remove the foil, plastic, or parchment, and score the meat into 4-inch squares. Alternatively, load the seasoned ground meat into a jerky gun, and shoot 4- to 5-inch strips onto the baking sheets.

3. Bake until the pork reaches an internal temperature of 160°F, 8 to 10 minutes.

4. **FOR THE HONEY GLAZE,** while the meat is baking, in a small bowl, combine the honey, hoisin, and soy sauce.

5. Preheat a food dehydrator to 130° to 140°F. Transfer cooked meat strips to towels and pat dry. Arrange the pieces on the drying trays without touching. Brush the meat with half of the honey glaze. After 1 hour, turn the meat over and brush with the remaining glaze. Continue to dry the meat until thin strips are crisp or thick strips feel soft to the touch but are firm and flexible, another 3 to 5 hours.

6. Turn off the dehydrator and expose the trays to the air. Remove any visible oil beads by patting the meat with towels. If desired, cut into 2-inch squares. Cool until no longer warm, about 30 minutes.

STORAGE: 1 to 2 weeks at room temperature (68°F) in a dark, dry location in an airtight container, 1 to 2 months refrigerated, or 6 months frozen.

CAJUN-STYLE TURKEY JERKY

Prep Time (including marination): 7 to 25 hours | **Drying Temp & Time:** 165° to 185°F for 4 to 6 hours | **Yield:** 14 to 20 (1-ounce) servings

Cajun flavor begins with the holy trinity of green pepper, celery, and onion. Of course, I add a kick of hot pepper and some zing from vinegar to punch up these smoky turkey strips. Turkey breast meat is very lean and makes great jerky without a lot of preparation. I like it sliced quite thin and then cut into squares or wide strips.

1 tablespoon green bell
pepper powder

2 teaspoons celery salt

1 teaspoon onion powder

1 teaspoon garlic powder

1 teaspoon ground
black pepper

1 teaspoon hot chile powder,
such as cayenne

½ cup cider vinegar

¼ cup water or turkey broth

2 tablespoons liquid smoke

2½ pounds turkey breast
or tenders

1. In a large bowl or container, combine the bell pepper powder, celery salt, onion powder, garlic powder, black pepper, chile powder, vinegar, and water. Cover and refrigerate until ready to use. May be prepared up to 3 days in advance.

2. Trim and cut the meat into squares or strips as described in step 2 of Classic Beef Jerky (page 69). Add the meat to the marinade and toss until evenly coated. Cover and refrigerate for 6 to 24 hours.

3. Preheat a food dehydrator to 165° to 185°F. Remove the meat strips from the marinade, drain, and pat dry. Place on the drying trays without touching. Within the first 2 hours of drying, confirm the poultry has reached a safe internal temperature of 165°F. Test the temperature of at least one meat strip on every tray by wrapping it around an instant-read thermometer. If the meat is under 165°F, consider a pasteurization step (see Drying Meat Safely, page 66) after drying is complete. Continue to dry the meat until the strips crack when bent but do not break, another 2 to 4 hours.

4. Turn off the dehydrator and expose the trays to the air. Remove any visible oil beads by patting the meat with towels. Cool until no longer warm, about 30 minutes.

STORAGE: 1 to 2 weeks at room temperature (68°F) in a dark, dry location in an airtight container, 1 to 2 months refrigerated, or 6 months frozen.

CRANBERRY-ORANGE TURKEY JERKY

Prep Time (including marination): 7 to 25 hours | Drying Temp & Time: 165° to 185°F for 4 to 6 hours | Yield: 14 to 20 (1-ounce) servings

This recipe uses the same flavors found in the cranberry-orange sauce that graces many Thanksgiving tables. I give this jerky a kick with hot pepper, then tame the heat with a honey glaze. It makes a great snack for holiday adventures, whether you are shopping for gifts, trimming the tree, or caroling with friends and family. You can also change up the flavors with other berry powders and citrus. Perhaps blueberry and lemon, strawberry and pineapple, or blackberry and lime. You really can't go wrong with this one.

2 tablespoons cranberry powder

2 tablespoons chopped dried orange zest

2 tablespoons brown sugar

1½ teaspoons table salt or 1 tablespoon kosher salt

½ teaspoon hot chile powder such as cayenne

2½ pounds turkey breast or tenders

¼ cup honey, thinned with 1 tablespoon water

1. In a large bowl or container, combine the cranberry powder, orange zest, brown sugar, salt, and chile powder. Trim and cut the meat into squares or strips as described in step 2 of Classic Beef Jerky (page 69). Add the meat to the marinade and toss until evenly coated. Cover and refrigerate for 6 to 24 hours.

2. Preheat a food dehydrator to 165° to 185°F. Remove the meat strips from marinade and pat dry. Place the strips on the drying trays without touching. Brush half the thinned honey over the strips. Within the first 2 hours of drying, confirm the poultry has reached a safe internal temperature of 165°F. Test the temperature of at least one meat strip on every tray by wrapping it around an instant-read thermometer. If the meat is under 165°F, consider a pasteurization step (see Drying Meat Safely, page 66) after drying is complete. Turn the strips over and brush with the remaining thinned honey. Continue to dry the meat until the strips crack when bent but do not break, another 2 to 4 hours.

3. Turn off the dehydrator and expose the trays to the air. Remove any visible oil beads by patting the meat with towels. Cool until no longer warm, about 30 minutes.

STORAGE: 1 to 2 weeks at room temperature (68°F) in a dark, dry location in an airtight container, 1 to 2 months refrigerated, or 6 months frozen.

SPICY CURRY GROUND TURKEY JERKY

Prep Time: 1 hour | Drying Temp & Time: 130° to 140°F for 4 to 6 hours | Yield: 7 to 10 (1-ounce) servings

This ground meat jerky uses Madras curry powder, the British-style curry spice blend with its vibrant yellow color and distinct flavor of fenugreek. Madras is an interpretation of garam masala, the spice blend that has many regional variations throughout India—even household to household! If you are familiar with yellow curry powder from the grocer's shelf, you'll feel right at home with this recipe. Because it's a ground meat jerky, I recommend the use of curing salt. Since the meat is precooked, it is dried at a much lower temperature.

2 teaspoons Madras Curry Spice Mix (page 51)

1 teaspoon tomato powder

1 teaspoon onion powder

1 teaspoon crushed dried thyme leaves

¾ teaspoon table salt or 1½ teaspoons kosher salt

½ teaspoon garlic powder

½ teaspoon ginger powder

½ teaspoon habanero or cayenne chile powder

¼ teaspoon pink curing salt #1

1¼ pounds boneless, skinless turkey breast meat

1 to 2 tablespoons cold water, chicken broth, or white wine

1. In a large bowl, combine the curry spice mix, tomato powder, onion powder, thyme, salt, garlic powder, ginger powder, habanero powder, and curing salt. Set aside until ready to use. Line two rimmed baking sheets with silicone baking mats or parchment paper.

2. Dry the turkey breast with towels to eliminate excess moisture. Cut into ½-inch cubes, add to the bowl with the curry mixture, and toss until evenly coated. Place in a single layer on the baking sheets, cover, and freeze for 30 minutes. Also freeze your meat-grinder parts or food-processor blade to keep the meat as cold as possible during preparation. With a meat grinder or in a food processor, grind the turkey. Add the water as needed to create a smooth, uniform mixture—too coarse, and the jerky will fall apart.

3. Preheat a conventional oven to 300°F. Line 2 baking sheets with silicone baking mats or parchment paper. Flatten the mixture, place on the lined baking sheet, and cover with a piece of foil, plastic wrap, or parchment paper. Use a rolling pin to flatten the meat mixture to ¼ inch thick. Remove the foil, plastic, or parchment, and score the meat into strips 1 to 2 inches wide and any length. Alternatively, load the seasoned ground meat into a jerky gun, and shoot 4- to 5-inch strips onto the prepared baking sheets.

4. Bake the ground meat strips until they reach an internal temperature of 165°F, 8 to 10 minutes.

5. Preheat a food dehydrator to 130° to 140°F. Using an offset spatula, transfer the turkey strips to towels and pat dry. Arrange on the drying trays without touching. Dry the meat until it feels soft to the touch, is not hard on the outside, and bends without breaking in half, 4 to 6 hours.

6. Turn off the dehydrator and expose the trays to the air. Remove any visible oil beads by patting the meat with towels. Cool until no longer warm, about 30 minutes.

STORAGE: 1 to 2 weeks at room temperature (68°F) in a dark, dry location in an airtight container, 1 to 2 months refrigerated, or 6 months frozen.

COCONUT-CURRY GROUND CHICKEN JERKY

Prep Time: 1 hour | Drying Temp & Time: 130° to 140°F for 4 to 6 hours | Yield: 7 to 10 (1-ounce) servings

This ground chicken jerky is seasoned with my coconut curry spices, an Indian spice blend known as *goda masala*. For safety's sake, grind the chicken yourself and use curing salt. Like all ground meat jerkies, this one is precooked, allowing it to dry at a much lower temperature.

2½ teaspoons Coconut Curry Spices (page 51)

1¼ teaspoons kosher salt or ¾ teaspoon table salt

1¼ teaspoons brown sugar

½ teaspoon ginger powder

¼ teaspoon hot chile powder (optional)

¼ teaspoon pink curing salt #1

1¼ pounds boneless, skinless chicken breast meat

1 to 2 tablespoons cold cashew, almond, or coconut milk

1. In a large bowl or container, combine the coconut curry spices, salt, brown sugar, ginger powder, chile powder (if using), and curing salt. Line two rimmed baking sheets with silicone baking mats or parchment paper.

2. Cut, season and grind the chicken with the milk as described in step 2 of Spicy Curry Ground Turkey Jerky (page 92).

3. Preheat a conventional oven to 300°F. Line 2 baking sheets with silicone baking mats or parchment paper. Flatten the mixture, place on the lined baking sheet, and cover with a piece of foil, plastic wrap, or parchment paper. Use a rolling pin to flatten the meat mixture to ¼ inch thick. Remove the foil, plastic, or parchment, and score the meat into strips 1 to 2 inches wide and any length. Alternatively, load the seasoned ground meat into a jerky gun, and shoot 4- to 5-inch strips onto the prepared baking sheets.

4. Bake the ground meat strips until they reach an internal temperature of 165°F, 8 to 10 minutes.

5. Preheat a food dehydrator to 130° to 140°F. Using an offset spatula, transfer the chicken strips to towels and pat dry. Arrange on the drying trays without touching. Dry the meat until it feels soft to the touch, is not hard on the outside, and bends without breaking in half, 4 to 6 hours.

6. Turn off the dehydrator and expose the trays to the air. Remove any visible oil beads by patting the meat with towels. Cool until no longer warm, about 30 minutes.

STORAGE: 1 to 2 weeks at room temperature (68°F) in a dark, dry location in an airtight container, 1 to 2 months refrigerated, or 6 months frozen.

CARIBBEAN-STYLE GOAT JERKY

Prep Time (including marination): 7 to 25 hours | Drying Temp & Time: 165° to 185°F for 4 to 6 hours | Yield: 14 to 20 (1-ounce) servings

Goat meat seems to be enjoyed almost everywhere in the world except the United States. Approximately 70 percent of the world's people regularly consume goat meat. And why not? Kid meat is lean, environmentally sustainable, tender, and mild tasting. This goat jerky uses flavors found in Cuban and Jamaican cuisines. The recipe works equally well with pork, chicken, lamb, or game meat. The fruity, herbal marinade can be as spicy as you like with habanero pepper.

¼ cup orange powder

3 tablespoons brown sugar

2 tablespoons Pickapeppa or Worcestershire sauce

1 tablespoon fresh lime zest or 1 teaspoon chopped dried lime zest or ⅛ teaspoon lime zest powder

2 teaspoons shallot powder

2 teaspoons scallion powder

1½ teaspoons crushed dried thyme leaves

1½ teaspoons table salt or 1 tablespoon kosher salt

1½ teaspoons garlic powder

1 teaspoon ground coriander

1 teaspoon ground cumin

½ teaspoon ginger powder

½ teaspoon habanero or other hot chile powder

2½ pounds lean goat meat such as leg, rump, loin, or backstrap

1. In a large bowl or container, combine the orange powder, brown sugar, Pickapeppa sauce, lime zest, shallot powder, scallion powder, thyme, salt, garlic powder, coriander, cumin, ginger powder, and habanero powder. Trim and cut the meat into squares or strips as described in step 2 of Classic Beef Jerky (page 69). Add the meat to the marinade and toss until evenly coated. Cover and refrigerate for 6 to 24 hours.

2. Preheat a food dehydrator to 165° to 185°F. Remove the meat strips from the marinade and pat dry. Place the strips on the drying trays without touching. Within the first 2 hours of drying, confirm the meat has reached a safe internal temperature of 160°F. Test the temperature of at least one meat strip on every tray by wrapping it around an instant-read thermometer. If the meat is under 160°F, consider a pasteurization step (see Drying Meat Safely, page 66) after drying is complete. Continue to dry meat until the strips crack when bent but do not break, another 2 to 4 hours.

3. Turn off the dehydrator and expose the trays to the air. Remove any visible oil beads by patting the meat with towels. Cool until no longer warm, about 30 minutes.

STORAGE: 1 to 2 weeks at room temperature (68°F) in a dark, dry location in an airtight container, 1 to 2 months refrigerated, or 6 months frozen.

BASIC DRIED FISH FOR MEALS

Prep Time (including marination): 2 to 5 hours | Drying Temp & Time: 155° to 165°F for 4 hours | Yield: 14 to 20 (1-ounce) servings

Lean, skinless dried fish fillets are best for dehydrated meals. These include fish such as cod, flounder, grouper, mahi mahi, and tilapia. Although fish with higher oil content are often used to make jerky, including tuna, trout, and salmon, lean fish jerkies can be stored longer. Brine the fish before dehydrating to protect the flavor and texture. A few optional seasonings are suggested, and you can add any other spices or aromatics that you wish. Or keep the brine simple so you can use the dried fish in any recipe.

2 quarts water

½ cup kosher salt

Optional flavorings: ½ cup packed brown sugar, ¼ cup soy sauce, 2 tablespoons black peppercorns, or 1 teaspoon dried chopped garlic

2½ pounds lean, skinless fish fillets, such as cod, flounder, grouper, mahi mahi, or tilapia

1. In a shallow container, combine the water, salt, and any optional ingredients, stirring until salt is completely dissolved. Cover and refrigerate until ready to use. May be prepared up to 3 days in advance.

2. Run your fingers over the fillets to feel for pin bones and use needle-nose pliers to pull them out. Place the fish in the freezer for 30 minutes to firm it up. Slice lengthwise into ½-inch strips. Cut the strips into 1-inch lengths. Place the strips in a shallow layer in the marinade, then turn gently to coat. Cover and refrigerate for 1 to 4 hours.

3. Preheat a food dehydrator to 155° to 165°F. Remove the strips from the brine and pat dry. Place the strips slightly apart on the drying trays. Within the first 2 hours of drying, confirm the fish has reached a safe internal temperature of 145°F using an instant-read thermometer between two strips. If under 145°F, consider a pasteurization step (see Drying Meat Safely, page 66) after drying is complete. Continue to dry the fish until the strips crack when bent but do not break, about another 2 hours.

4. Turn off the dehydrator and expose the trays to the air. Remove any visible oil beads by patting the fish with towels. Cool until no longer warm, about 30 minutes.

STORAGE: 1 to 2 weeks at room temperature (68°F) in a dark, dry location in an airtight container, 1 to 2 months refrigerated, or 6 months frozen.

HAWAIIAN-STYLE TUNA JERKY

Prep Time (including marination): 3 to 9 hours | Drying Temp & Time: 155° to 165°F for 4 hours | Yield: 7 to 10 (1-ounce) servings

This tuna jerky recipe uses flavors common in huli-huli sauce, most often used on chicken. *Huli* means "turn" in Hawaiian and refers to the method of putting the chicken between two grill racks that were flipped over during cooking. The soy sauce, brown sugar, garlic, tomato, and tropical fruit flavors complement tuna nicely, which "turns" it into this deliciously sweet glazed jerky.

½ cup soy sauce

2 tablespoons brown sugar

1 tablespoon pineapple or mango powder

1 teaspoon tomato powder

½ teaspoon hot chile powder

⅛ teaspoon garlic powder

⅛ teaspoon ginger powder

1¼ pounds skinless ahi, yellowtail, or bluefin tuna with no bloodline

1. In a large shallow container, combine the soy sauce, brown sugar, pineapple powder, tomato powder, chile powder, garlic powder, and ginger powder. Place the tuna in the freezer for 30 minutes to firm it up. Slice into ¼- to ½-inch strips. Cut the strips into 3- to 4-inch or shorter lengths.

2. Place the strips in a shallow layer in the marinade, then turn gently to coat. Cover and refrigerate for 2 to 8 hours.

3. Preheat a food dehydrator to 155° to 165°F. Remove the tuna strips from the marinade and pat dry. Place the strips slightly apart on the drying trays. Within the first 2 hours of drying, confirm the fish has reached a safe internal temperature of 145°F using an instant-read thermometer between two strips. If under 145°F, consider a pasteurization step (see Drying Meat Safely, page 66) after drying is complete. Continue to dry the tuna until it darkens and the strips crack when bent but do not break, about another 2 hours.

4. Turn off the dehydrator and expose the trays to the air. Remove any visible oil beads by patting the tuna with towels. Cool until no longer warm, about 30 minutes.

STORAGE: 1 to 2 weeks at room temperature (68°F) in a dark, dry location in an airtight container, 1 to 2 months refrigerated, or 6 months frozen.

LEMON-PEPPER TROUT JERKY

Prep Time (including marination): 3 to 9 hours | Drying Temp & Time: 155° to 165°F for 4 hours | Yield: 7 to 10 (1-ounce) servings

Use this lemon-pepper jerky recipe to flavor any type of saltwater or freshwater trout. These seasonings complement the strong flavor of trout jerky. But they will also work for lean fish, such as cod, flounder, grouper, mahi mahi, and tilapia.

1¼ pounds skin-on trout fillets

½ cup soy sauce

1 tablespoon fresh lemon zest or 2 teaspoons chopped dried lemon zest or ¼ teaspoon lemon zest powder

1 teaspoon honey

½ teaspoon kosher salt

⅛ teaspoon garlic powder

1 tablespoon Lemon-Pepper Seasoning (page 50)

1. Leave the skin on the trout during preparation. If desired, remove it after drying or before eating. Run your fingers over the trout to feel for pin bones, and use needle-nose pliers to pull them out. Place the trout in the freezer for 30 minutes to firm it up. Slice the trout lengthwise into ¼- to ½-inch strips. Cut the strips into 3- to 4-inch lengths.

2. In a large shallow container, combine the soy sauce, lemon zest, honey, salt, and garlic powder. Place the strips in a shallow layer in the marinade, then turn gently to coat. Cover and refrigerate for 2 to 8 hours.

3. Preheat a food dehydrator to 155° to 165°F. Remove the trout strips from the marinade and pat dry. Sprinkle with the lemon pepper and press lightly to adhere to the trout. Place the strips slightly apart on the drying trays. Within the first 2 hours of drying, confirm the fish has reached a safe internal temperature of 145°F using an instant-read thermometer between two strips. If under 145°F, consider a pasteurization step (see Drying Meat Safely, page 66) after drying is complete. Continue to dry the trout until it darkens and the strips crack when bent but do not break, about another 2 hours.

4. Turn off the dehydrator and expose the trays to the air. Remove any visible oil beads by patting the trout with towels. Cool until no longer warm, about 30 minutes.

STORAGE: 1 to 2 weeks at room temperature (68°F) in a dark, dry location in an airtight container, 1 to 2 months refrigerated, or 6 months frozen.

GLAZED SALMON CANDY

Prep Time (including marination): 1½ to 4½ hours | **Drying Temp & Time:** 155° to 165°F for 3 to 6 hours | **Yield:** 7 to 10 (1-ounce) servings

Salmon "candy" refers to smoked fish glazed with something sweet—brown sugar, maple syrup, honey, or molasses. If you aren't smoking the fish, add some liquid smoke if you want to capture that flavor. Whether you remove the skin before eating is up to you, but leave it on during preparation to keep the thin strips intact while you marinate and dry the fish.

1¼ pounds skin-on salmon fillets

1 cup packed dark brown sugar

½ cup kosher salt

¼ cup maple syrup or honey

2 tablespoons dark rum

1 to 2 teaspoons liquid smoke (optional)

1 tablespoon coarsely ground black pepper (optional)

1. Run your fingers over the fillet to feel for pin bones, and use needle-nose pliers to pull them out. Place the salmon in the freezer for 30 minutes to firm it up. Slice lengthwise into ¼- to ½-inch strips. Cut the strips into 3- to 4-inch lengths.

2. Make a curing mix by combining the brown sugar and salt. Spread a ¼-inch layer of the mixture on the bottom of a marinating container. Lay the salmon strips over the cure, close together without overlapping. Spread the remaining cure over the strips. Cover and refrigerate for 30 minutes or no longer than 3 hours. The cure will dissolve, form a brine, and firm up the fish. In a small bowl, combine the maple syrup, rum, and liquid smoke to taste (if using).

3. Preheat a food dehydrator to 155° to 165°F. Remove the salmon strips from the brine, rinse well with water, and pat dry. Sprinkle with the pepper (if using) and press lightly to help it adhere to the salmon. Place the strips skin-side down, slightly apart on the drying trays. Brush the salmon flesh (not the skin) with half of the syrup mixture. Within the first 2 hours of drying, confirm the salmon has reached a safe internal temperature of 145°F using an instant-read thermometer between two strips. If under 145°F, consider a pasteurization step (see Drying Meat Safely, page 66) after drying is complete. Brush the salmon with the remaining syrup mixture. Continue to dry the salmon until it darkens and the strips crack when bent but do not break, another 1 to 4 hours.

continued

4. Turn off the dehydrator and expose the trays to the air. Remove any visible oil beads by patting the salmon with towels. Brush the strips with the remaining glaze. Cool until no longer warm, about 30 minutes.

STORAGE: 1 to 2 weeks at room temperature (68°F) in a dark, dry location in an airtight container, 1 to 2 months refrigerated, or 6 months frozen.

NATIVE AMERICAN PEMMICAN

Prep Time: 3 to 4 hours | **Yield:** 8 to 12 (1-ounce) servings

Pemmican is prepared by mixing dried meat with rendered fat. The mixture is then cooled and cut into serving pieces. One of the original "superfoods," this nutritious survival and trail food dates back hundreds of years. This recipe is adapted from the North American Cree tribe, who made pemmican from dried buffalo, elk, or other available game. To use this recipe, first make any plain or seasoned jerky or dried meat and dried berries of your choice.

2 cups (about 4 ounces) very dry beef or game, such as venison, preferably smoked

¼ cup dried berries, such as blueberries or Saskatoon berries (optional)

½ to 2 cups (4 to 14 ounces) tallow or lard (rendered animal fat)

1. Use dried meat and berries that are brittle, not partially dried or pliable. Cut the dried meat into small pieces or shreds to facilitate grinding. Using a food processor, high-speed blender, or mortar and pestle, grind the meat and dried berries (if using) into a powder, then place in a bowl. In a small saucepan over medium heat, melt the tallow. Strain any solids (crackling) if present, and in batches pour the melted fat over the powder, using enough fat to coat the meat well. In summer or warmer climates, use less fat; in winter or temperate climates, you may use more, if desired. Stir until the mixture is well combined.

2. Line a small rimmed baking sheet with foil, plastic wrap, or parchment paper. Spread the meat mixture in the pan to about ½ inch thick. Refrigerate until the mixture is firm and holds its shape, about 1 hour.

3. Before the mixture becomes too hard, remove from the pan, and cut into 8 to 12 small bars. Dry the bars on a cooling rack at room temperature (<70°F), or in the refrigerator if it is a warmer day, until completely cooled. When the bars are hard, bring to room temperature, and wrap each one in foil, plastic wrap, or parchment paper.

STORAGE: Up to 1 year in an airtight container in a cool, dark place. Correctly made and stored, pemmican has been known to last for 50 years.

MIXED BERRY LEATHER, PAGE 110

Fruit and Veggie Leathers and Chips

Dried fruit and vegetable leathers and chips make tasty, healthful, portable snacks. There are many ways to get creative when making leathers and chips. The recipes in this chapter will provide you with a range of ideas. But don't stop there. Feel free to swap fruits, vegetables, and seasonings to suit your taste.

For leathers, you can use less-than-perfect produce: "seconds," misshapen or scarred, slightly overripe or bruised, or the pulp leftover from juicing. Just don't use spoiled produce—anything heavily bruised, moldy, or rotting goes in the compost. When making fruit and vegetable chips, do use flawless produce that is perfectly ripe and slightly firm.

Peeling skins for leathers or chips is optional for fruits and vegetables that are usually eaten with their peels on, such as apples and cucumbers. Peeling is also optional for root vegetables such as carrots and beets—just be sure they are well-scrubbed.

ORANGE-SCENTED APPLE LEATHER

Prep Time: 30 to 60 minutes | **Drying Temp & Time:** 125° to 135°F for 4 to 8 hours | **Yield:** 8 servings

This recipe makes apple leather from freshly made applesauce, flavored with a little orange and cinnamon. You can also use frozen or canned apples or store-bought applesauce. Many people do not add sugar to fruit leathers, because drying intensifies the fruit's natural sweetness. But depending on your preference or the type of apple used, you may add sweetener if you wish. A splash of cider vinegar can also enhance the apple flavors. When making homemade applesauce, a blend of two or three varieties usually results in a more flavorful sauce. Some recommended apples for sauce making are Cortland, Crispin (Mutsu), Empire, Gala, Golden Delicious, Fuji, Gravenstein, Honeycrisp, Ida Red, Jonathan, Macoun, McIntosh, and Winesap. This is by no means a complete list; there are thousands of apple varieties, and local orchards may offer you something unique and delicious. Ask them for "seconds," and you'll save a little money.

8 medium apples (2 to 2½ pounds), or 6 cups frozen apple slices, thawed, or 4 cups drained canned apples, or 4 cups unsweetened applesauce

1 teaspoon orange zest powder

½ teaspoon ground cinnamon

1 to 2 teaspoons honey or maple syrup (optional)

½ to 1 teaspoon cider vinegar (optional)

1. Preheat a food dehydrator to 125° to 135°F. Wash the apples, peel if desired, core, cut into chunks, and pretreat for browning; see Steam Blanching and Acidulating (page 6–7). In a blender or food mill, process the fresh apple chunks, thawed frozen slices, canned apples, or applesauce with the orange zest, cinnamon, honey or maple syrup to taste (if using), and cider vinegar to taste (if using) into a smooth puree.

2. Spread the puree on lined drying trays in an even layer, ¼ to ⅜ inch thick. Dry the leather until firm but pliable, 4 to 8 hours. Press lightly in several places to check for soft or sticky spots and continue drying if needed.

3. Turn off the dehydrator and peel the leather from the liner while still warm. When almost cool, cut the leather into 8 pieces, and roll each portion in a piece of parchment or wax paper.

STORAGE: Up to 3 months, wrapped, in an airtight container in a cool, dry place.

QUICK TIPS FOR PERFECT CHIPS AND LEATHERS

- Use only perfectly ripe produce for dried chips, but less-than-perfect produce for leathers is okay.
- Wash the produce well and trim away bruised portions or imperfections.
- Peeling skins is optional; scrubbing root vegetables is not.
- Add small amounts of liquids only as needed to facilitate pureeing or to enhance flavor (for example, with citrus juice).
- Fruit flavor is concentrated when dried, so sweetener is not usually needed but is optional.
- Add flavorings as desired, such as lemon juice or zest, spices, or a pinch of salt.
- After drying, it's easiest to peel the leather from the liner while still warm.
- Wrap the leathers individually to prevent them from the sticking together.
- Like all dried foods, store leathers and chips in an airtight container where it's cool and dry.
- Leathers may also be dried until crisp and enjoyed like crackers.
- To soften a crisp leather, lightly brush it with plain water and let stand until supple again, about 30 minutes.

BANANA-ORANGE LEATHER

Prep Time: 30 minutes | **Drying Temp & Time:** 125° to 135°F for 4 to 8 hours | **Yield:** 8 servings

Although bananas are often combined with other juicy fruits such as strawberries or pineapple, you can make fruit leather out of nothing but bananas and a bit of lemon juice to prevent browning. Here I combine bananas with fresh orange segments and orange zest for another boost of flavor and suggest adding cocoa powder. Other flavors instead of orange and cocoa that would work with bananas include lime segments and zest, strawberries and ground peanuts, pineapple and coconut, or bananas Foster–style with rum, brown sugar, and Greek yogurt.

7 medium bananas (about 1¾ pounds)

1 seedless orange

2 to 4 tablespoons unsweetened cocoa powder (optional)

1 to 2 tablespoons brown sugar (optional)

1. Preheat a food dehydrator to 125° to 135°F. Peel the bananas and slice. Zest the orange and finely chop the zest. Peel the orange and separate the segments. In a blender or food mill, process the banana slices, orange segments and zest, cocoa to taste (if using), and brown sugar to taste (if using) into a smooth puree.

2. Spread the puree on lined drying trays in an even layer, ¼ to ⅜ inch thick. Banana puree takes longer to dry, so spread thinner for faster drying. Dry the leather until firm but pliable, 4 to 8 hours. Press lightly in several places to check for soft or sticky spots and continue drying if needed.

3. Turn off the dehydrator and peel the leather from the liner while still warm. When almost cool, cut the leather into 8 pieces, and roll each portion in a piece of parchment or wax paper.

STORAGE: Up to 3 months, wrapped, in an airtight container in a cool, dry place.

TROPICAL FRUIT LEATHER

Prep Time: 30 to 60 minutes | **Drying Temp & Time:** 125° to 135°F for 4 to 8 hours | **Yield:** 8 servings

This fruit leather is like having a bit of paradise in your pocket for a getaway any time you need it, even if you don't happen to live on a tropical island. You can use just one fruit such as mango or pineapple or combine several. If you want that Hawaiian Punch flavor, you need to add passion fruit or guava, which are hard to find fresh, unless you do live on a tropical island. But frozen tropical fruit purees without added sugar are available and might be found in markets that focus on Southeast Asian or Caribbean foods. You can use a pinch of salt to enhance the flavor of tropical fruits, as well as melons and pears.

4 cups chopped fresh or frozen tropical fruit (such as banana, kiwi fruit, mango, papaya, or pineapple)

1 to 2 tablespoons fresh lime juice

Pinch salt

¼ cup grated coconut or finely chopped macadamia nuts (optional)

1. Preheat a food dehydrator to 125° to 135°F. In a blender or food mill, puree the fruit, lime juice to taste, and salt into a smooth puree.

2. Spread the puree on lined drying trays in an even layer, ¼ to ⅜ inch thick. Sprinkle evenly with the coconut (if using). Dry the leather until firm but pliable, 4 to 8 hours. Press lightly in several places to check for soft or sticky spots and continue drying if needed.

3. Turn off the dehydrator and peel the leather from the liner while still warm. When almost cool, cut the leather into 8 pieces, and roll each portion in a piece of parchment or wax paper.

STORAGE: Up to 3 months, wrapped, in an airtight container in a cool, dry place.

STRAWBERRY-RHUBARB LEATHER

Prep Time: 30 to 45 minutes | Drying Temp & Time: 125° to 135°F for 4 to 8 hours | Yield: 8 servings

If you love strawberry-rhubarb pie, you are going to like this fruit leather. It's got everything but the piecrust, and you can take it anywhere. I suggest cooking the rhubarb just until it softens. However, rhubarb can be eaten raw, so this step isn't entirely necessary. Just be sure to cut off any rhubarb leaves—they contain relatively high levels of oxalic acids and can cause nausea and vomiting. We all eat many foods containing oxalic acids, including spinach, beets, berries, cocoa, nuts, bran, and many other foods. But rhubarb leaves contain very high levels, so be sure to discard them.

8 medium stalks fresh rhubarb (1¼ to 1⅓ pounds)

2 tablespoons water

2 pints fresh strawberries

2 tablespoons sugar or honey

1 tablespoon fresh lemon juice or 1 teaspoon chopped dried lemon zest (optional)

1. Preheat a food dehydrator to 125° to 135°F. Trim and discard the rhubarb leaves, wash the stalks, and cut into ½-inch-thick slices. In a medium saucepan over medium heat, combine the rhubarb and water and cook, covered, until the rhubarb softens, 3 to 5 minutes. Remove from heat and allow to cool. Wash the strawberries, remove the hulls, and cut in half. In a blender or food mill, process the rhubarb, strawberries, sugar, and lemon juice (if using) to a smooth puree.

2. Spread the puree on lined drying trays in an even layer, ¼ to ⅜ inch thick. Dry the leather until firm but pliable, 4 to 8 hours. Press lightly in several places to check for soft or sticky spots and continue drying if needed.

3. Turn off the dehydrator and peel the leather from the liner while still warm. When almost cool, cut the leather into 8 pieces, and roll each portion in a piece of parchment or wax paper.

STORAGE: Up to 3 months, wrapped, in an airtight container in a cool, dry place.

PEACH MELBA LEATHER

Prep Time: 30 to 60 minutes | **Drying Temp & Time:** 125° to 135°F for 4 to 8 hours | **Yield:** 8 servings

Peach Melba is a classic dessert of peaches, raspberry sauce, and vanilla ice cream created in 1893 by famed French chef Auguste Escoffier (1846–1935) to honor Australian opera singer Nellie Melba (1861–1931). The ingredients in Peach Melba combine deliciously in this fruit leather, which you can prepare in true operatic form with dramatic effects, except no one dies—though they may swoon when they taste this colorful creation. If you want to take it up a notch, sauté the peach slices in butter until lightly browned before pureeing.

6 medium peaches (1½ to 2 pounds), or 6 cups frozen peach slices, or 4 cups drained canned peaches

1 cup fresh raspberries

1 to 2 tablespoons brown sugar (optional)

1 cup plain yogurt (nonfat or 1-percent or 2-percent low-fat)

1. Preheat a food dehydrator to 125° to 135°F. Wash the peaches, peel if desired, halve, remove the pits, cut into chunks, and pretreat for browning; see Steam Blanching or Acidulating (pages 6–7). In a blender or food mill, process the peaches into a smooth puree. Place in a bowl. In the same blender or food mill, process the raspberries with the brown sugar to taste (if using) into a smooth puree. Whisk the yogurt until smooth and pourable.

2. Spread the peach puree evenly on lined drying trays to ¼ to ⅜ inch thick. Drizzle with the raspberry puree and then with the yogurt. If desired for additional effect, use a table knife or chopstick to swirl the raspberry puree and yogurt through the peach puree. Alternatively, the purees and yogurt may be blended into a homogeneous puree. Dry the leather until firm but pliable, 4 to 8 hours. Press lightly in several places to check for soft or sticky spots and continue drying if needed.

3. Turn off the dehydrator and peel the leather from the liner while still warm. When almost cool, cut the leather into 8 pieces, and roll each portion in a piece of parchment or wax paper.

STORAGE: Up to 3 months, wrapped, in an airtight container in a cool, dry place.

MIXED BERRY LEATHER

Prep Time: 15 to 30 minutes | **Drying Temp & Time:** 125° to 135°F for 4 to 8 hours | **Yield:** 8 servings

Berries make luscious, mouthwatering leathers. Mix sweet and tart berries such as blueberries and raspberries to balance cloying and sharp flavors. If desired, remove the seeds from blackberries, raspberries, and strawberries—or leave them in for texture, your choice. (Seedless varieties are also available.) To leave the seeds in, mash the berries into a puree with a fork or in a food processor or blender. To remove the seeds, press the berries through a fine mesh strainer or food mill. It can be easier to strain the seeds after heating the berries. To heat the berries, place in a saucepan and crush lightly using a potato masher or the back of a large spoon, and cook over medium heat until the berries soften. If needed, add a small amount of water to prevent sticking. Press the hot berries through a sieve or food mill.

8 cups berries (strawberries, raspberries, black-berries, blueberries, or other berries)

2 tablespoons sugar

1 tablespoon fresh lemon juice or 1 teaspoon chopped dried lemon zest (optional)

1. Preheat a food dehydrator to 125° to 135°F. Wash the berries; pick over and remove stems or moldy berries. Hull the strawberries and cut in half. Leave the other berries whole. In a blender or food mill, process the berries, sugar to taste, and lemon juice (if using) into a smooth puree.

2. Spread the puree on lined drying trays in an even layer, ¼ to ⅜ inch thick. Dry the leather until firm but pliable, 4 to 8 hours. Press lightly in several places to check for soft or sticky spots and continue drying if needed.

3. Turn off the dehydrator and peel the leather from the liner while still warm. When almost cool, cut the leather into 8 pieces, and roll each portion in a piece of parchment or wax paper.

STORAGE: Up to 3 months, wrapped, in an airtight container in a cool, dry place.

COCONUT-CURRY PUMPKIN LEATHER

Prep Time: 15 minutes | **Drying Temp & Time:** 125° to 135°F for 4 to 8 hours | **Yield:** 8 servings

This delicious leather is made with canned ingredients. It's a great recipe when you need a healthy snack in a hurry. Of course, feel free to substitute fresh pumpkin and homemade apple puree. The savory nature of this leather is a nice change from fruity leathers. But you can easily take it to the sweet side; just swap out the curry and savory spices for cinnamon, nutmeg, or pumpkin-pie spice. The sesame seeds won't mind one bit. Pumpkin puree marries well with many other flavors. Try chopped peanuts and bacon bits, orange zest and dried cranberries, or rosemary and balsamic vinegar.

2 cups pumpkin puree

2 cups unsweetened applesauce

¼ cup honey or maple syrup

2 teaspoons Coconut Curry Spices (page 51)

½ teaspoon turmeric powder

¼ teaspoon hot chile powder (optional)

2 tablespoons sesame seeds, toasted (page 30)

1. Preheat a food dehydrator to 125° to 135°F. In a blender or food mill, process the pumpkin, applesauce, honey to taste, coconut curry spices, turmeric powder, and chile powder (if using) into a smooth puree.

2. Spread the puree on lined drying trays in an even layer, ¼ to ⅜ inch thick. Sprinkle evenly with the sesame seeds. Dry the leather until firm but pliable, 4 to 8 hours. Press lightly in several places to check for soft or sticky spots and continue drying if needed.

3. Turn off the dehydrator and peel the leather from the liner while still warm. When almost cool, cut the leather into 8 pieces, and roll each portion in a piece of parchment or wax paper.

STORAGE: Up to 3 months, wrapped, in an airtight container in a cool, dry place.

GREEN SMOOTHIE LEATHER

Prep Time: 1 hour | Drying Temp & Time: 125° to 135°F for 4 to 8 hours | Yield: 2 servings

Yes, you can dry a smoothie. Starting with a green vegetable juice (I suggest avocado), Greek yogurt or coconut cream, and seeds or nuts for body, plus apple and citrus peel. You can include some of the white part of the peel, called the pith; it contains pectin, which can help hold the leather together, but it's also bitter, so this is optional. You could substitute almost any other vegetable, such as carrots, squash, beets, or corn. Or prepare your favorite smoothie recipe. Dry until chewy for healthy breakfasts or snacks on the go. Dry until crisp and munch like crackers, or grind to a powder and then rehydrate with water—though the consistency will be different from a freshly made smoothie.

2 cups loosely packed chopped spinach or kale leaves

2 medium stalks celery, thinly sliced (about 1 cup)

1 medium avocado, halved, pitted, and scooped out (about 1¼ cups)

1 medium green apple or pear, cored and grated (about ¾ cup)

½ medium cucumber (4 ounces), seeded and grated (about ½ cup)

1 cup Greek yogurt or coconut cream

1 tablespoon seeds or nuts (such as sesame seeds, pumpkin seeds, peanuts, or cashews)

1 tablespoon dried orange peel (zest and pith, if desired)

1 teaspoon grated lemon zest

1. Preheat a food dehydrator to 125° to 135°F. In a blender or food mill, process the spinach, celery, avocado, apple, cucumber, yogurt, seeds, orange peel, and lemon zest to a smooth puree.

2. Spread the puree on lined drying trays in an even layer, ¼ to ⅜ inch thick. Dry the leather until firm but pliable, 4 to 8 hours. Press lightly in several places to check for soft or sticky spots and continue drying if needed. Alternatively, continue to dry the leather until crisp, if desired.

3. Turn off the dehydrator and peel the pliable leather from the liner while still warm. Crispy leather should release on its own. When almost cool, cut pliable leather into 8 pieces, and roll each portion in a piece of parchment or wax paper. Break crisp leather into cracker-size portions.

STORAGE: Up to 3 months, wrapped, in an airtight container in a cool, dry place.

SAVORY TOMATO LEATHER

Prep/Cook Time: 2 to 3 hours | Drying Temp & Time: 125° to 135°F for 4 to 8 hours | Yield: 12 snack servings, or 4 cups tomato sauce if rehydrated

Tomato leather can be enjoyed as a snack food. But it can also be rehydrated and used in recipes calling for tomato sauce, such as soups, stews, pasta sauces, and pizza. To rehydrate, combine the leather with an equal amount of water or just barely cover torn pieces of leather. You can also use a piece of tomato leather as a sandwich or burger topping that won't slide out when you take a big bite. Or try a piece inside a grilled cheese sandwich. If tomato sauce is your primary purpose, you might want to puree plain tomatoes without any other vegetables, seasoning, or salt. For snacking, use any seasonings you wish. You can also dry the leather until crisp—in this case, a small amount of vegetable oil can improve texture. Vegetable crisps are very delicate and make a nice topping when crushed and sprinkled over soups, salads, eggs, or what-have-you.

12 cups halved, seeded, and chopped tomatoes, or 3 quarts drained canned diced tomatoes

2 to 4 tablespoons water

1 tablespoon onion powder

1 teaspoon Italian Herb Seasoning Blend (page 50)

½ teaspoon celery powder

½ teaspoon salt

½ teaspoon vegetable or olive oil (optional)

⅛ teaspoon garlic powder

1. In a heavy-bottomed, medium saucepan over low heat, cook the tomatoes, covered, until softened, 15 to 20 minutes, adding the water if needed to prevent sticking. Process in a blender or food mill into a smooth puree. Return to the saucepan and add the onion powder, seasoning blend, celery powder, salt, oil (if using), and garlic powder and simmer, uncovered, over low heat until thickened and reduced by half, 1 to 2 hours.

2. Preheat a food dehydrator to 125° to 135°F. Spread the puree on lined drying trays in an even layer, ¼ to ⅜ inch thick—use the thinner amount when drying until crisp. Dry the leather until firm but pliable, 4 to 8 hours. Press lightly in several places to check for soft or sticky spots and continue drying if needed. Alternatively, continue to dry the leather until crisp, if desired.

3. Turn off the dehydrator and peel pliable leather from the liner while still warm. Crisp leather should release on its own. When almost cool, cut pliable leather into 8 pieces, and roll each portion in a piece of parchment or wax paper. Gently break crisp leather into cracker-size portions.

STORAGE: Up to 3 months, wrapped, in an airtight container in a cool, dry place.

APPLE, PEAR, OR BANANA CHIPS

Prep Time: 30 minutes | **Drying Temp & Time:** 125° to 135°F for 4 to 8 hours | **Yield:** 8 servings

Thinly sliced fruits dried until crisp make supremely satisfying snacks—they're crunchy, sweet, and mouthwatering. Be sure to pretreat apples, pears, and bananas for browning, so toss with fresh lemon or lime juice or dip in acidulated water with ascorbic acid or commercial anti-oxidant. For apples, you can seek out a variety that is slow to turn brown—check with a local orchard for recommendations or simply cut different types of apples and leave at room temperature for 30 minutes. An apple that hasn't turned significantly brown is a good candidate for drying with no pretreatment. Note that these apples will eventually turn brown in storage, but I've had them last several months.

8 medium apples, pears, or bananas

2 quarts acid dip (page 7)

1. Preheat a food dehydrator to 125° to 135°F. Wash the apples. Peel if desired; unpeeled apples take longer to dry. Use a corer to remove the core, or cut in half to trim the core with a paring knife. Cut into rings or half slices ⅛ to ¼ inch thick. Pretreat for browning using the acid dip (see page 7). Drain the apples and pat dry with towels.

2. Arrange the apples on the drying trays in a single layer without overlapping. Dry until crisp, 4 to 8 hours.

STORAGE: Up to 1 year at room temperature in an airtight container.

ROASTED PINEAPPLE CRISPS

Prep/Cook Time: 30 to 45 minutes | **Drying Temp & Time:** 125° to 135°F for 4 to 8 hours | **Yield:** 6 servings

A 2-pound pineapple will yield about 1 pound of fruit. You can dry fresh pineapple slices as is or roast them as suggested here with a sprinkle of brown sugar, which turns the pineapple into a candy-like treat when dried. If you want them crisp, be sure to slice them thin. Other complementary seasonings you can sprinkle on pineapple slices before drying include chili seasoning, curry powder, ground lime zest, or sea salt.

1 medium pineapple (about 2 pounds)

2 to 6 tablespoons brown sugar

1. Preheat the oven to 400°F. Line a rimmed baking sheet with foil.

2. Scrub the pineapple, cut a 1-inch slice from the top and bottom, trim around the sides to remove the peel, and trim any remaining "eyes." Use a pineapple coring tool or cut into round slices and cut out the core with a paring knife or pastry tip, or cut the pineapple lengthwise into quarters and trim the core; cut whole, half, or quarter slices to ⅛ to ¼ inch thick.

3. Arrange the pineapple on the baking sheet and sprinkle with the brown sugar to taste. Bake until the pineapple is golden and the sugar is bubbly and caramelized, 10 to 15 minutes. Be careful not to let the sugar burn.

4. Preheat a food dehydrator to 125° to 135°F. Arrange the pineapple slices on the drying trays in a single layer without overlapping. Dry until crisp, 4 to 8 hours.

STORAGE: Up to 1 year at room temperature in an airtight container.

MARCO'S MELON SLICES

Prep Time: 30 minutes | **Drying Temp & Time:** 125° to 135°F for 4 to 10 hours | **Yield:** 8 servings

Marco Polo is said to have described dried melon as "sweet as honey." Whether he said this or not, it's quite true. Drying intensifies the aromatic, musky flavors of cantaloupe, honeydew, and watermelon, providing a distinctive, ethereal taste you won't forget. It's easy to eat a lot of crisp dried melon. White or light-green melon flesh may turn slightly brown when dried, especially if sliced thin and dried until very crisp, whereas orange- and red-fleshed varieties better retain their original color. Don't throw out the seeds, either. As with pumpkin seeds, you can dry melon seeds for snacks or use them to make the Mexican beverage Horchata with Melon (page 23).

1 medium fresh melon, any variety (about 3 pounds) or 1 small seedless watermelon (about 3 pounds)

¼ to ½ teaspoon kosher or sea salt (optional)

1. Preheat a food dehydrator to 125° to 135°F. Wash the melon. Cut in half and scoop out the seeds. Cut the melon into quarters, then slice across into ⅛- to ¼-inch-thick slices. Trim the rind from each slice. Pat the slices dry to remove excess moisture.

2. Arrange the slices on the drying trays in a single layer without overlapping. Lightly sprinkle with the salt to taste (if using). Dry until crisp, 4 to 10 hours.

STORAGE: Up to 1 year at room temperature in an airtight container.

PARMESAN TOMATO CRISPS

Prep Time: 15 to 30 minutes | **Drying Temp & Time:** 125° to 135°F for 6 to 10 hours | **Yield:** 8 servings

Dried tomato slices for snacks need nothing more than a sprinkle of salt. You might be astonished at the rich tomato flavor—better than anything you can buy and worth the price of a dehydrator. However, you can dress them up with herbs and cheese, as done in this recipe. Almost any tomato will work, from big beefsteaks to hothouse salad tomatoes or big heirlooms. Plum tomatoes can also work and make a petite chip.

8 medium or 5 to 6 large tomatoes (2½ to 3 pounds)

¼ cup grated Parmesan cheese

1 tablespoon Italian Herb Seasoning Blend (page 50)

½ teaspoon kosher or coarse sea salt

¼ teaspoon ground black pepper

1. Preheat a food dehydrator to 125° to 135°F. Wash the tomatoes and remove the core with a paring knife or tomato "shark" tool. Cut into ⅛- to ¼-inch-thick slices. In a small bowl, combine the cheese, seasoning blend, salt, and pepper.

2. Arrange the tomato slices on the drying trays in a single layer without overlapping. Sprinkle evenly with the cheese mixture. Dry until crisp, 6 to 10 hours.

STORAGE: 1 to 2 weeks at room temperature or 1 to 2 months in the refrigerator in an airtight container.

HERBED CARROT CHIPS

Prep Time: 15 to 30 minutes | **Drying Temp & Time:** 125° to 135°F for 6 to 10 hours | **Yield:** 8 servings

Thin slices of carrots can be dried to make delightful, healthy snacks at a fraction of the cost of store-bought chips. Carrot chips shrink a lot, so find the largest carrots you can. Diagonal slices are especially useful if the carrots are not large, so the slices will be longer. Steam-blanching slices will retain color, but the chips will shrink more. A variety of vegetables makes for a colorful mélange. This recipe will work for any root vegetable, including beet, rutabaga, radish or daikon, sweet potato, or turnip.

3 to 4 large carrots (1½ to 1¾ pounds)

2 to 3 tablespoons Ranch Dressing Seasoning Mix (page 51) or seasoning of your choice such as dried oregano, Italian herbs, salt, and pepper

Olive oil, lemon juice, or water, as needed

1. Preheat a food dehydrator to 125° to 135°F. Cut off the green carrot tops if present. Wash the carrots. Peel if desired. If not peeling the carrots, scrub with a stiff brush under running water. Cut the carrots crosswise into thin coins or diagonally into ⅛-inch-thick slices. Most vegetables benefit from blanching; see Steam Blanching (page 6). Steam-blanch in a shallow layer (1 to 2 inches) over boiling water about 1 minute for thin chips. Pat dry.

2. In a large bowl, toss the carrot slices with the seasoning to taste until well coated. If the slices are very dry, use a drizzle of the oil to help the seasonings stick. A small amount of oil can also help make the vegetables crisp, but don't overdo it.

3. Arrange the slices on the drying trays in a single layer without overlapping. Dry until crisp, 6 to 10 hours. Raw carrots will take longer to dry than blanched.

STORAGE: Up to 1 year at room temperature in an airtight container.

SWEET AND SOUR ROOT VEGETABLE CHIPS

Prep/Cook Time (including marination): 3 to 25 hours | Drying Temp & Time: 125° to 135°F for 2 to 8 hours | Yield: 8 servings

Dried root vegetable chips are crunchy and toothsome, though denser and less crisp than those fried in oil. For a crisper texture, precook the vegetables and slice as thin as possible, less than ⅛ inch if you have a mandoline. Use any type of beet (red, yellow, or striped Chioggia). Feel free to include any other root vegetable such as carrot, radish or daikon, sweet potato, or turnip.

8 medium beets or
    2 average rutabagas or
    1½ to 1¾ pounds any
    combination of root
    vegetables

½ cup apple cider vinegar

½ cup honey

1 teaspoon chopped dried
    orange or lemon zest

½ teaspoon kosher or coarse
    sea salt

¼ teaspoon ground
    black pepper

1. Wash root vegetables under running water; peel if desired. If drying unpeeled roots, scrub well with a stiff brush. Peeling the rutabaga is recommended if the vegetable is waxed. Dry vegetables raw, or cook before drying by roasting or steam-blanching.

2. To roast the vegetables, preheat the oven to 400°F. Place the whole, unpeeled or peeled vegetables in a baking dish, cover, and bake until tender but still slightly firm in the center, about 15 to 30 minutes, depending on size. Allow to cool at least 30 minutes before slicing.

3. To steam-blanch the vegetables, slice the raw unpeeled or peeled vegetables (see step 4). Steam-blanch in a shallow layer (1 to 2 inches) over boiling water for 30 to 60 seconds; pat dry.

4. Slice the raw or roasted vegetables to 1/16 to ⅛ inch thick. You may wish to cut large roots (more than 3 inches in diameter) in halves or quarters before slicing.

5. In a large bowl or container, combine the vinegar, honey, orange zest, salt, and pepper. Add the raw or cooked slices, turn until evenly coated, cover, and refrigerate for 2 to 24 hours. Drain and pat dry.

6. Preheat a food dehydrator to 125° to 135°F. Arrange the slices on the drying trays in a single layer without overlapping. Dry until crisp, 2 to 8 hours. Raw vegetables will take longer to dry than cooked.

STORAGE: Up to 1 year at room temperature in an airtight container.

LEMON-PEPPER PARSNIP CHIPS

Prep Time: **30 minutes** | Drying Temp & Time: **125° to 135°F for 6 to 10 hours** | Yield: **8 servings**

Although parsnips look like ivory-colored carrots, their flavor is zesty like a radish when raw but sweet like a carrot when cooked. Like carrots, beets, and other root vegetables, parsnips will make a tasty snack chip. Since they turn brown when peeled or cut, you need to treat them for browning before drying. Use this recipe to prepare dehydrated chips from other root vegetables that turn brown when peeled or cut, including celeriac and potato.

8 medium parsnips
(1¾ to 2 pounds)

2 to 3 tablespoons
Lemon-Pepper
Seasoning (page 50) or
seasoning of your choice
such as dried dill, chives,
salt, and pepper

Olive oil, lemon juice, or
water, as needed

1. Preheat a food dehydrator to 125° to 135°F. Cut off the green parsnip tops if present. Wash the parsnips and peel if desired. If not peeling the parsnips, scrub with a stiff brush under running water. If the parsnips contain a woody core, they're very mature and not the best choice for dehydrating. Cut the parsnips crosswise into thin coins or diagonally into ⅛-inch-thick slices. Alternatively, slice lengthwise into long, thin strips. Pretreat for browning; see Steam Blanching or Acidulating (pages 6–7). Steam blanching also helps create crisper chips; to steam-blanch, steam thin slices for 30 to 60 seconds, then pat dry.

2. In a large bowl, toss the parsnip slices with the seasoning to taste until well coated. If the slices are very dry, use a drizzle of the oil, lemon juice, or water to help the seasonings stick. A small amount of oil can help make the vegetables crisp, but don't overdo it.

3. Arrange the slices on the drying trays in a single layer without overlapping. Dry until crisp, 6 to 10 hours. Raw parsnips will take longer to dry than cooked.

STORAGE: Up to 1 year at room temperature in an airtight container.

CRISPY GARLIC KALE

Prep Time: 30 minutes | **Drying Temp & Time:** 125° to 135°F for 2 to 4 hours | **Yield:** 8 servings

Dried kale is a popular crunchy snack because it's both tasty and healthy. Season the kale leaves before drying with a small amount of salt, or take it up a notch or two with some of the seasoning suggestions in this recipe. They turn out reliably crunchy if you don't overdo the liquid ingredients. So toss the leaves well and add more liquid only if necessary. Don't just eat dried kale as a snack; use dried kale to crumble on soup or salads, or layer on burgers and sandwiches.

3 bunches kale, any variety (1¼ to 1½ pounds total)

½ teaspoon salt

1 to 2 tablespoons seasoning (optional), such as those found on pages 50–52, or ground nuts or seeds (peanuts, almonds, sesame seeds, etc.), or any other seasonings of your choice, such as onion powder, garlic powder, celery powder, citrus powder, coconut powder, or black pepper

1 to 2 teaspoons olive oil, soy sauce, Worcestershire sauce, lemon juice, honey, or a combination

1. Preheat a food dehydrator to 125° to 135°F. Fold the kale leaves in half and cut or tear away the tough central stem. Swish the leaves in a large sink or basin of cold water, let stand for 5 minutes, lift the leaves from the water, and drain in a colander. If there is sand in the basin, repeat the process until the leaves are completely clean. Cut the leaves into palm-size or smaller pieces. Dry the leaves with towels or in a salad spinner.

2. In a large bowl, toss the dry kale leaves with the salt, seasoning to taste, and 1 teaspoon of oil until well coated. If needed, add more oil, but don't overdo it—too little is better than too much.

3. Arrange the kale leaves on the drying trays in a single layer without overlapping. Dry until crisp, 2 to 4 hours.

STORAGE: Up to 1 year at room temperature in an airtight container.

SALTED CUCUMBER OR ZUCCHINI CHIPS

Prep Time: 30 minutes | **Drying Temp & Time:** 125° to 135°F for 4 to 8 hours | **Yield:** 8 servings

If you garden, cucumbers, zucchini, and other summer squash can grow faster than you can use them. Fortunately, thin slices can be dried as chips, which you can use as if they were fresh for salads and sandwich toppings. Like other dried vegetable chips, cucumbers and summer squash make a great crunchy snack that you can season any way you wish. Dry any type of cucumber, including salad, seedless, or lemon, or any type of summer squash or zucchini, from gold to green. Don't slice them too thinly, or they may nearly disappear when dried.

4 to 5 medium zucchini or summer squash or 3 medium salad cucumbers (1¼ to 1½ pounds total)

1 teaspoon Lemon-Pepper Seasoning (page 50), dill salt, or celery salt

1. Preheat a food dehydrator to 125° to 135°F. Wash the squash or cucumbers. If desired, score the sides using a fork or zesting tool to create decorative ridges. Cut crosswise or on the diagonal into ⅛-inch-thick slices, discarding the ends.

2. Arrange the slices on the drying trays in a single layer without overlapping. Sprinkle evenly with the seasoning. Dry until crisp, 4 to 8 hours.

STORAGE: Up to 1 year at room temperature in an airtight container.

SNAP PEA SNACKS

Prep Time: 15 minutes | **Drying Temp & Time:** 125° to 135°F for 4 to 8 hours | **Yield: 4 servings**

This is one of the easiest dried vegetable snacks you can make. Pea pods require almost no preparation, just a quick wash and they're ready to go in the dehydrator. Here we've added some simple seasoning suggestions. Like other dried vegetables, they make great alternative munchies to fried chips, often seasoned with too much salt, sugar, or other ingredients you may not want. If you are craving a cheesy snack, toss them with nutritional yeast. Vegans know this is a clever way to get a "cheesy" taste. Try it on other vegetable chips such as potatoes and kale, too.

4 cups fresh sugar snap or snow pea pods

3 to 4 tablespoons nutritional yeast (optional)

½ teaspoon kosher or coarse sea salt

1 to 2 teaspoons olive oil, soy sauce, hot sauce, or water

1. Preheat a food dehydrator to 125° to 135°F. Wash the pea pods, drain, and pat dry. In a large bowl, toss the peas with the yeast to taste (if using), salt, and 1 teaspoon oil, soy sauce, hot sauce, or water until well coated. If needed, add more oil, but don't overdo it if using oil, or your vegetables will be soggy instead of crisp—too little is better than too much. If using soy sauce, hot sauce, or water, use as much as you need to get the seasonings evenly distributed.

2. Arrange the pods on the drying trays in a single layer without overlapping. Dry until crisp, 4 to 8 hours.

STORAGE: Up to 1 year at room temperature in an airtight container.

SPICED PUMPKIN CHIPS

Prep Time: 30 minutes | Drying Temp & Time: 125° to 135°F for 4 to 10 hours | Yield: 4 to 16 servings

Thin slices of pumpkin or winter squash can be dried much like apples. You can even leave the rind on the pumpkin as you do apple peel; it's up to you. Small, tender varieties are generally easier to handle. Try acorn, butternut, carnival, delicata, or sugar pumpkin. Season them with savory or sweet spices, using a complimentary liquid to help the seasonings stick: coconut oil with cinnamon, lemon juice with black pepper, or honey with hot chile powder.

1 small squash such as acorn (1 to 4 pounds)

1 to 4 teaspoons coconut oil, lemon juice, or honey

1 to 4 tablespoons ground cinnamon, black pepper, or hot chile powder

1. Preheat a food dehydrator to 125° to 135°F. Wash the squash. Cut in half and scoop out the soft pulp and seeds, which can be dried separately (page 30). Cut the squash into ⅛- to ¼-inch-thick slices. If desired, trim the rind from the flesh.

2. In a large bowl, toss the slices with the oil. Use just enough to moisten the slices. Add the cinnamon to taste and toss until evenly coated.

3. Arrange the slices on the drying trays in a single layer without overlapping. Dry until crisp, 4 to 10 hours.

STORAGE: Up to 1 year at room temperature in an airtight container.

THAI-STYLE RED CURRY WITH CHICKEN, PAGE 144

CHAPTER 5

Just Add Water

The recipes in this chapter include fully cooked entrées and side dishes that are dried and can be rehydrated to make complete meals for breakfast, lunch, and dinner.

In addition, you'll find meal kits—formulas or recipes that can be assembled from the dried fruits, vegetables, meats, and seasonings in your dehydrated pantry. Use these formulas and suggested combinations to create many different types of customized meals to suit your needs and tastes.

Whether you are going backpacking in the wilderness, planning a family camping trip, building an emergency kit, or simply looking for everyday meals that are homemade and easy to prepare, these recipes can become the heart of your dehydrated larder.

VEGETARIAN SUBSTITUTES FOR GROUND MEAT

You can substitute any of these for 1 pound of ground beef:

- 16 ounces firm tofu, wrapped in a towel and weighted for 15 minutes to remove excess moisture, then chopped
- 1 (16-ounce) can black, pinto, soy or other beans or chickpeas, drained and rinsed
- 1 pound dried red lentils, rinsed under running water (soaking is not needed, since they will break down readily in soups and stews)
- 1 cup white, red, or tri-color quinoa cooked until tender in 2 cups water
- 1 pound mushrooms, finely chopped, sautéed dry (without oil) until lightly browned and seasoned with a pinch of thyme and ground black pepper

CLASSIC WESTERN GROUND BEEF CHILI

Prep/Cook Time: 2½ hours | **Drying Temp & Time:** 140° to 160°F for 8 to 12 hours | **Yield:** 6 servings

Chili is a wonderful meal to have on hand. This recipe is a classic Western-style chili made with ground beef, peppers, tomatoes, and beans. Season it with Taco and Chili Seasoning Blend (page 51) or purchased seasoning.

1 pound lean or extra lean (90 percent or higher) ground beef

½ cup finely ground cracker or bread crumbs (optional)

1 medium red bell pepper, seeded and diced (1 cup)

1 medium onion, chopped (1 cup)

2 garlic cloves, minced

2 tablespoons chili seasoning blend

½ to 1 teaspoon salt

½ teaspoon red pepper flakes or hot chile powder

½ teaspoon ground black pepper

1 (15-ounce) can pinto or black beans, undrained

1 (15-ounce) can diced or stewed tomatoes

1 (8-ounce) can tomato sauce

1 to 2 cups beef broth or water, as needed

1 bunch scallions, chopped

1. In a medium bowl, stir together the beef and cracker crumbs (if using). In a large skillet or sauté pan over medium-high heat, cook until browned, 10 to 15 minutes.

2. Reduce the heat to medium, add the bell pepper, onion, garlic, chili seasoning, salt to taste, red pepper flakes, and black pepper. Sauté until soft, 3 to 5 minutes. Add the beans, tomatoes, tomato sauce, and enough of the broth to cover the ingredients. Reduce the heat to low, cover, and simmer for 1 hour.

3. Stir in the scallions. Taste and adjust the salt and heat level with more chili seasoning, red pepper flakes, or black pepper. Allow the chili to cool, uncovered, for 30 minutes.

4. Preheat a food dehydrator to 140° to 160°F. Spread the chili on lined drying trays in an even layer. After 4 to 6 hours, when firm but still moist, turn it over and break into clumps. Continue to check every 1 to 2 hours, breaking clumps into smaller pieces. Dry for 4 to 6 hours longer, until the pieces break with a snap with no visible signs of moisture.

STORAGE: If desired, divide into individual servings. You may also package it with dried pasta or rice to be rehydrated together. Store for up to 2 weeks at room temperature, 2 months refrigerated, or 1 year frozen in an airtight container.
TO REHYDRATE: Combine 1 portion of chili (with or without side dish) with an equal portion of water, bring to a boil, cover, and simmer, until fully hydrated, 5 to 8 minutes.
MAKE IT VEGETARIAN: Replace the beef with a vegetarian substitute (see page 128) added in step 2.

TIPS FOR COOKING GROUND MEAT

- To avoid spoilage of dehydrated meats or dishes containing meat, use lean or extra lean meat, preferably 10 percent fat or less.

- For more tender ground meat, add ½ cup of finely ground cracker or bread crumbs to every 1 pound of ground meat.

- Cook the meat over medium-high heat until it turns from pink to gray and all the moisture has evaporated, 5 to 8 minutes. Stir and break up the meat as it cooks into pebble-size or smaller pieces.

- To prevent rancidity of dehydrated meats that will be stored at room temperature, after cooking the meat, rinse it well under hot running water to remove any residual fat.

- To develop more flavor, after rinsing, continue to cook the meat over medium-high heat until it browns lightly, an additional 5 to 8 minutes. If needed to prevent sticking, add 1 to 2 tablespoons of water to scrape up any browned bits from the bottom of the pan—do not add oil.

- To dehydrate, scatter fully cooked ground meat on drying trays and dry at 140° to 160°F until hard, 6 to 10 hours. Break up any clumps during drying; the dried meat should look like pebbles or gravel.

HUNGARIAN BEEF GOULASH WITH PAPRIKA

Prep/Cook Time: 2 hours | **Drying Temp & Time:** 140° to 160°F for 8 to 12 hours | **Yield:** 4 to 6 servings

Hungarian goulash is a simple beef and tomato stew flavored with paprika. Paprika is available in several styles: Spanish paprika is labeled *dulce* (sweet), *agridulce* (bittersweet), and *picante* (hot). Serve goulash with buttered noodles, rice, or mashed potatoes.

1¼ to 1½ pounds lean or extra lean (90 percent or higher) ground beef

1 medium yellow onion, chopped (about 1 cup)

1 medium carrot, diced (about ½ cup)

1 medium turnip, peeled and diced (about ½ cup)

2 garlic cloves, chopped

1 (15-ounce) can diced tomatoes, undrained

1 (15-ounce) can tomato sauce

1 cup beef broth or water

1 tablespoon sweet paprika

½ teaspoon hot paprika, hot chile powder, or ground black pepper

1 teaspoon crushed dried parsley or oregano leaves or Italian Herb Seasoning Blend (page 50)

½ teaspoon salt

½ teaspoon caraway seeds (optional)

1 tablespoon cider or red wine vinegar (optional)

1 tablespoon brown sugar, or to taste (optional)

1. In a large skillet or sauté pan over medium-high heat, cook the ground beef until browned, 10 to 15 minutes.

2. Reduce the heat to medium. Add the onion, carrot, turnip, and garlic, and sauté until soft, 3 to 5 minutes. Add the diced tomatoes, tomato sauce, broth, sweet paprika, hot paprika, parsley, salt to taste, and caraway. Bring to a simmer, reduce the heat to low, cover, and simmer for 1 hour. Taste and season with the vinegar to taste, brown sugar, and additional salt or pepper to taste. Allow the goulash to cool, uncovered, for 30 minutes.

3. Preheat a food dehydrator to 140° to 160°F. Spread the goulash on lined drying trays in an even layer. After 4 to 6 hours, when the goulash is firm but still moist, turn it over and break into clumps. Continue to check every 1 to 2 hours, breaking clumps into smaller pieces. Dry for 4 to 6 hours longer, until the pieces break with a snap with no visible signs of moisture.

STORAGE: If desired, divide into individual servings. You may also package it with dried pasta, rice, or potatoes to be rehydrated together. Store for up to 2 weeks at room temperature, 2 months refrigerated, or 1 year frozen in an airtight container.

TO REHYDRATE: Combine 1 portion of goulash (with or without side dish) with an equal portion of water, bring to a boil, cover, and simmer, stirring occasionally, until fully hydrated, 5 to 8 minutes.

MAKE IT VEGETARIAN: Replace the beef with 1½ portions of a vegetarian substitute (see page 128) added in step 2.

REHYDRATION 101

There are several methods you can use to rehydrate foods. Which method you choose is a matter of preference. Some people want to save time, and others want to save fuel (such as when camping or backpacking). Here are the primary considerations:

Ratio of water. As a rule, use equal parts water for most foods, including salads, stir-fries and curries, grain dishes such as rice pilaf and for saucy stews. Use twice the volume of water to food for soups. Start with a smaller amount—you can always add more water if needed.

- For example: ½ cup of water to 1 cup of salad or stir-fry vegetables, 1 cup of water to 1 cup of dehydrated stew, and 2 cups of water to 1 cup of soup mix.

Cold soaking. This method is used for foods such as salads, cereals, and smoothies. Grain and vegetable dishes, such as pilafs, can also be soaked and eaten cold. Place the food and water in a jar, cover, and stir or shake every few minutes for 20 minutes to 2 hours, or longer if kept refrigerated, or in a thermos. For example, soak breakfast cereal overnight, and it's ready in the morning when you are. Or soak grain pilaf in the morning, and it's ready for lunch or dinner.

Heating food in water. Do this to rehydrate soups, stews, and one-pot meals using any of the following methods. Presoaking foods in cold water that will be heated is optional but has the dual benefit of reducing the heating time and saving fuel.

- For the fastest heating, in a saucepan, combine the dehydrated food and the water. Heat to boiling over high heat, reduce the heat to low, cover, and simmer, stirring occasionally, until fully hydrated, 5 to 8 minutes.
- In a microwave, in a microwave-safe bowl, combine the food and water. Microwave on high for 2 minutes or until boiling. Remove, cover, and let stand until fully hydrated, 6 to 10 minutes.
- To conserve fuel, heat water to boiling. In an insulated container, stir the water into the dehydrated food, cover, and let stand until fully hydrated, 10 to 15 minutes.

Food is ready when there are no crunchy bits. If needed, add more hot water and allow to soak until fully hydrated.

MADRAS-STYLE BEEF AND TOMATO CURRY

Prep/Cook Time: 40 minutes | Drying Temp & Time: 140° to 160°F for 8 to 12 hours | Yield: 4 to 6 servings

This beef jerky stew is flavored with Madras-style hot curry powder, lightened with yogurt. Two more curry recipes follow later in this chapter, each in a very different style. Curry is a great dish for dehydrated meals because the spices lose nothing in the process. The result is a satisfying one-dish meal chock-full of meat, vegetables, and flavor and as easy to make as it is warm and comforting. This tomato curry is particularly good served with potatoes.

1 to 2 tablespoons vegetable oil

1 medium onion, chopped (about 1 cup)

2 garlic cloves, minced

1 to 3 teaspoons Madras Curry Spice Mix (page 51)

1 teaspoon minced peeled fresh ginger

1 (15-ounce) can crushed tomatoes

1 cup beef broth or water

1 cup chopped cauliflower

1 to 2 serrano or other hot chiles, seeded and diced (optional)

Salt

Freshly ground black pepper

1 cup frozen green peas

7 to 10 ounces Nepalese-Style Smoked Dried Meat (page 80) or any teriyaki-style meat jerky, shredded

½ cup low-fat or nonfat yogurt

1. In a large skillet or sauté pan over medium-high heat, heat the oil until very hot. Add the onion, garlic, spice mix to taste, and ginger, and sauté until fragrant, 1 to 2 minutes. Add the tomatoes, broth, and cauliflower, and bring to a boil. Reduce the heat to low and simmer until the cauliflower is tender, 8 to 10 minutes. Taste and adjust the seasoning with salt, pepper, and spice mix. Remove from the heat. Stir in the chiles (if using), peas, meat, and yogurt.

2. Preheat a food dehydrator to 140° to 160°F. Spread the curry on lined drying trays in an even layer. After 4 to 6 hours, when the curry is firm but still moist, turn it over and break into clumps. Continue to check every 1 to 2 hours, breaking clumps into smaller pieces. Dry for 4 to 6 hours longer, until the pieces break with a snap with no visible signs of moisture.

STORAGE: If desired, divide into individual servings. You may also package it with dried rice or potatoes to be rehydrated together. Store for up to 2 weeks at room temperature, up to 2 months refrigerated, or up to 1 year frozen in an airtight container.

TO REHYDRATE: Combine 1 portion of curry (with or without side dish) with an equal portion of water, bring to a boil, cover, and simmer, stirring occasionally, until fully hydrated, 5 to 8 minutes.

MAKE IT VEGETARIAN: Replace the beef with one 16-ounce can of chickpeas, drained and rinsed, or 1 pound of red lentils, rinsed, or any other vegetarian substitute (see page 128) added in step 1 with the tomatoes.

CUBAN ROPA VIEJA BEEF AND PEPPER STEW

Prep/Cook Time: 1¾ hours | **Drying Temp & Time:** 140° to 160°F for 8 to 12 hours | **Yield:** 4 to 6 servings

This simple stew is a national dish of Cuba. The name means "old clothes" and refers to the way the meat and vegetables look when strewn on a platter. It is typically made with flank steak, but shredded dried beef makes a very acceptable stand-in when you want to preserve *ropa vieja* by dehydrating. Serve it over rice or with tortillas for wrapping and garnishes such as fried plantains, sliced green olives, sour cream, and fresh cilantro leaves.

1 tablespoon vegetable oil

1 medium yellow onion, chopped (about 1 cup)

1 medium green bell pepper, seeded and diced (1 cup)

1 medium red bell pepper, seeded and diced (1 cup)

1 medium yellow bell pepper, seeded and diced (1 cup)

2 garlic cloves, minced

1 cup white wine

1 (8-ounce) can tomato sauce

1 cup beef broth or water

1 tablespoon white vinegar

1 teaspoon ground cumin

7 to 10 ounces Mexican Dried Beef (page 81) or Hot Chile Pepper Beef Jerky (page 71) or any beef jerky, shredded

3 tablespoons chopped fresh parsley

1. In a large skillet or sauté pan over medium-high heat, heat the oil until hot, Add the onion, green pepper, red pepper, yellow pepper, and garlic, and sauté until well browned, 15 to 20 minutes. Stir in the wine and cook until almost evaporated, about 2 minutes. Stir in the tomato sauce, broth, vinegar, and cumin. Reduce the heat to low, cover, and simmer for 10 minutes. Uncover and simmer until the liquid is reduced by half, 20 to 30 minutes. Stir in the beef and parsley. Allow the stew to cool, uncovered, for 30 minutes.

2. Preheat a food dehydrator to 140° to 160°F. Spread the stew on lined drying trays in an even layer. After 4 to 6 hours, when the stew is firm but still moist, turn it over and break into clumps. Continue to check every 1 to 2 hours, breaking clumps into smaller pieces. Dry for 4 to 6 hours longer, until the pieces break with a snap with no visible signs of moisture.

STORAGE: If desired, divide into individual servings. You may also package it with dried rice or quinoa to be rehydrated together. Store for up to 2 weeks at room temperature, 2 months refrigerated, or 1 year frozen in an airtight container.

TO REHYDRATE: Combine 1 portion of stew (with or without side dish) with an equal portion of water, bring to a boil, cover, and simmer, stirring occasionally, until fully hydrated, 5 to 8 minutes.

MAKE IT VEGETARIAN: Replace the beef with a vegetarian substitute (see page 128) added in step 1 with the tomato sauce.

KOREAN BULGOGI BEEF OR PORK STEW

Prep/Cook Time: 1½ hours | Drying Temp & Time: 140° to 160°F for 8 to 12 hours | Yield: 4 to 6 servings

Bulgogi is a Korean dish of thinly grilled beef that has been marinated in soy, sesame, and black pepper. It is often enjoyed as part of a hot-pot meal with an array of vegetables around a steaming bowl of broth. Bulgogi is also great in lettuce wraps or over a bowl of rice.

1 pound mushrooms, sliced

3 garlic cloves, minced

1 medium yellow onion, chopped (about 1 cup)

1 medium carrot, diced (about ½ cup)

½ green bell pepper, seeded and diced (about ½ cup)

2 tablespoons all-purpose flour, rice flour, or dried ground rice

1 cup beef broth or water

¼ cup soy sauce

1 tablespoon honey or brown sugar (optional)

½ teaspoon ground black pepper

7 to 10 ounces Bulgogi-Style Dried Beef or Pork (page 76) or any teriyaki-style meat jerky, shredded

2 scallions, thinly sliced

2 tablespoons sesame seeds

1. In a large skillet or sauté pan, over medium-high heat, cook the mushrooms in a single layer until lightly browned, 5 minutes. Do not crowd; cook in batches if needed.

2. Reduce the heat to medium. Add the garlic, onion, carrot, and bell pepper, and sauté until soft, 3 to 5 minutes. Sprinkle with the flour and cook for 2 minutes, stirring constantly. Stir in the broth, soy sauce, honey (if using), and black pepper. Cover and bring to a boil, about 10 minutes. Uncover and cook until the liquid is reduced by about half, 20 to 30 minutes. Stir in the beef, scallions, and sesame seeds. Allow to cool, uncovered, for 30 minutes.

3. Preheat a food dehydrator to 140° to 160°F. Spread the stew on lined drying trays in an even layer. After 4 to 6 hours, when the stew is firm but still moist, turn it over and break into clumps. Continue to check every 1 to 2 hours, breaking clumps into smaller pieces. Dry for 4 to 6 hours longer, until the pieces break with a snap with no visible signs of moisture.

STORAGE: If desired, divide into individual servings. You may also package it with dried rice or bulgur to be rehydrated together. Store for up to 2 weeks at room temperature, 2 months refrigerated, or 1 year frozen in an airtight container.

TO REHYDRATE: Combine 1 portion of bulgogi (with or without side dish) with an equal portion of water, bring to a boil, cover, and simmer, stirring occasionally, until fully hydrated, 5 to 8 minutes.

MAKE IT VEGETARIAN: Replace the beef with a vegetarian substitute (see page 128) added in step 2 with the broth.

INDIAN LENTILS WITH LAMB (DAL GOSHT)

Prep/Cook Time: 1 hour 10 minutes | Drying Temp & Time: 140° to 160°F for 8 to 12 hours | Yield: 4 to 6 servings

Dal gosht simply means lentils and lamb. It's very quick to put together. Use a purchased curry powder if you haven't made your own. If you've made curries before, you'll feel right at home. If you haven't, this is a great recipe to introduce you to these wonderful, comforting flavors.

1 pound ground lamb, from lean leg or chops, trimmed of all fat

1 medium onion, chopped (about 1 cup)

2 serrano or other green chiles, seeded and minced

2 garlic cloves, minced

1 teaspoon minced peeled fresh ginger

1 tablespoon Madras or Coconut Curry Spices (page 51)

1 teaspoon sweet or smoked paprika

1 teaspoon ground coriander

1 teaspoon ground cumin

½ teaspoon salt

¼ teaspoon ground black pepper

1 (15-ounce) can chickpeas, drained and rinsed

1 (15-ounce) can diced tomatoes, undrained

½ cup dried red lentils (masoor dal)

3 tablespoons chopped fresh parsley or 1 tablespoon dried

1 cup water, or as needed

1. In a large skillet or sauté pan over medium-high heat, cook the lamb, onion, chiles, garlic, and ginger until the lamb turns from pink to gray, 5 to 8 minutes. Stir in the curry seasoning, paprika, coriander, cumin, salt, and pepper and cook until fragrant, 1 minute. Stir in the chickpeas, tomatoes, lentils parsley, and enough water to just cover the ingredients. Bring to a boil, reduce the heat to low, cover, and simmer until the lentils are soft (red lentils break down easily), about 15 minutes. Allow the mixture to cool, uncovered, for 30 minutes.

2. Preheat a food dehydrator to 140° to 160°F. Spread the dal on lined drying trays in an even layer. After 4 to 6 hours when the dal is firm but still moist, turn it over on and break into clumps. Continue to check every 1 to 2 hours, breaking clumps into smaller pieces. Dry for 4 to 6 hours longer, until the pieces break with a snap with no visible signs of moisture.

STORAGE: If desired, divide into individual servings. You may also package it with dried rice or potatoes to be rehydrated together. Store for up to 2 weeks at room temperature, 2 months refrigerated, or 1 year frozen in an airtight container.

TO REHYDRATE: Combine 1 portion of dal (with or without side dish) with an equal portion of water, bring to a boil, cover, and simmer, stirring occasionally, until fully hydrated, 5 to 8 minutes.

MAKE IT VEGETARIAN: Replace the lamb in step 1 with 12 to 16 ounces of drained and diced tofu. Alternatively, cook the aromatics without meat and add another can of chickpeas or drained red beans, or any other vegetarian substitute (see page 128).

RISOTTO WITH PANCETTA, PEAS, AND MUSHROOMS

Prep/Cook Time: 1 hour | Drying Temp & Time: 140° to 160°F for 8 to 12 hours | Yield: 6 to 8 servings

Risotto is a creamy rice dish made with arborio, a large, short-grained rice that contains more starch than long-grain rice. Short-grain sushi rice, pearled barley, or farro also make a creamy risotto. You can add vegetables, meats, or seafood to make a more substantial dish. It's a good dish to make ahead and dehydrate—without the butter and cheese, which you can stir in along with the water for rehydrating.

1 to 2 tablespoons olive or vegetable oil

1 medium leek (white and light-green parts), diced (1 cup)

4 ounces mushrooms (5 or 6 whole), chopped (1 to 1½ cups)

1 teaspoon salt

¼ teaspoon ground white or black pepper

2 cups arborio rice

½ cup white wine

4 to 5 cups hot chicken broth or water, divided, or as needed

6 to 12 ounces thinly sliced pancetta or deli meat, such as ham or turkey

1 cup frozen peas, chopped

1. In a large skillet or sauté pan over medium-high heat, heat the oil until hot. Add the leeks, mushrooms, salt, and pepper, and sauté until lightly browned, 5 to 8 minutes. Stir in the rice and wine; cook until the wine is nearly evaporated. Stir in ½ cup of broth, reduce the heat to medium, and cook, stirring, until the liquid is nearly evaporated. The liquid should simmer gently; adjust the heat as needed. Repeat, adding ½ cup of broth each time. When the rice is al dente, remove from the heat and stir in the pancetta and peas.

2. Preheat a food dehydrator to 140° to 160°F. Spread the risotto on lined drying trays in an even layer. After 4 to 6 hours, when the risotto is firm but still moist, turn it over and break into clumps. Continue to check every 1 to 2 hours, breaking clumps into smaller pieces. Dry for 4 to 6 hours longer, until the pieces break with a snap with no visible signs of moisture.

STORAGE: If desired, divide into individual servings. Store for up to 2 weeks at room temperature, 2 months refrigerated, or 1 year frozen in an airtight container.

TO REHYDRATE: Combine 1 portion of risotto with an equal portion of water, bring to a boil, cover, and simmer, stirring occasionally, until fully hydrated, 5 to 8 minutes. If desired, stir in 1 tablespoon of grated Parmesan cheese and 1 to 2 teaspoons of soft butter per serving.

MAKE IT VEGETARIAN: Replace the pancetta with a vegetarian substitute (see page 128) and use water or vegetable broth.

CAJUN-STYLE DIRTY RICE

Prep/Cook Time: 1½ hours | Drying Temp & Time: 140° to 160°F for 8 to 12 hours | Yield: 4 to 6 servings

Traditional dirty rice is flecked with meat, chicken livers and the Cajun holy trinity: onions, bell peppers, and celery. Ground beef, pork, or turkey can be used, with or without chicken livers. It was originally concocted by slaves and sharecroppers in the South, who made use of the spare ingredients available to them. It's now a regional favorite enjoyed across the country.

2 cups chicken broth or water

1 cup long-grain white rice

1 teaspoon salt

1 pound lean or extra lean (90 percent or higher) ground beef, pork, or turkey, or ½ pound lean ground meat and ½ pound chicken livers (6 to 10 average-size), ground together

1 small onion, chopped (½ cup)

1 small green bell pepper, seeded and diced (½ cup)

1 stalk celery, diced (½ cup)

2 garlic cloves, minced

1 to 2 teaspoons Taco and Chili Seasoning Blend (page 51)

½ teaspoon dried thyme

½ teaspoon salt

¼ teaspoon red pepper flakes or ground black pepper

¼ cup thinly sliced scallions or chopped fresh parsley

1. In a medium saucepan over high heat, bring the broth to a boil, stir in the rice and salt, reduce the heat to low, cover, and cook for 15 minutes. Turn off the heat, stir and fluff the rice, cover, and let stand until ready to use.

2. In a large skillet or sauté pan over medium-high heat, cook the meat until it turns from pink to gray, 5 to 8 minutes.

3. Reduce the heat to medium, add the onion, bell pepper, celery, garlic, seasoning blend to taste, thyme, salt, and red or black pepper and sauté until lightly browned, 3 to 5 minutes. Reduce the heat to medium-low, cover, and cook until the vegetables are soft and browned, 15 to 20 minutes. Stir in the rice and scallions. Taste and add more seasoning if needed. Allow the rice to cool, uncovered, for 30 minutes.

4. Preheat a food dehydrator to 140° to 160°F. Spread the rice on lined drying trays in an even layer. After 4 to 6 hours drying flip over on drying trays and break up clumps. Continue to check every hour and break up clumps into smaller pieces. Dry until the pieces break with a snap with no visible signs of moisture, 8 to 12 hours.

STORAGE: If desired, divide into individual servings. Store for up to 2 weeks at room temperature, 2 months refrigerated, or 1 year frozen in an airtight container.

TO REHYDRATE: Combine 1 portion of rice with an equal portion of water, bring to a boil, cover, and simmer, stirring occasionally, until fully hydrated, 5 to 8 minutes.

MAKE IT VEGETARIAN: Skip step 2. Replace the meat with chopped cooked mushrooms or any vegetarian substitute (see page 128) added in step 3.

UN-FRIED RICE WITH CHICKEN AND PORK

Prep/Cook Time: **1 hour 15 minutes** | Drying Temp & Time: **140° to 160°F for 8 to 12 hours** | Yield: **4 to 6 servings**

I call this un-fried rice because I've left out the egg, which can produce undesirable texture and shorten the storage life of the meal. If you want to try it, whisk 1 or 2 eggs. After the vegetables have browned in step 3, push them aside and pour in the egg. Allow the eggs to set for one minute, and then stir and cook until they start to scramble, about another minute, before finishing the dish.

8 ounces lean or extra lean (90 percent or higher) ground pork

8 ounces lean or extra lean (90 percent or higher) ground chicken or turkey

1 small onion, chopped (½ cup)

1 to 2 garlic cloves, minced

1 teaspoon minced peeled fresh ginger

1 small red bell pepper, seeded and diced (½ cup)

2 or 3 mushrooms, chopped (½ cup)

1 to 2 teaspoons soy sauce

½ teaspoon red pepper flakes or ground white or black pepper

1 cup frozen peas and carrots

1 or 2 scallions, thinly sliced

2 to 3 cups cooked rice

1. In a large skillet or sauté pan over medium-high heat, cook the ground pork, ground chicken, onion, garlic to taste, and ginger until the meat turns from pink to gray, 5 to 8 minutes.

2. Reduce the heat to medium, add the bell pepper and mushrooms, and sauté until the vegetables are soft and the mixture is beginning to brown, 5 to 8 minutes. Stir in the soy sauce to taste, pepper to taste, peas and carrots, and scallions to taste. Stir in the rice. Taste and add more soy sauce if needed. Allow the rice to cool, uncovered, for 30 minutes.

3. Preheat a food dehydrator to 140° to 160°F. Spread the rice on lined drying trays in an even layer. After 4 to 6 hours, when the rice is firm but still moist, turn it over and break into clumps. Continue to check every 1 to 2 hours, breaking clumps into smaller pieces. Dry for 4 to 6 hours longer, until the pieces break with a snap with no visible signs of moisture.

STORAGE: If desired, divide into individual servings. Store for up to 2 weeks at room temperature, 2 months refrigerated, or 1 year frozen in an airtight container.

TO REHYDRATE: Combine 1 portion of rice with an equal portion of water, bring to a boil, cover, and simmer, stirring occasionally, until fully hydrated, 5 to 8 minutes.

MAKE IT VEGETARIAN: Replace lean ground meat with chopped cooked mushrooms or any vegetarian substitute for meat (see page 128) added in step 2.

HAPPY FAMILY SWEET AND SOUR STIR-FRY

Prep/Cook Time: 1 hour | Drying Temp & Time: 140° to 160°F for 8 to 12 hours | Yield: 4 to 6 servings

"Happy family" in Chinese cooking refers to cooking several types of meat and seafood together with vegetables. Here is a stir-fry of pork, chicken, and shrimp in a homemade sweet and sour sauce with an array of colorful vegetables. It's a highly adaptable dish. You can change it up with different meats, seafood, or vegetables, as well as a different sauce such as teriyaki, bulgogi, or huli-huli or any bottled Asian cooking sauce.

FOR THE SWEET AND SOUR SAUCE:

1 tablespoon cornstarch

2 tablespoons water

¼ cup rice, white, or cider vinegar

¼ cup pineapple or orange juice

¼ cup tomato sauce or ketchup, or 1 teaspoon tomato powder whisked into ¼ cup water

2 tablespoons white or brown sugar

1 tablespoon soy sauce

FOR THE STIR-FRY:

8 ounces lean or extra lean (90 percent or higher) ground pork

1 small onion, chopped (½ cup)

1 or 2 garlic cloves, minced

1 teaspoon minced peeled fresh ginger

1 small red bell pepper, seeded and cut into strips (½ cup)

1. **FOR THE SWEET AND SOUR SAUCE:** In a medium bowl, whisk together the cornstarch and water; stir in the vinegar to taste, pineapple juice, tomato sauce, sugar to taste, and soy sauce. Set aside.

2. **FOR THE STIR-FRY:** In a large skillet or sauté pan over medium-high heat, cook the ground pork, onion, garlic to taste, and ginger until the pork turns from pink to gray, 5 to 8 minutes. Add the bell pepper, carrots, and mushrooms, and sauté until the vegetables are lightly browned, 5 to 8 minutes. Stir in the sweet and sour sauce, bring to a boil, and cook until the sauce thickens, about 2 minutes. Add the chicken, shrimp, cooked or frozen vegetables, pineapple, and scallions to taste, stirring until the chicken and vegetables are evenly coated with the sauce. Allow the stir-fry to cool, uncovered, for 30 minutes.

3. Preheat a food dehydrator to 140° to 160°F. Spread the stir-fry on lined drying trays in an even layer. After 4 to 6 hours, when the stir-fry is firm but still moist, turn it over and break into clumps. Continue to check every 1 to 2 hours, breaking clumps into smaller pieces. Dry for 4 to 6 hours longer, until the pieces break with a snap with no visible signs of moisture.

2 medium carrots, thinly
sliced (1 cup)

4 ounces mushrooms
(5 or 6 whole), thinly
sliced (1 to 1½ cups)

1 (5-ounce) can chicken,
drained if desired and
shredded or cut into
¼-inch dice

4 ounces cooked shrimp
(10 to 12 medium), sliced

½ cup cooked or frozen
vegetables, such as snow
peas, chopped broccoli,
peas, or peas and carrots

¼ cup diced pineapple
or mango

1 or 2 scallions, thinly sliced

STORAGE: If desired, divide into individual servings. You may also package it with dried rice to be rehydrated together. Store for up to 2 weeks at room temperature, 2 months refrigerated, or 1 year frozen in an airtight container.

TO REHYDRATE: Combine 1 portion of stir-fry (with or without side dish) with an equal portion of water, bring to a boil, cover, and simmer, stirring occasionally, until fully hydrated, 5 to 8 minutes.

MAKE IT VEGETARIAN: In step 2, omit browning the meat and begin by browning the bell pepper, carrots, and mushrooms. Replace the meats and shrimp with tofu or beans (see page 128) added with the cooked or frozen vegetables and pineapple in step 2.

CONVENIENCE FOODS TO DEHYDRATE

You can dry a variety of canned and frozen foods to save time when preparing basic supplies for your dehydrated pantry. Since prepared meats and seafood are already cooked, and vegetables are already blanched, dehydrating is a simple task.

In a few cases, drying prepared foods results in a better dried product than one that is homemade. For example, canned chicken and canned beans rehydrate more successfully after drying than home-cooked products, which often remain hard or pebbly.

MEAT AND SEAFOOD

Store dried meat or seafood in an airtight container for 1 to 2 weeks at room temperature or 1 to 2 months refrigerated, or up to 1 year frozen.

- **Lean deli meats (10 percent fat or less),** such as beef, turkey, or ham, cut into thin bite-size pieces. Dry at 135° to 145°F until hard, 4 to 6 hours. Remove any visible oil beads by patting meat with paper towels.
- **Canned chicken or seafood** (such as water-packed tuna, pink salmon, crabmeat, or imitation crab), drained. Shred or cut into ¼-inch or smaller dice. Dry at 135° to 145°F until crisp, 4 to 6 hours. Store for 1 to 2 weeks at room temperature or 1 to 2 months refrigerated.
- **Peeled and deveined medium shrimp** (40/50 count—do not get them any larger—they won't dry well). Thaw in the refrigerator if necessary and slice across into 4 or 5 coins. Dry at 135° to 145°F until hard, 4 to 6 hours.

DAIRY AND EGGS

Store dried yogurt in an airtight container for 1 to 2 days at room temperature or 1 to 2 months refrigerated.

- **Nonfat or low-fat yogurt (2 percent fat or less).** Greek-style yogurt has less water and takes less time to dry. Stir the yogurt to a smooth consistency, then spread thinly (⅛ inch) on lined drying trays. Dry at 125° to 135°F until brittle, 6 to 8 hours, or longer at 115° to 125°F to prevent discoloring. Grind into powder, or it will not rehydrate to a smooth consistency. Rehydrate 1 part yogurt powder to 1 to 3 parts liquid. The texture may be slightly gritty compared to the fresh product, but the dehydrated version tastes great.
- **Milk, cheese, and eggs are not recommended for home drying.** Commercially dried products are readily available.

BEANS AND LEGUMES

Store dried tofu, beans, and bean powders in an airtight container for 1 to 2 weeks at room temperature or 1 to 2 months refrigerated, or up to 1 year frozen.

- **Firm or extra-firm tofu.** Drain, then cut into ¼-inch slabs or ½-inch strips or cubes. Remove excess moisture to shorten drying time by pressing between towels for up to 30 minutes. If desired, brush the tofu with soy sauce or marinade, or toss with spices. Dry at 125° to 135°F until leathery, 6 to 8 hours.
- **Canned beans (drained), refried beans, or prepared hummus (made without oil).** Spread in a single layer on lined drying trays, no more than ¼ inch thick. Dry at 125° to 135°F until hard, 8 to 10 hours. Canned beans often split when dried; to avoid split beans, dry at a lower temperature (95° to 115°F).

FRUITS AND VEGETABLES

Store pliable fruits and vegetables in an airtight container for 1 to 2 weeks at room temperature or 1 to 2 months refrigerated. Store crisp dried produce or powders for 1 to 2 months at room temperature, up to 6 months refrigerated, and 1 year frozen.

- **Frozen fruits and vegetables, including hash browns.** For best results, dry one type of fruit or vegetable per tray or mixed pieces of uniform size. Partially thaw larger pieces such as broccoli florets and whole strawberries and cut into ½-inch or smaller pieces. Spread the frozen food on the drying trays in a single layer. Dry at 125° to 135°F until leathery or crisp, depending on intended use, 4 to 8 hours.
- **Bagged washed fresh sturdy greens (collards, kale, etc.).** Spread the fresh greens on the drying trays in a single layer (overlapping slightly). Dry at 125° to 135°F until crisp, 2 to 3 hours.
- **Canned beets or potatoes.** Shred or cut into uniform pieces ½ inch or smaller, pat dry, and dry at 125° to 135°F until leathery or crisp, 6 to 10 hours. Other canned vegetables contain a lot of moisture, so they are not optimal for drying.
- **Canned, jarred, or pouched sauerkraut or kimchi.** Drain, pat dry, and dry at 125° to 135°F until crisp, 3 to 6 hours.
- **Canned sauces (applesauce, tomato, or pasta sauce—without meat, cheese, or oil).** Spread thinly on lined drying trays. Dry at 125° to 135°F until leathery or crisp, 4 to 20 hours.
- **Canned fruit such as peach halves and pineapple slices**. Dry at 125° to 135°F until leathery, 6 to 10 hours.

THAI-STYLE RED CURRY WITH CHICKEN

Prep/Cook Time: 1 hour | Drying Temp & Time: 140° to 160°F for 8 to 12 hours | Yield: 4 to 6 servings

Canned chicken rehydrates better than dehydrated roasted or sautéed chicken. So save yourself some time and use canned chicken in this recipe. Whether you rinse the chicken or not is up to you. If you don't rinse it, you may want to leave out the additional salt. Cut the chicken into small pieces by pulling it apart in threads or cutting into ¼-inch or smaller dice. Substitute any vegetables in this recipe; you want about 3 to 4 cups total of chopped vegetables.

1 to 2 tablespoons vegetable oil

4 ounces mushrooms, chopped (1½ cups)

2 garlic cloves, minced

1 teaspoon minced peeled fresh ginger

1 large shallot or 1 small red onion, diced (½ cup)

1 medium carrot, diced (½ cup)

½ medium red bell pepper, seeded and diced (½ cup)

1 (13-ounce) can unsweetened coconut milk

1 cup chicken broth or water

1 tablespoon red curry paste

1 tablespoon fish sauce

1 tablespoon palm sugar

1 teaspoon sea salt

½ teaspoon ground white pepper

1 (12.5-ounce) can chicken, drained (if desired) and shredded or cut into ¼-inch dice

1 cup fresh spinach leaves, coarsely chopped

1. In a large skillet or sauté pan over medium-high heat, heat the oil until very hot. Add the mushrooms, garlic, and ginger, and sauté for 1 to 2 minutes. Add the shallot, carrot, and bell pepper, and sauté until lightly browned, 1 to 2 minutes. Stir in the coconut milk, broth or water, curry paste, fish sauce, sugar, salt, and pepper to taste. Bring to a boil and add the chicken and spinach. Reduce the heat to low, cover, and simmer until the flavors blend, 3 to 5 minutes. Allow the curry to cool, uncovered, for 30 minutes.

2. Preheat a food dehydrator to 140° to 160°F. Spread the curry on lined drying trays in an even layer. After 4 to 6 hours, when the curry is firm but still moist, turn it over and break into clumps. Continue to check every 1 to 2 hours, breaking clumps into smaller pieces. Dry for 4 to 6 hours longer, until the pieces break with a snap with no visible signs of moisture.

STORAGE: If desired, divide into individual servings. You may also package it with dried rice to be rehydrated together. Store for up to 2 weeks at room temperature, 2 months refrigerated, or 1 year frozen in an airtight container.

TO REHYDRATE: Combine 1 portion of curry (with or without side dish) with an equal portion of water, bring to a boil, cover, and simmer, stirring occasionally, until fully hydrated, 5 to 8 minutes.

MAKE IT VEGETARIAN: Replace the chicken in step 1 with tofu or any other vegetarian substitute (see page 128).

CHICKEN CACCIATORE HUNTER STEW

Prep/Cook Time: 1 hour 10 minutes | Drying Temp & Time: 140° to 160°F for 8 to 12 hours | Yield: 4 to 6 servings

Since *cacciatore* means hunter in Italian, some believe the original dish by this name was likely made with rabbit or game meat rather than chicken as is common today. This rustic stew is also a popular French bistro dish, where it goes by the name *chasseur*. The typical ingredients include chicken and mushrooms in a tomato sauce spiked with wine and flavored with herbs. It's a simple, adaptable, and economical dish that is always a crowd pleaser.

1 tablespoon olive oil

1 medium onion, chopped (1 cup)

1 medium (any color) bell pepper, seeded and diced (1 cup)

3 garlic cloves, minced

4 ounces mushrooms (5 or 6 whole), chopped (1 to 1½ cups)

½ cup dry red or white wine

1 (15-ounce) can diced tomatoes, undrained

1 (8-ounce) can tomato sauce

1 cup chicken broth or water

1 tablespoon Italian Herb Seasoning Blend (page 50)

1 (12.5-ounce) can chicken, drained if desired and shredded or cut into ¼-inch dice

½ teaspoon salt

¼ teaspoon ground black pepper

1. In a large skillet or sauté pan over medium-high heat, heat the oil until very hot. Add the onion, bell pepper, and garlic, and sauté until soft, 3 to 5 minutes. Add the mushrooms and cook until the vegetables begin to brown, 5 to 8 minutes. Stir in the wine and simmer until nearly evaporated. Add the tomatoes, tomato sauce, broth, seasoning blend, salt and pepper and bring to a boil. Stir in the chicken, reduce the heat to low, cover, and simmer until the flavors blend, 10 to 15 minutes. Allow the stew to cool, uncovered, for 30 minutes.

2. Preheat a food dehydrator to 140° to 160°F. Spread the stew on lined drying trays in an even layer. After 4 to 6 hours, when the stew is firm but still moist, turn it over and break into clumps. Continue to check every 1 to 2 hours, breaking clumps into smaller pieces. Dry for 4 to 6 hours longer, until the pieces break with a snap with no visible signs of moisture.

STORAGE: If desired, divide into individual servings. You may also package it with dried rice, polenta, or potatoes to be rehydrated together. Store for up to 2 weeks at room temperature, 2 months refrigerated, or 1 year frozen in an airtight container.

TO REHYDRATE: Combine 1 portion of stew (with or without side dish) with an equal portion of water, bring to a boil, cover, and simmer, stirring occasionally, until fully hydrated, 5 to 8 minutes.

MAKE IT VEGETARIAN: Replace the chicken in step 1 with tofu, or any other vegetarian substitute (see page 128).

SPANISH CHICKPEA AND SPINACH STEW

Prep/Cook Time: 1 hour | Drying Temp & Time: 140° to 160°F for 8 to 12 hours | Yield: 6 servings

This popular Spanish tapas dish comes together very easily. It's the kind of dish that improves when reheated, so it's a great choice for the dehydrated pantry. I specify sweet paprika, but you can replace some or all of it with hot or smoked paprika. This dish is typically made with cod, but canned chicken replaces the fish here. If you prefer a vegetarian dish, leave out the chicken, and if desired, add more chickpeas, beans, or any other vegetarian substitute for meat (see page 128).

1 to 2 tablespoons vegetable oil

1 medium red onion, diced (about 1 cup)

1 medium red or green bell pepper, seeded and diced (about 1 cup)

3 garlic cloves, minced

1 (15-ounce) can diced tomatoes, undrained

1 (8-ounce) can tomato sauce, or 1 tablespoon tomato powder whisked into 1 cup water

1 (15-ounce) can chickpeas, drained and rinsed

1 (12.5-ounce) can chicken, drained if desired and shredded or cut into ¼-inch dice

1 to 2 teaspoons sweet paprika

½ teaspoon ground cumin

½ teaspoon salt

¼ teaspoon red pepper flakes or cayenne pepper

2 cups (2 to 3 ounces) fresh spinach leaves, coarsely chopped

1. In a large skillet or sauté pan over medium-high heat, heat the oil until hot. Add the onion, bell pepper, and garlic, and sauté until soft, 3 to 5 minutes. Stir in the tomatoes, tomato sauce, chickpeas, chicken, paprika to taste, cumin, salt to taste, and red pepper flakes. Add water if needed to barely cover the ingredients. Bring to a boil, stir in the spinach, reduce the heat to low, and simmer for 10 minutes. Taste and adjust the seasonings with more salt or red pepper as needed. Allow the stew to cool, uncovered, for 30 minutes.

2. Preheat a food dehydrator to 140° to 160°F. Spread the stew on lined drying trays in an even layer. After 4 to 6 hours, when the stew is firm but still moist, turn it over and break into clumps. Continue to check every 1 to 2 hours, breaking clumps into smaller pieces. Dry for 4 to 6 hours longer, until the pieces break with a snap with no visible signs of moisture.

STORAGE: If desired, divide into individual servings. You may also package it with dried rice, quinoa, or potatoes to be rehydrated together. Store for up to 2 weeks at room temperature, 2 months refrigerated, or 1 year frozen in an airtight container.

TO REHYDRATE: Combine 1 portion of stew (with or without side dish) with an equal portion of water, bring to a boil, cover, and simmer, stirring occasionally, until fully hydrated, 5 to 8 minutes.

MAKE IT VEGETARIAN: Leave out the chicken in step 1. If desired, add more chickpeas or another vegetarian substitute (see page 128).

MOROCCAN CHICKEN AND VEGETABLE STEW

Prep/Cook Time: 1 hour 10 minutes | Drying Temp & Time: 140° to 160°F for 8 to 12 hours | Yield: 4 to 6 servings

This recipe is based on the Moroccan tagine or maraq. There are many variations for this stew-like dish. So feel free to make any meat, vegetable, and seasoning substitutions you wish. Serve as a soup or with rice, quinoa, or flatbread for a heartier meal.

1 to 2 tablespoons olive oil

2 medium carrots, diced

½ medium onion, chopped

2 garlic cloves, minced

1 to 2 teaspoons Berbere Ethiopian Spice Blend (page 50)

½ teaspoon salt

1 (14.5-ounce) can diced tomatoes, undrained

1 (15- to 16-ounce) can chickpeas, drained and rinsed

2 tablespoons fresh lemon juice or chopped preserved lemon

1 (12.5-ounce) can chicken, drained if desired and shredded or cut into ¼-inch dice

1 medium zucchini, diced (about 1 cup)

½ cup slivered almonds, toasted (see page 30)

½ cup dried fruit, such as raisins, apricots, or prunes, larger fruit cut ¼ inch or smaller

3 tablespoons minced fresh cilantro or parsley

2 tablespoons minced fresh mint (optional)

1. In a large skillet or sauté pan over medium-high heat, heat the oil until very hot. Add the carrots and onion, and sauté until soft and lightly browned, 8 to 10 minutes. Add the garlic, spice blend to taste, and salt to taste, and cook, stirring, until fragrant, 1 minute. Stir in the tomatoes, chickpeas, and lemon juice. Add water as needed to almost cover the ingredients. Remove 1 cup of the mixture and puree in a blender or food processor until smooth. Return the puree along with the chicken and zucchini to the pan. Cover and bring to a simmer, reduce the heat to low, and cook until the chicken is heated through and the carrots are tender, 3 to 5 minutes. Remove from the heat. Stir in the almonds, dried fruit, and cilantro. Allow the stew to cool, uncovered, for 30 minutes.

2. Preheat a food dehydrator to 140° to 160°F. Spread the stew on lined drying trays in an even layer. After 4 to 6 hours of drying, when the stew is firm but still moist, turn it over on the drying trays and break into clumps. Continue to check every 1 to 2 hours, breaking clumps into smaller pieces. Dry for 4 to 6 hours longer, until the pieces break with a snap with no visible signs of moisture.

STORAGE: If desired, divide into individual servings. Store for up to 2 weeks at room temperature, 2 months refrigerated, or up to 1 year frozen in an airtight container.

TO REHYDRATE: Combine 1 portion of stew with an equal portion of water, bring to a boil, cover, and simmer, stirring occasionally, until fully hydrated, 5 to 8 minutes.

MAKE IT VEGETARIAN: Omit the chicken in step 1. If you would like additional protein, add diced tofu or any other vegetarian substitute (see page 128).

WEST AFRICAN PEANUT STEW

Prep/Cook Time: 1 hour 10 minutes | Drying Temp & Time: 140° to 160°F for 8 to 12 hours |
Yield: 6 servings

According to cookbooks of the day, peanuts were popularly known as groundnuts in the first half of the 19th century. You can find many variations of West African groundnut or peanut stew or soup that include seasonal vegetables, herbs, and garnishes. In this recipe, collard greens, sweet potatoes, and chicken are added to the aromatic sauce.

1 tablespoon vegetable oil

1 medium red onion, chopped (1 cup)

4 garlic cloves, minced

2 tablespoons minced peeled fresh ginger

1 bunch (1 pound) collard greens or kale, stemmed and roughly chopped (about 6 cups)

1 quart chicken or vegetable broth or water, or as needed

1 pound sweet potatoes, peeled and diced

1 (8-ounce) can tomato sauce

1 teaspoon salt

¼ teaspoon Berbere Ethiopian Spice Blend (page 50) or hot chile powder

¼ cup peanut butter

1 (12.5-ounce) can chicken, drained if desired and shredded or cut into ¼-inch dice

1. In a large skillet or sauté pan over medium heat, heat the oil until hot. Add the onion, garlic, and ginger, and sauté until soft and fragrant, 3 to 5 minutes. Add the collards and stir until they wilt, 5 to 10 minutes. Increase the heat to high and add the broth or water, sweet potatoes, tomato sauce, salt, and spice blend. Add more water as needed to cover the ingredients. Bring to a boil, reduce the heat to low, and simmer until the sweet potatoes are tender, 8 to 10 minutes. Stir in the peanut butter and chicken. Taste and adjust the flavor with more salt, berbere, or peanut butter as needed. Allow the stew to cool, uncovered, for 30 minutes.

2. Preheat a food dehydrator to 140° to 160°F. Spread the stew on lined drying trays in an even layer. After 4 to 6 hours of drying, when the stew is firm but still moist, turn it over on the drying trays and break into clumps. Continue to check every 1 to 2 hours, breaking clumps into smaller pieces. Dry for 4 to 6 hours longer, until the pieces break with a snap with no visible signs of moisture.

STORAGE: If desired, divide into individual servings. You may also package it with dried rice, bulgur, or quinoa to be rehydrated together. Store for up to 2 weeks at room temperature, 2 months refrigerated, or 1 year frozen in an airtight container.
TO REHYDRATE: Combine 1 portion of stew (with or without side dish) with an equal portion of water, bring to a boil, cover, and simmer, stirring occasionally, until fully hydrated, 5 to 8 minutes.
MAKE IT VEGETARIAN: Replace the chicken with tofu, black-eyed peas, chickpeas, or any vegetarian substitute (see page 128).

HAWAIIAN-STYLE SHRIMP CURRY

Prep/Cook Time: 50 minutes | Drying Temp & Time: 140° to 160°F for 8 to 12 hours |
Yield: 4 to 6 servings

This is based on an old-school Hawaiian curry. It's served with toppings such as nuts and pineapple, which I suggest you add to the sauce before drying. Use medium-size (40/50 count) shrimp and cut into 4 to 5 slices; smaller shrimp dry too small and larger shrimp can take too long to dry.

1 to 2 tablespoons vegetable oil

½ medium onion, minced (½ cup)

3 garlic cloves, minced

2 teaspoons minced peeled fresh ginger

1 (14-ounce) can coconut milk

1 cup chicken broth or water

8 ounces yard-long beans or green beans, cut into 1-inch pieces (about 1½ cups)

1 tablespoon Madras Curry Spice Mix (page 51)

½ teaspoon salt

12 ounces medium (40/50 count) shrimp, peeled, deveined, and each cut into 4 or 5 slices

2 or 3 scallions, thinly sliced

¼ cup chopped macadamia nuts, cashews, almonds, or peanuts

¼ cup finely chopped fresh or canned crushed pineapple (optional)

2 tablespoons unsweetened shredded coconut (optional)

1. In a large skillet or sauté pan over medium-high heat, heat the oil until very hot. Add the onion, garlic, and ginger, and sauté until fragrant, 1 to 2 minutes. Add the coconut milk, broth, beans, spice mix, and salt, and bring to a boil. Reduce the heat to low, cover, and simmer for 5 minutes. Add the shrimp and simmer until the beans are tender-crisp and the shrimp are cooked through, 2 to 4 minutes. Remove from the heat and stir in the scallions, nuts, pineapple (if using), and coconut (if using). Allow the curry to cool, uncovered, for 30 minutes.

2. Preheat a food dehydrator to 135° to 145°F. Spread the curry on lined drying trays in an even layer. After 4 to 6 hours of drying, when the curry is firm but still moist, turn it over on the drying trays and break into clumps. Continue to check every 1 to 2 hours, breaking clumps into smaller pieces. Dry for 4 to 6 hours longer, until the pieces break with a snap with no visible signs of moisture.

STORAGE: If desired, divide into individual servings. You may also package it with dried rice or potatoes to be rehydrated together. Store for up to 2 weeks at room temperature, 2 months refrigerated, or 1 year frozen in an airtight container.

TO REHYDRATE: Combine 1 portion of curry (with or without side dish) with an equal portion of water, bring to a boil, cover, and simmer, stirring occasionally, until fully hydrated, 5 to 8 minutes.

MAKE IT VEGETARIAN: Replace the shrimp in step 1 with diced extra-firm tofu, or add 1 medium potato, peeled and diced, along with the broth and simmer until tender.

CHILEAN BEAN AND VEGETABLE STEW

Prep/Cook Time: 1½ hours | Drying Temp & Time: 140° to 160°F for 8 to 12 hours | Yield: 4 to 6 servings

Porotos granados is a traditional Chilean bean stew made with the "three sisters," the indigenous crops of the Americas: beans, corn, and winter squash. Depending on whose grandmother you talk to, the dish is made with yellow canary beans or mottled cranberry beans (also known as Roman beans). But pinto or white beans make a fine stand-in. Serve this thick and hearty dish with a fresh salsa made from diced tomato, banana pepper, and chopped cilantro, dressed with lime juice, oil, and hot pepper sauce. Or serve with standard chili accompaniments such as fresh cilantro leaves, cheese, and sour cream.

1 to 2 tablespoons vegetable oil

1 medium onion, chopped (1 cup)

2 garlic cloves, minced

1 teaspoon ground coriander

1 teaspoon ground cumin

1 teaspoon dried oregano

1 (15-ounce) can Romana, pinto, or white beans, undrained

1 (15-ounce) can diced or stewed tomatoes, undrained

1 cup frozen corn kernels or 1 (8-ounce) can corn, undrained

1 cup diced peeled winter squash (any variety such as butternut or acorn)

1 poblano pepper, roasted (see page 151), peeled, seeded, and diced

½ teaspoon salt

3 tablespoons chopped fresh parsley

1. In a large skillet or sauté pan over medium heat, heat the oil until hot. Add the onion, garlic, coriander, cumin, and oregano, and sauté until soft, 3 to 5 minutes. Add the beans, tomatoes, corn, squash, pepper, and salt, bring to a simmer, reduce the heat to low, cover, and simmer until the squash is tender, 10 to 15 minutes. Stir in the parsley and season to taste with more salt. Allow the stew to cool, uncovered, for 30 minutes.

2. Preheat a food dehydrator to 140° to 160°F. Spread the stew on lined drying trays in an even layer. After 4 to 6 hours of drying, when the stew is firm but still moist, turn it over on the drying trays and break into clumps. Continue to check every 1 to 2 hours, breaking clumps into smaller pieces. Dry for 4 to 6 hours longer, until the pieces break with a snap with no visible signs of moisture.

STORAGE: If desired, divide into individual servings. You may also package it with dried rice or quinoa to be rehydrated together. Store for up to 2 weeks at room temperature, 2 months refrigerated, or 1 year frozen in an airtight container.

TO REHYDRATE: Combine 1 portion of beans (with or without side dish) with an equal portion of water, bring to a boil, cover, and simmer, stirring occasionally, until fully hydrated, 5 to 8 minutes.

MEAT OPTION: Add 7 to 10 ounces of dried beef or jerky, shredded, with the parsley in step 1. Alternatively, prepare as for Classic Western Ground Beef Chili (page 129) with ground beef.

HOW TO ROAST PEPPERS

For one or two peppers, it is usually easiest to roast peppers on the stovetop or a gas grill. Place the peppers directly over a gas flame or grill, or place in a grill pan.

For more than two peppers, it is easier to oven-broil. Preheat the broiler on high. Place the peppers on a parchment- or foil-lined baking sheet on the upper rack, at least 6 inches from the broiler.

For either method, roast until charred on all sides, soft, and collapsing, 20 to 25 minutes. Use tongs to turn the peppers every 4 to 5 minutes.

Put the charred peppers in a paper bag or wrap loosely in aluminum foil and let stand for 10 minutes, to steam and loosen the skins. Peel, stem, seed, and dice the peppers, or prepare as directed in your recipe.

PUERTO RICAN PINK BEANS

Prep/Cook Time: 1 hour | Drying Temp & Time: 140° to 160°F for 8 to 12 hours | Yield: 6 servings

Puerto Rican creole cooking is a blend of native, Spanish, and African influences. These beans are a step away from the national dish *arroz con gandules* made with pigeon peas and an aromatic sofrito. Here, more familiar pinto and red beans are featured, but feel free to substitute other beans. Serve as a vegetarian meal with rice or plantains, garnished with green olives. As a side dish, these flavorful beans complement a platter of ribs, roast chicken, or grilled fish.

1 to 2 tablespoons vegetable oil

1 small onion, chopped (½ cup)

1 small green bell pepper, seeded and diced (½ cup)

3 or 4 garlic cloves, minced

2 teaspoons minced fresh cilantro

2 (15-ounce) cans pink, red, or pinto beans, undrained

1 (8-ounce) can tomato sauce

1 medium potato, peeled and diced

1 teaspoon ground coriander

1 teaspoon ground cumin

½ teaspoon dried oregano

½ teaspoon salt

¼ teaspoon ground black pepper

2 tablespoons chopped fresh parsley

1. In a large skillet or sauté pan over medium heat, heat the oil until hot. Add the onion, bell pepper, garlic to taste, and cilantro, and sauté until soft, 3 to 5 minutes. Add the beans, tomato sauce, potato, coriander, cumin, oregano, salt, and pepper, bring to a simmer, reduce the heat to low, cover, and simmer until the potato is tender, 10 to 15 minutes. Stir in the parsley. Allow the beans to cool, uncovered, for 30 minutes.

2. Preheat a food dehydrator to 135° to 145°F. Spread the beans on lined drying trays in an even layer. After 4 to 6 hours of drying, when the beans are firm but still moist, turn them over on the drying trays and break into clumps. Continue to check every 1 to 2 hours, breaking clumps into smaller pieces. Dry for 4 to 6 hours longer, until the pieces break with a snap with no visible signs of moisture.

STORAGE: If desired, divide into individual servings. You may also package the beans with dried rice, potatoes, or plantains to be rehydrated together. Store for up to 2 weeks at room temperature, 2 months refrigerated, or 1 year frozen in an airtight container.

TO REHYDRATE: Combine 1 portion of beans (with or without side dish) with an equal portion of water, bring to a boil, cover, and simmer, stirring occasionally, until fully hydrated, 5 to 8 minutes.

MEAT OPTION: Instead of vegetable oil, use 2 slices (2 ounces) of lean ham, chopped and sautéed with the vegetables in step 1. Add 7 to 10 ounces of carne seca (page 81), shredded, with the tomato sauce and beans in step 1.

DRIED RICE

Prep Time: 40 to 65 minutes | Drying Temp & Time: **125° to 135°F for 3 to 6 hours** | Yield: **4 to 6 servings**

There are a few tricks to cooking and dehydrating rice. To boost flavor, cook it in broth instead of water, but make sure the broth is fat-free. You want to decrease the water and slightly under-cook the rice, since it finishes cooking when rehydrated. Break up clumps before it finishes drying to avoid clumps that won't break up once rehydrated. Use dehydrated rice as a side dish or to assemble ready-to-reheat meals. Swap out the broth for milk (regular or dairy-free) and add sugar for a rice porridge suitable for breakfast or dessert (see variation below).

1 cup long-grain white or brown rice

1½ cups (for white rice) to 1¾ cups (for brown rice) water or fat-free beef, chicken, or vegetable broth

½ teaspoon salt (optional)

1. In a medium saucepan, combine the rice, water, and salt (if using). Bring to a boil over high heat. Reduce the heat to low, cover with a tight-fitting lid, and simmer gently for 15 minutes for white rice and 40 minutes for brown rice. Remove from the heat and keep the lid on to finish steaming for 10 minutes. The rice should be firm and dry and fluff up easily with a fork.

2. Preheat a food dehydrator to 125° to 135°F. Spread the rice on lined drying trays in a loose, even layer. Every hour or so, rub any clumps between your fingers to break them up. Dry the rice until hard, 3 to 6 hours.

STORAGE: Up to 3 months at room temperature, 6 months refrigerated, or 1 year frozen in an airtight container.

TO REHYDRATE: Pour 1 part (½ cup) boiling water over 1 part (½ cup) dehydrated rice, cover, and let stand until fully rehydrated, 10 to 15 minutes.

RICE PORRIDGE: Use low-fat milk, coconut milk, or almond milk in place of the water or broth, and add 1 to 2 tablespoons of sugar and ½ teaspoon of salt (optional).

DRIED QUINOA

Prep/Cook Time: **35 minutes** | Drying Temp & Time: **125° to 135°F for 3 to 6 hours** | Yield: **4 servings**

Quinoa (pronounced KEEN-wa) is a seed that is prepared and used like other grains such as rice and bulgur. The ancient grain is a popular staple in Peru and Bolivia, where it has been cultivated for thousands of years. Quinoa is a high-fiber, high-protein, gluten-free food with a delicious, nutty taste. Cook it for a side dish, use it in salads, soups, or pilafs, or prepare it as a breakfast porridge. White or ivory quinoa is most common, but yellow, red, brown, and black varieties are grown and can be found packaged together as a multi-color blend.

1 cup white, red, or tri-color quinoa

1⅓ cups water or fat-free beef, chicken, or vegetable broth

½ teaspoon salt (optional)

1. Place the quinoa in a fine mesh strainer and rinse under cold water until the water runs clear. In a medium saucepan, combine the quinoa, water, and salt (if using). Bring to a boil over high heat. Reduce the heat to low, cover with a tight-fitting lid, and simmer gently for 15 minutes. Remove from the heat and keep the lid on to finish steaming until firm and dry, about 5 minutes.

2. Preheat a food dehydrator to 125° to 135°F. Spread the quinoa on lined drying trays in a loose, even layer. Every hour or so, rub any clumps between your fingers to break them up. Dry the quinoa until hard, 3 to 6 hours.

STORAGE: Up to 3 months at room temperature, 6 months refrigerated, or 1 year frozen in an airtight container.

TO REHYDRATE: Pour 1 part (½ cup) boiling water over 1 part (½ cup) dehydrated quinoa, cover, and let stand until fully rehydrated, 10 to 15 minutes.

QUINOA PORRIDGE: Use low-fat milk, coconut milk, or almond milk in place of the water or broth, and add 1 to 2 tablespoons of sugar and ½ teaspoon of salt (optional).

DRIED BULGUR WHEAT

Prep/Cook Time: 35 to 45 minutes | Drying Temp & Time: 125° to 135°F for 3 to 6 hours | Yield: 4 servings

Bulgur is precooked cracked wheat berries, making it a quick-cooking whole grain. You may be familiar with bulgur as the grain in tabbouleh salad. Use bulgur in the same way you do rice, as a side dish as well as in soups, salads, and pilafs. Bulgur can be purchased in different grades from fine to coarse. For the most flexibility, choose a medium bulgur. As with other grains, cook bulgur until the water is absorbed but the grains are firm but chewy for best texture when it is rehydrated later.

1 cup medium bulgur

1¾ cups water or fat-free beef, chicken, or vegetable broth

½ teaspoon salt (optional)

1. In a medium saucepan, combine the bulgur, water, and salt (if using). Bring to a boil over high heat. Reduce the heat to low, cover with a tight-fitting lid, and simmer gently for 15 minutes. Remove from the heat and keep the lid on to finish steaming until the bulgur is firm but chewy, about 5 minutes.

2. Preheat a food dehydrator to 125° to 135°F. Spread the bulgur on lined drying trays in a loose, even layer. Every hour or so, rub any clumps between your fingers to break them up. Dry the bulgur until hard, 3 to 6 hours.

STORAGE: Up to 3 months at room temperature, 6 months refrigerated, or 1 year frozen in an airtight container.

TO REHYDRATE: Pour 1 part (½ cup) boiling water over 1 part (½ cup) dehydrated bulgur, cover, and let stand until fully rehydrated, 10 to 15 minutes.

BULGUR WHEAT PORRIDGE: Use low-fat milk, coconut milk, or almond milk in place of the water or broth, and add 1 to 2 tablespoons of sugar and ½ teaspoon of salt (optional).

DRIED POLENTA OR GRITS

Prep/Cook Time: **30 minutes** | Drying Temp & Time: **125° to 135°F for 3 to 6 hours** | Yield: **4 servings**

You can easily prepare homemade instant grits from whole-grain coarsely ground cornmeal. They'll rehydrate just like store-bought instant grits but taste much better with great corn flavor. You can dehydrate them as a savory side with broth or for porridge with milk and sugar. Stir in dried fruits and nuts for a delicious breakfast. Serve savory polenta instead of potatoes, rice, or pasta, dressed up if you like with dried tomatoes or mushrooms, herbs, and seasonings. Top polenta with stew, stir-fry, or marinara sauce.

1 cup coarsely ground white or yellow polenta or grits

3 cups water or fat-free beef, chicken, or vegetable broth

½ teaspoon salt (optional)

1. In a medium saucepan, combine the polenta, water, and salt (if using). Bring to a boil over high heat and cook for 5 minutes. Reduce the heat to low, cover with a tight-fitting lid, and simmer gently for 10 minutes. Remove from the heat and keep the lid on to finish steaming, 10 minutes.

2. Preheat a food dehydrator to 125° to 135°F. Polenta is sticky, and rinsing or dipping your hands or spoons in cold water makes it easier to handle. Drop small clumps onto lined drying trays. Every hour or so, check the polenta and pull apart clumps to break them up into smaller pieces. Dry the polenta until hard, 3 to 6 hours. Rub handfuls of it between your palms to break any remaining clumps into pebble-size or smaller pieces. You can also pulse in a food processor or blender to make it fine again, but small clumps are okay, too.

STORAGE: Up to 3 months at room temperature, 6 months refrigerated, or 1 year frozen in an airtight container.

TO REHYDRATE: Pour 1 part (½ cup) boiling water over 1 part (½ cup) dehydrated polenta, cover, and let stand for 10 to 15 minutes or until fully rehydrated. Stir to break up any lumps. For softer polenta, stir in more hot water to the consistency desired.

SWEET GRITS PORRIDGE: Use low-fat milk, coconut milk, or almond milk in place of the water or broth, and add 1 to 2 tablespoons of sugar and ½ teaspoon of salt (optional).

DRIED PASTA

Prep/Cook Time: 15 minutes | Drying Temp & Time: 125° to 135°F for 3 to 6 hours, longer for "nests" | Yield: 3 to 4 servings for entrées served with a sauce, 5 to 8 servings for soups or sides

Dehydrated cooked pasta rehydrates quickly in hot water, soups, or sauces. This saves fuel when you are camping or hiking and saves time wherever you might be. It can also be added to convenience meals—with other dried ingredients and will rehydrate at the same rate. Be sure to undercook pasta slightly, firmer than "al dente," because it will finish cooking when reheated. Short, small pasta shapes such as elbows, shells, fusilli, and farfalle present fewer challenges in cooking and drying. If you want to dehydrate long pastas such as spaghetti, linguine, or angel hair, swirl the cooked strands on the drying trays into serving-size "nests" to hide the sharp ends that can pierce plastic bags. To facilitate drying, make sure the nests are flat and loose. Flip the nests over when mostly dried to ensure the underside and center are fully dried.

1 pound pasta

1 teaspoon salt

1. In a stockpot over high heat, bring 4 to 6 quarts water to a boil. Add the pasta and salt, stir, cover, and start timing immediately. After a few minutes, the water will return to a boil; uncover the pot to prevent it from boiling over and stir the pasta again to break up any clumps.

2. Start checking the pasta's doneness after 4 minutes by spooning out a piece and cutting or biting it in two. Cook the pasta until slightly underdone. Most pasta is ready in 6 to 10 minutes. Pasta is ready when showing a sliver of white in the center. Drain and rinse briefly with cold water to stop the cooking and separate the individual pieces for drying.

3. Preheat a food dehydrator to 125° to 135°F. Spread the pasta on the drying trays in a single, loose layer without overlapping. For long pasta such as spaghetti, swirl each serving into a nest to prevent sharp corners. Dry the pasta until hard, 3 to 6 hours.

STORAGE: Up to 3 months at room temperature, 6 months refrigerated, or 1 year frozen in an airtight container.
TO REHYDRATE: Pour 1 part (½ cup) boiling water over 1 part (½ cup) dehydrated pasta, cover, and let stand until al dente, 8 to 12 minutes. Thinner pastas (such as farfalle) take less time to rehydrate than thicker pasta (such as rigatoni).

DRIED MASHED POTATOES

Prep/Cook Time: 30 minutes | **Drying Temp & Time:** 125° to 135°F for 3 to 6 hours | **Yield:** 4 servings

There are several ways to make dehydrated mashed potatoes, but I like the following method best, because it is easy and relatively foolproof, takes less time, and produces a more reliable product for rehydration compared to drying soupy or thick mashed potatoes. For best results, choose baking or all-purpose potatoes such as russet or Yukon Gold. This same process also works for sweet potatoes, turnips, rutabagas, and winter squash.

2 pounds baking or
    all-purpose potatoes

1 teaspoon salt

1. Wash the potatoes, peel, trim any blemishes or green areas, and cut into quarters. Place in a medium saucepan, cover with cold water, and bring to a boil over high heat. Reduce the heat to low, add the salt, and simmer until the potatoes are tender when pierced with a knife, 10 to 15 minutes. It is important that the potatoes be fully cooked but not soft or falling apart. Drain, cover with cold water, and let stand until cool enough to handle, about 10 minutes.

2. Preheat a food dehydrator to 125° to 135°F. Drain the potatoes and pat dry. Shred using a grater or mandoline. Spread the potato shreds on the drying trays in a loose, even layer. Dry until hard, 3 to 6 hours. For use as mashed potatoes, grind the potato shreds to a powder.

STORAGE: Up to 3 months at room temperature, 6 months refrigerated, or 1 year frozen in an airtight container.

TO REHYDRATE: Pour 1 part (½ cup) boiling water over 1 part (½ cup) potato powder. If desired, add salt, pepper, and 1 tablespoon butter with the boiling water to season the mashed potatoes as they rehydrate, cover, and let stand until fully rehydrated, 10 to 15 minutes. Stir to break up any lumps. For softer potatoes, stir in more hot water to the consistency desired.

SWEET AND SAVORY RICE PILAF

Prep/Cook Time: 1¾ hours | Drying Temp & Time: 125° to 135°F for 3 to 6 hours | Yield: 4 to 6 servings

A rice pilaf combines vegetables and grains into one great side dish. It's a great accompaniment to have on hand for grilled meats, or even as a lighter or vegetarian meal all by itself. This is a basic recipe that you can adapt. Change up the vegetables, fruits, nuts, and seasonings to suit your taste. Be sure to adjust the cooking time if you substitute longer-cooking grains such as bulgur or farro. In this case, either soak the grain to shorten the cooking time, or wait to add the vegetables, fruits, and nuts until halfway through the cooking time. I suggest baking in the oven, but you can also steam the pilaf on the stovetop as you would when cooking plain rice or grains.

2 tablespoons olive or vegetable oil or butter

1 small onion, shallot, or leek, chopped (½ cup)

1 cup long-grain white rice

1 small garlic clove, minced

1 teaspoon salt

½ teaspoon curry powder

¼ teaspoon turmeric powder

¼ teaspoon crushed dried thyme leaves

2 cups fat-free beef, chicken, or vegetable broth

½ cup frozen peas and carrots

¼ cup slivered almonds or chopped pecans, toasted (see page 30)

¼ cup raisins or finely chopped dried apricots or pineapple

1. Preheat the oven to 375°F. In a flameproof covered casserole over medium heat, heat the oil until hot. Add the onion and sauté until soft, 3 to 5 minutes. Stir in the rice and cook until it starts to brown, 3 to 5 minutes. Add the garlic, salt, curry powder, turmeric powder, and thyme, and cook, stirring, until fragrant, about 30 seconds. Add the broth, peas and carrots, almonds or pecans, and raisins. Bring to a simmer, cover, and transfer to the oven. Bake, covered, until the broth is completely absorbed, 15 to 20 minutes.

2. Uncover, fluff with a fork, and let the pilaf cool for 30 minutes.

3. Preheat a food dehydrator to 125° to 135°F. Spread the pilaf on the drying trays in a loose, even layer no more than ½ inch thick. Every hour or so, rub any clumps between your fingers to break them up. Dry until hard, 3 to 6 hours.

STORAGE: Up to 2 weeks at room temperature, 2 months refrigerated, and 1 year frozen in an airtight container.
TO REHYDRATE: Pour 1 part (½ cup) boiling water over 1 part (½ cup) dehydrated pilaf, cover, and let stand until fully rehydrated, 10 to 15 minutes.

SHREDDED VEGETABLE SALAD

Prep Time (including marination): 25 hours | **Drying Temp & Time:** 125° to 135°F for 10 to 14 hours | **Yield:** 7 to 9 servings

Here's a great technique for anyone to use who wants freshly made vegetable salads from your dried pantry. Simply prepare the vegetables as you would for coleslaw, draw out moisture with a salt-sugar marinade, replace that moisture with a seasoned vinegar, and then dehydrate the dressed vegetables. I suggest typical coleslaw vegetables, but feel free to substitute almost any shredded vegetable or fruit, such as beets, cucumbers, summer squash, celery, fennel, radish or daikon, bell peppers, hot peppers, apples, mango, or pineapple. To help you gauge quantities, 2 cups of fresh vegetables dries to 1 cup, or 3 servings of ⅓ cup each. You can turn the slaw into a quick meal by adding chicken or beef or a vegetarian protein and use it as a filling for tortillas, raw "flaxi-wraps," or lettuce wraps.

½ medium cabbage head, cored and sliced ¹⁄₁₆ inch thick (4 to 5 cups)

1 medium carrot, shredded (½ cup)

½ medium red onion, quartered and sliced ¹⁄₁₆ inch thick (½ cup)

2 tablespoons roughly chopped fresh parsley

½ cup sugar

¼ cup kosher salt or ½ cup table salt

½ cup apple cider vinegar or red wine vinegar

¼ cup honey or packed brown sugar

½ teaspoon mustard or celery seeds

½ teaspoon garlic powder

½ teaspoon black pepper

1. In a large heatproof bowl, combine the cabbage, carrot, onion, and parsley and sprinkle with the sugar and salt. Toss the vegetables until well combined. Let stand for 5 minutes. Transfer the vegetables to a colander and rinse thoroughly under cold running water. Dry in a salad spinner or spread loosely on towels and blot with more towels. Dry the bowl and return the vegetables to it.

2. In a small saucepan, stir together the vinegar, honey, mustard seeds, garlic powder, and pepper. Bring to a boil over high heat and cook, stirring, until the honey is dissolved. Pour over the vegetables and toss until evenly coated. Cover and refrigerate for 24 hours, tossing the vegetables every few hours to redistribute the dressing.

3. Preheat a food dehydrator to 125° to 135°F. Arrange the vegetables on the drying trays in a loose, even layer no more than ½ inch thick. Dry until crunchy but not brittle, 10 to 14 hours.

STORAGE: Up to 1 year at room temperature in an airtight container.

TO REHYDRATE: For each serving, cover ⅓ cup of salad with ⅓ cup of water and let stand 30 minutes or until fully rehydrated.

MEAL KITS

These are template recipes you can use to make many different types of meals. Once you put them together in a bag or jar, they can sit in your dry pantry, ready to rehydrate at home or to take along to the office or on a trip.

Each recipe makes 1 serving and includes a separate meat or vegetarian option. Since protein foods have a shorter storage life, you may want to add them at the last minute—before preparing your meal at home or to go.

The recipes list volume, but if you are using a food scale to weigh your servings, aim for a dehydrated ingredient weight of 3 to 4 ounces of vegetables, fruits, or grains, and if you are including a protein, a weight of 1 to 2 ounces, for a total weight of 4 to 6 ounces per serving.

INSTANT CEREAL WITH FRUIT AND NUTS

You can enjoy hot or cold cereal in an instant by combining your favorite grains, fruits, nuts, and seasonings. It's great for busy mornings, breakfast at the office, or any time of day you want a delicious, healthy, comforting snack.

Dehydrated ingredients:
½ cup dried porridge (rice, quinoa, bulgur wheat, or grits) or instant oats or chopped rolled oats (pulse 10 times in a food processor)

¼ cup dried chopped fruit (apples, blueberries, cranberries, mango, raisins, peaches, etc.)

¼ cup dried nuts or seeds (walnuts, almonds, pumpkin, sesame, chia, flax, etc.)

2 tablespoons dried milk or yogurt powder (optional if porridge was prepared with milk)

Optional flavorings:
1 tablespoon dried shredded coconut

1 tablespoon chopped dried orange zest

1 to 3 teaspoons brown sugar (optional if porridge is sweetened), to taste

Dash ground cinnamon

Pinch sea salt

If you'd like more protein:
1 to 2 tablespoons protein powder (whey, pea, hemp, spirulina, etc.), to taste

To rehydrate: Stir ¾ cup of boiling water into the cereal and let stand until full hydrated, about 5 minutes. Add more boiling water if needed to desired consistency. You can also eat cereal mix as a dry snack.

Suggested combinations:
Rice cooked in coconut milk, blueberries, almonds, and coconut

Bulgur, cranberries, pumpkin seeds, dairy milk powder, orange zest, brown sugar, and cinnamon

Oats, apples, walnuts, flaxseed, chia seed, and brown sugar

FRUIT AND VEGETABLE SMOOTHIE

Smoothies are many people's favorite way to enjoy a healthy drinkable meal packed with flavor and nutrients. They are typically made with fresh produce, but you can also enjoy the same ingredients by combining dried fruits and vegetables with seasonings, protein powder, and other ingredients.

Dehydrated ingredients:

¼ to ½ cup dried chopped greens or 2 to 4 tablespoons dried powder (kale, spinach, etc.)

¼ cup dried chopped fruit (apples, blueberries, cranberries, mango, raisins, peaches, etc.)

10 to 20 dehydrated banana slices or ¼ cup dried vegetable slices (carrots, beets, cucumber, celery)

2 tablespoons dried milk or yogurt powder

1 tablespoon dehydrated grains (rice, quinoa, grits, etc.) or dried seeds (sesame, chia, hemp, flaxseed, etc.), optional

Optional flavoring combos:

1 teaspoon unsweetened cocoa powder and ⅛ teaspoon cayenne pepper

¼ teaspoon ground cinnamon and ¼ teaspoon vanilla powder

1 teaspoon chopped dried orange zest and ⅛ teaspoon ginger or turmeric powder

If you'd like more protein:

1 to 2 tablespoons protein powder (whey, pea, hemp, spirulina, etc.)

To rehydrate: Shake the mix with 1 cup of cold water or milk (dairy or nondairy) until smooth. Alternatively, blend with 1 cup of ice cubes and water.

Suggested combinations:

Spinach, apple, beets, or blueberries, cucumber, celery, and yogurt powder

Spinach, avocado, carrot, pineapple, and flaxseed

Kale, banana, avocado, mango, rice, and orange zest

CITRUS-SCENTED DRIED FRUIT COMPOTE

Fruit compote is nothing more than fruit chunks cooked or stewed with sweetener, spices, and other flavorings. Classic recipes include apples, plums, figs, and rhubarb, but almost any fruit can be used to make compote.

Dehydrated ingredients:

½ cup (about 3 ounces) dried sliced or chopped fruits and whole berries

1 tablespoon dried shredded coconut

1 teaspoon chopped dried orange zest

¼ teaspoon chopped dried lemon or lime zest

Flavorings:

1 teaspoon brown sugar

Dash ground cinnamon

Pinch vanilla powder

Pinch ginger powder

Pinch salt

If you'd like protein:

2 to 3 tablespoons dried milk or yogurt powder and/or 2 to 3 tablespoons chopped dried nuts

To rehydrate: Stir ½ cup of hot water into the fruit and let stand until fully hydrated, about 5 minutes. Serve warm with yogurt, cereal, or ice cream. If the fruit is very dry, add more water as needed and let stand for another 5 minutes. If you add dried milk or yogurt powder and/or dried nuts, you may need to add an additional ¼ to ½ cup of water.

Suggested combinations:
Apple and fig with lemon zest and ground cinnamon
Pear and cranberry with orange zest and ginger powder
Pineapple and kiwi with lime zest and dried shredded coconut

HERB AND VEGETABLE SOUP CUP

Why buy instant soup cups that often contain too much salt and unpronounceable ingredients, when it's so easy to make your own? The sky's the limit. Customize just-add-water soups with vegetables, seasonings, and other simple ingredients--even meat jerky— from your dried pantry.

Dehydrated ingredients:
½ cup mixed dried chopped vegetables

Flavorings:
1 teaspoon dehydrated broth or
    soup base
1 teaspoon tomato powder
½ teaspoon crushed dried herbs of
    your choice

Dash salt
Dash onion powder, garlic powder, citrus
    powder, or ground black pepper
1 to 2 tablespoons milk powder (dairy,
    coconut, nut, rice), potato flakes,
    bean powder, or cheese powder for
    creamy soups

If you'd like meat:
1 ounce shredded dried meat or jerky

To rehydrate: Stir 1 cup of boiling water into ½ cup of soup mix, cover, and let stand until rehydrated, 8 to 10 minutes. Add additional hot water as needed for desired consistency.

Suggested combinations:
Chunky Tomato Basil: diced tomatoes, tomato powder, milk or potato powder, dried basil, marjoram or oregano, onion powder, garlic powder, salt, and black pepper
Three Sisters Chilean Bean: beans, winter squash, corn, tomatoes, bell peppers, onion powder, garlic powder, ground coriander, ground cumin, dried oregano, salt, and black pepper
Thai-Style Coconut Curry: vegetable broth powder or soup base, mushrooms, shallots, carrots, red bell peppers, spinach, Coconut Curry Spices (page 51), red bell pepper powder, garlic powder, ginger powder, sugar, salt, white and/or hot chile

HEARTY VEGETABLE SOUP BOWL

Make a more substantial vegetable soup by adding dried beans, grains, or potatoes to a basic recipe.

Dehydrated ingredients:
½ cup dried starches (beans, pasta, rice or grains, diced potatoes or flakes, winter squash)
½ cup dried chopped vegetables (onions, carrots, celery, cabbage, corn, beets, asparagus, green beans, zucchini, tomatoes, cauliflower, etc.)

Flavorings:
1 to 2 teaspoons dehydrated broth or soup base
1 sheet dried seaweed (nori, kombu, kelp, dulse, wakame), or to taste, crushed (about 2 teaspoons crushed, or 3 grams)
1 to 2 teaspoons crushed, dried herbs of choice, to taste
Dash onion or garlic powder
Pinch salt or ground black pepper
1 to 2 tablespoons milk powder (dairy, coconut, nut, rice), potato flakes, bean powder, or cheese powder for creamy soups

If you'd like meat:
1 to 2 ounces shredded dried meat or jerky

To rehydrate: Stir 2 cups of boiling water into 1 cup of soup mix, cover, and let stand until rehydrated, 10 to 12 minutes. Add additional hot water as needed for desired consistency.

Suggested combinations:
Old-Fashioned Beef and Vegetable: potatoes, mushrooms, onions, carrots, celery, dried beef, beef soup base, parsley, thyme, garlic powder, salt, and black pepper
Chicken Noodle: pasta, onions, carrots, celery, peas, dried chicken, chicken soup base, onion powder, garlic powder, poultry seasoning, salt, and white or black pepper
U.S. Senate Bean and Ham: beans, onion, celery, dried diced ham, parsley, potato flakes, garlic powder, salt, and black pepper
Italian Minestrone: pasta, beans, onions, carrots, peas, zucchini, tomato powder, Italian Herb Seasoning Blend (page 50), garlic powder, salt, and red or black pepper

CHOPPED VEGETABLE SALAD

Yes, it is possible to make salad from dried ingredients. The trick is to add ample seasoning and rehydrate the ingredients with an acidic ingredient such as lemon juice or vinegar rather than plain water. The dried vegetables become crunchy, delicious, and healthy.

Dehydrated ingredients:

½ to 1 cup dried shredded or chopped vegetables such as carrots, turnips, beets, corn, celery, daikon or radish, cucumber, zucchini, tomatoes, bell pepper, green beans, peas, broccoli, cauliflower, mushrooms, green or red onion, cabbage, or kale

For heartier salads, include up to half dry beans, grain (rice, quinoa, etc.), or pasta

1 to 2 tablespoons dried fruit, such as apples, raisins, pineapple, or mango (optional)

Flavorings:

1 tablespoon (1 sheet) crushed seaweed strands or flakes (nori, wakame, kombu, kelp, dulse, etc.)

1 to 2 teaspoons tomato powder, to taste

¼ to ½ teaspoon crushed dried herbs of your choice, to taste

Pinch dry mustard or celery seed

Pinch chopped dried lemon zest

Dash onion or garlic powder

Dash sugar

Dash celery salt or table salt

Dash red pepper flakes or ground black pepper

1 tablespoon yogurt powder (for a creamy dressing)

If you'd like meat:

1 to 2 ounces shredded dried meat or jerky

To add after rehydration:

1 to 2 tablespoons chopped nuts or seeds (almonds, pecans, sunflower seeds, sesame seeds, etc.)

To rehydrate: In a small saucepan, combine equal parts vinegar or citrus juice and water (for ½ cup of salad mix, use ¼ cup each of vinegar and water for a total of ½ cup of liquid), bring to a boil, and pour over the salad mix; let stand until rehydrated, about 30 minutes. Sprinkle with the nuts or seeds. *Note:* Shredded vegetables rehydrate faster than diced vegetables.

Suggested combinations:

Greek Salad: chopped tomato, cucumber, yellow bell peppers, green bell peppers, red onion, parsley, oregano or mint, garlic powder, salt, and black pepper. Rehydrate with water, red wine vinegar, or lemon juice.

Fiesta Bean Salad: black beans, corn, chopped tomatoes, green bell pepper, red onion, parsley or cilantro, ground cumin, and salt. Rehydrate with water, apple cider vinegar, or lime juice.

CREAMY PASTA CASSEROLE MIX

Just as you can make instant soup, you can make instant pasta bowls, from the comforting Chili Mac to the trendy Salmon Pesto.

Dehydrated ingredients:
½ to ¾ cup dried pasta (page 157)
½ cup dried chopped vegetables, such as peas and mushrooms
1 teaspoon dried chopped onion

Flavorings:
1 tablespoon all-purpose flour, potato flakes or powder, yogurt powder, or cheese powder
½ teaspoon crushed dried herbs
Pinch garlic powder
Dash salt
Dash ground black pepper

If you'd like meat:
1 to 2 ounces dried ground beef or chicken

To rehydrate: Pour 1 cup boiling water over the casserole mix, cover, and let stand until hydrated, 10 to 12 minutes. Stir and add additional hot water if needed for desired consistency.

Suggested combinations:
Mushroom Stroganoff: egg noodles, mushrooms, potato flakes, yogurt powder, and onion, with or without shredded beef
Chili Mac: elbow macaroni, chili, cheddar cheese powder, and scallions, with or without ground beef or turkey

Salmon Pesto: curly pasta (fusilli, cavatappi, or rotini), shredded salmon jerky, green peas, chopped mushrooms, chopped onions or shallots, basil, ground roasted walnuts or pine nuts, cheese powder, salt, and black pepper

STIR-FRIED RICE BLEND

Usually a stir-fry takes lots of prep; with your dried pantry, it comes together in a snap.

Dehydrated ingredients:
½ cup dried vegetables, such as carrots, bell pepper, zucchini, bamboo shoots, spinach, snow peas, daikon, scallions, or shallots, plus green peas or corn
½ cup dried rice (page 153)

Flavorings:
1 to 2 teaspoons commercial stir-fry seasoning mix, or make your own: 1 tablespoon (1 sheet) crushed seaweed strands or flakes (nori, wakame, kombu, kelp, dulse, etc.), 1 to 3 crushed dried shrimp, dash onion or garlic powder, dash sugar or salt, pinch ground mustard seed, and pinch red or black pepper

If you'd like meat:
1 to 2 ounces shredded or finely diced dried beef or chicken

To rehydrate: Rehydrate the vegetables and rice separately. Pour ½ cup of boiling water over the vegetables and ½ cup of boiling water over rice, cover, and let stand until the liquid is absorbed, 8 to 10 minutes. Stir-fry the vegetables over high heat in 1 to 2 teaspoons of oil for 1 to 2 minutes or until steaming. If desired, push the vegetables aside, add a beaten egg to the pan, cook until scrambled and set, 1 to 2 minutes. Stir in the rice and toss until hot, 3 to 5 minutes.

Suggested combinations:
Chicken and Vegetable Stir-Fry: carrot, broccoli, mushroom, chicken, tomato powder, brown sugar, garlic powder, salt, and black pepper
Shrimp and Pineapple Stir-Fry: broccoli, red bell pepper, pineapple, shrimp, and stir-fry seasoning

MEAT OR VEGETABLE CURRY MIX

Curries are familiar and comforting dishes that can take too much time to make when you need a quick meal. Put together your curry kit using dried vegetables and seasonings, plus meat or vegan protein for a more substantial meal, and you can have a delicious curry ready in no time at all.

Dehydrated ingredients:
½ cup shredded or thinly sliced vegetables, such as onions, tomato, eggplant, squash, spinach, green peas, sweet peppers, or hot chiles

Flavorings:
1 to 2 teaspoons curry powder of your choice, to taste
Dash salt
Dash red pepper flakes or ground black pepper

If you'd like meat or protein:
1 to 2 ounces shredded or finely diced dried beef, chicken, fish, tofu, or beans

To rehydrate: In a saucepan, combine the curry mix with an equal portion of water, bring to a boil, cover, and simmer, stirring occasionally, until fully hydrated with no crunchy bits, 5 to 8 minutes. If needed, add more hot water while reheating. Serve with rice or potatoes.

Suggested combinations:
Madras-Style Curry: onions, tomato, eggplant, spinach, Madras Curry Spice Mix (page 51), salt, and black pepper, with optional meat, fish, tofu, or beans
Coconut Curry: shallots, spinach, winter squash, Coconut Curry Spices (page 51), salt, and red pepper flakes, with optional meat, fish, tofu, or beans

CHOCOLATE CHIP COOKIES, PAGE 202

Fresh from the Dehydrator

These recipes for flourless breads, crackers, cookies, cereals, snack foods, and more are made to be eaten as soon as they come out of the dehydrator. All are suitable for raw diets, where food is not heated above 115°F. Recipes include both a low-temperature drying range and a standard setting for drying vegetables, fruits, and grains at a higher temperature.

If you are drying at the lower temperature setting, it is recommended that you preheat the dehydrator to the higher setting given in the recipe and dry at this temperature for the first hour, and then turn down to the lower setting. A high-temperature start is especially recommended for dense foods such as breads, patties, and cookies. Doing this will save energy by decreasing the drying time, as well as inhibit microbial growth in the early stages when the food is still quite moist and its internal temperature is still low.

SWEET AND SALTY DRIED ALMONDS

Prep Time: 2 to 8 hours | Drying Temp & Time: 95° to 115°F for 12 to 24 hours | Yield: 6 to 8 servings of nuts, or 12 to 18 servings of trail mix

This recipe combines sweet and salty seasonings for a flavor-balanced snack. Feel free to use a different sweetener, such as maple or "yacon" syrup, honey, or coconut or rapadura sugar in place of the brown sugar. You can also add other spices or herbs, such as cinnamon, cumin, curry powder, or rosemary. For trail mix, prepare two or three kinds of dehydrated nuts (such as almonds, pumpkin seeds, and macadamias) and mix with dried fruits (see variations below).

1 quart water

2 teaspoons kosher or sea salt, divided

8 ounces (1½ to 2 cups) shelled and rinsed almonds

2 tablespoons brown sugar

¼ teaspoon cayenne or other hot chile powder, or ground black pepper

2 teaspoons soy sauce, liquid aminos, or water, or as needed

1. In a large glass bowl or container, combine the water and 1½ teaspoons of salt, and stir until the salt dissolves completely. Stir in the almonds. Make sure the water covers the almonds completely. Soak for 2 hours at room temperature or up to 8 hours refrigerated. Drain and rinse the almonds thoroughly.

2. In a medium bowl, stir together the brown sugar, remaining ½ teaspoon of salt, and cayenne to taste. Add the almonds and toss, adding the soy sauce as needed until evenly coated.

3. Preheat a food dehydrator to 95° to 115°F. Spread the almonds on the drying trays in a single, even layer. Dry until crunchy with no sign of moisture, 12 to 24 hours. Optionally, the nuts may be roasted after drying at 350°F for 8 to 12 minutes, stirring once after 4 to 6 minutes, until fragrant and lightly browned.

STORAGE: Up to 3 months at room temperature, 6 months refrigerated, and 1 year frozen in an airtight container.

VARIATIONS: This recipe works well with Brazil nuts, cashews, hazelnuts, macadamias, peanuts, pecans, pine nuts, pistachios, pumpkin seeds, sunflower seeds, or walnuts. For trail mix, add 1 cup of chopped dried fruits such as apples, cranberries, or pineapple to the nuts after drying.

HOW AND WHY TO SOAK AND DEHYDRATE NUTS AND SEEDS

Raw recipes call for soaking raw nuts or seeds before drying at a low temperature. But they are already dry, so why is this step necessary?

Soaking germinates the nuts, usually to prepare them for sprouting, but it also improves the available nutrition and digestibility, and makes them crunchier when dehydrated or roasted. Dehydrating lets the creaminess of the nuts shine through, while roasting in the oven brings out the nutty flavor many people prefer. And of course, drying them out again by either method extends their storage life.

In the following recipes, I'm concerned only with making crunchy nuts, not sprouting. Therefore, the length of soaking isn't particularly important. You can use the same basic technique for any nuts or seeds: Rinse them and cover generously with salted water (1 to 2 inches), soak for 2 hours at room temperature or up to 8 hours refrigerated, drain, pat dry, and then dehydrate or roast as preferred. Be sure to dehydrate or roast within 24 hours, or the nuts or seeds may begin to sprout (or get moldy if left too wet).

SPICY CURRY CASHEWS

Prep Time: 3 to 9 hours | Drying Temp & Time: 95° to 115°F for 12 to 24 hours | Yield: 6 to 8 servings of nuts, or 12 to 18 servings of trail mix

These are a very flavorful spiced nuts. They're wonderful alone but also work especially well in a trail mix, paired with dried fruits to help tame the heat. Make this recipe with cashews or pecans for a wonderful and slightly decadent food gift; just pour them into a cellophane bag and tie with a pretty ribbon. For trail mix, prepare two or three kinds of dehydrated nuts (such as almonds, pecans, and cashews) and mix with dried fruits (see variations below).

1 quart warm water

1½ teaspoons kosher or sea salt

8 ounces (1½ to 2 cups) cashews

2 teaspoons sugar

½ teaspoon ground cumin

½ teaspoon ground coriander

½ teaspoon paprika

¼ teaspoon curry powder

¼ teaspoon cayenne pepper

2 teaspoons water, or as needed

1. In a large glass bowl or container, combine the water and salt, and stir until the salt dissolves completely. Add the cashews. Make sure the water covers the cashews completely. Soak for 2 hours at room temperature or up to 8 hours refrigerated. Drain and rinse the cashews thoroughly.

2. In a medium bowl, stir together the sugar, cumin, coriander, paprika, curry powder, and cayenne. Add the nuts and toss, adding the water as needed to help the seasonings evenly coat the nuts.

3. Preheat a food dehydrator to 95° to 115°F. Spread the cashews on the drying trays in a single, even layer. Dry until crunchy with no sign of moisture, 12 to 24 hours. Optionally, the nuts may be roasted after drying at 300°F until browned for a pleasant, nutty flavor, about 20 minutes.

STORAGE: Up to 3 months at room temperature, 6 months refrigerated, and 1 year frozen in an airtight container.
VARIATIONS: Other nuts may be soaked and dried, including almonds, Brazil nuts, hazelnuts, macadamias, peanuts, pecans, pine nuts, pistachios, pumpkin seeds, sunflower seeds, and walnuts. For trail mix, add 1 cup of chopped dried fruits such as cherries, peaches, or raisins, after the nuts come out of the dehydrator.

PEAR, CRANBERRY, AND ALMOND LEATHER

Prep Time: 30 to 60 minutes | **Drying Temp & Time:** 105° to 115°F for 8 to 12 hours or 125° to 135°F for 4 to 8 hours | **Yield:** 8 servings

Leathers studded with solid pieces such as dried fruit, nuts, seeds, or coconut may not roll up without breaking. You have several options: Grind these ingredients with the fruit until the mixture is a puree or grind the ingredients to a powder and mix them with the fruit puree, then dry as usual and roll up. To use large pieces, sprinkle the solid ingredients on top of the puree after you have spread it on the drying tray. Once dry, roll up the leather with the solids on the inside. Or mix the solid ingredients into the puree and dry, but cut the dried leather into strips or squares instead of rolling, as specified in this recipe for pear leather studded with dried cranberries and almonds.

6 medium pears
   (2½ to 3 pounds),
   or 6 cups drained
   canned pears

¼ cup dried cranberries

¼ cup toasted or
   dried almonds

Pinch salt (optional)

1. Preheat a food dehydrator to the temperature you prefer (see above). Wash the pears, peel if desired, core, cut into chunks, and pretreat for browning; see Steam Blanching or Acidulating (pages 6–7). Finely chop the cranberries and almonds by hand or using a nut grinder. In a blender or food mill, process the pears into a smooth puree. Stir in the cranberries, almonds, and salt (if using).

2. Spread the puree on lined drying trays in an even layer, ¼ to ⅜ inch thick. Dry the leather until firm but pliable; timing is dependent on the temperature range (see above). Press lightly in several places to check for soft or sticky spots and continue drying if needed.

3. Turn off the dehydrator and peel the leather from the liner while still warm. When almost cool, cut the leather into 8 or more pieces. Stack the pieces with a piece of parchment or wax paper between each one.

STORAGE: Up to 3 months in an airtight container in a cool, dry place.

TIPS FOR SUCCESSFUL RAW DEHYDRATING

The temperature for raw dehydrating is not universally agreed upon. The recipes in this section suggest a lower temperature setting between 105° and 115°F. A lower temperature may be selected and will increase the drying time slightly.

- When converting other recipes to a raw temperature, expect to increase drying time by at least one-third for recipes dried 20 degrees higher. For example, a food dried at 135°F for 6 hours can be expected to take 8 hours at 115°F. This is only a rough guide, as many factors can affect drying time. See also Factors That Can Affect Dehydration Times (page 10).

- Because the internal temperature of food rises gradually at the beginning of dehydration, a higher temperature of 125° to 145°F may be selected for the first 1 to 2 hours of drying, then turned down to 105° to 115°F.

- A higher temperature at the start will inhibit microbial growth in the early stages of dehydration, when the food is still quite moist and its internal temperature is still low.

- A high-temperature start is especially recommended for dense foods such as breads, patties, and cookies.

- Dehydrating foods at a low temperature for a raw-food diet adds satisfying crisp textures from crunchy snacks like raw chips and crackers.

- Don't dry savory and sweet recipes at the same time, since flavors can transfer between the two and ruin the enjoyment of both foods.

- Remember that recipes for breads can be dried longer for crackers, and cracker recipes can be dried for less time for a soft bread or wrap.

CHERRY CRACK SEED

Prep Time: 40 to 50 minutes | Drying Temp & Time: 105° to 115°F for 16 to 24 hours or 125° to 135°F for 12 to 16 hours | Yield: 8 servings

Historically, salty dried plums, called *li hing mui* or "traveling plum," were used for long-distance travel in China to restore salt lost from perspiration and to reduce muscle cramps. These types of salty snacks are popular today in Hawaii, where they are known as "crack seed." You can make crack seed from cherries as well as plums, apricots, peaches, lemons, mangoes, or ginger. The following recipe is a typical preparation.

1 quart water

1 cup packed brown sugar

3 to 8 tablespoons salt (see Tip below)

Juice from 2 medium lemons

½ to ¾ teaspoon Chinese five-spice powder (optional)

2 pounds fresh whole cherries (any variety), pitted

1. In a small saucepan, combine the water, brown sugar, salt, and lemon juice. Bring to a boil over high heat, reduce the heat to low, and simmer, stirring, until the brown sugar and salt dissolve, about 10 minutes. Raise the heat to high and add the five-spice powder to taste (if using) and cherries. Bring back to a boil. Reduce the heat to a gentle simmer and poach for 5 minutes. Remove from the heat and allow the fruit to cool in the syrup at least 2 hours (at room temperature) or up to 5 days (in the refrigerator) before drying.

2. Preheat a food dehydrator to the temperature you prefer (see above). Drain, pat the fruit dry with paper towels, and arrange on the drying trays in a single, even layer. Dry until the fruit is pliable and there is no visible moisture when squeezed or cut. Sweet varieties of cherries might remain slightly sticky.

STORAGE: Up to 1 year at room temperature in an airtight container.

TIP: The sweeter the fruit, the more salt you may want to use. For sour cherries, I would recommend using 3 tablespoons of salt, and for sweet cherries, ½ cup.

SPICED CITRUS WHEELS

Prep Time: 15 to 30 minutes | **Drying Temp & Time:** 105° to 115°F for 8 to 12 hours or 125° to 135°F for 4 to 8 hours | **Yield:** 8 servings

Dried citrus, including the fruit, pith, and zest, makes a surprisingly sweet snack alone or as part of a mix with other dried fruits, such as apples, bananas, pineapple, and strawberries. It's an unusually pleasant way to enjoy the whole fruit, instead of just the segments or juice. Dry it plain or with any of the seasonings suggested in the recipe below. Dried citrus is delicious in tea and water infusions, for garnishing cocktails and salads, added to stews or stir-fries, and ground into powder for seasoning baked goods and marinades.

8 small oranges, seedless if possible, or 8 mandarin oranges (clementine, tangerine, etc.), or 8 limes or lemons, or 4 medium grapefruits, or 2 large pomelo

1 to 2 tablespoons brown sugar or grated coconut (optional)

½ to 1 teaspoon ground cinnamon (optional)

Pinch of sea salt or ginger powder (optional)

1. Preheat a food dehydrator to the temperature you prefer (see above). Wash the fruit. Cut the unpeeled whole fruit crosswise into ⅛- to ¼-inch-thick slices. For grapefruit or pomelo, cut in half through the stem and then across for half slices; cut the half slices into quarters if the fruit is large. Remove any seeds before drying the fruit.

2. In a small bowl, combine the brown sugar, cinnamon, and/or salt to taste (if using).

3. Arrange the fruit slices on the drying trays in a single layer without overlapping. Sprinkle evenly with the sugar mixture (if using). Dry until crisp; timing is dependent on the temperature range (see above).

STORAGE: Up to 1 year at room temperature in an airtight container.

FRESH CORN CHIPS

Prep Time: 15 minutes | **Drying Temp & Time:** 105° to 115°F for 16 to 20 hours or 125° to 135°F for 6 to 10 hours | **Yield:** 4 servings

Ground flaxseed or flaxseed meal is optional in this recipe but helps give structure to dried corn chips. Sweet corn is easy to come by for this recipe. But cooked polenta also works well. Polenta can be difficult to spread thinly (especially if cold), so blend it with some water, just enough to soften to spreading consistency. A small amount of oil can help produce a crisper chip. Although any added oil will shorten the storage life, no one has had a batch of these long enough to confirm this.

2 cups fresh, frozen (thawed), or drained canned corn kernels

¼ cup ground flaxseed, flaxseed meal, or chia seeds

1 to 2 teaspoons olive or vegetable oil (optional)

½ teaspoon kosher or sea salt

¼ teaspoon onion powder

¼ teaspoon garlic powder

⅛ teaspoon smoked paprika or hot chile powder

1 to 4 tablespoons water, or as needed

1. In a food processor, process the corn, flaxseed, oil (if using), salt, onion powder, garlic powder, and paprika to taste into a smooth, thick paste. If too firm or dry to spread, add 1 tablespoon of water at a time and process for several seconds. Repeat until spreading consistency is achieved.

2. Preheat a food dehydrator to the temperature you prefer (see above). Spread the mixture ⅛ inch thick on lined drying trays. Score to make 24 to 36 crackers; if the mixture is very soft, score after it has dried for 2 hours or becomes firm enough to score. About halfway through the drying time at either temperature, when the mixture is firm, turn over to finish drying. Dry until crisp; timing is dependent on the drying temperature (see above).

3. Cut apart at scored sections or break the sheets into serving pieces. See also Tips for Successful Raw Breads, Wraps, Tortillas, and Crackers (page 185).

STORAGE: Up to 1 week at room temperature or 1 month refrigerated in an airtight container.

CHEESY ONION CRISPS

Prep Time: 20 minutes | **Drying Temp & Time:** 105° to 115°F for 16 to 20 hours or 125° to 135°F for 6 to 10 hours | **Yield:** 4 servings

These onion crisps get their cheesy flavor from the nutritional yeast. Enjoy them as a snack or to top burgers and wraps, soups, salads, or anywhere you want a crunchy flavorful topping. If your eyes get irritated when slicing onions, try putting them (the onions, not your eyes) in the freezer for 20 minutes before slicing, wearing ski goggles or sunglasses while cutting onions, and/or working fast (but safely) to get the job done quickly! If you don't have a mandoline, it's safer to cut the onion in half, place the flat side down on the cutting board, and cut thin slices with a sharp knife.

2 medium onions (about 1 pound), peeled

2 tablespoons soy sauce or liquid aminos

2 tablespoons cider vinegar

2 tablespoons nutritional yeast

½ teaspoon onion powder

¼ teaspoon salt

⅛ teaspoon garlic powder

⅛ teaspoon ground black pepper or hot chile powder

1. Slice the onions thinly, ⅛ to ¼ inch thick, and separate into strips. Thinner slices will dry faster. In a large bowl, combine the onion strips, soy sauce, and vinegar, and toss until evenly coated. In a small bowl, combine the yeast, onion powder, salt, garlic powder, and pepper. Sprinkle evenly over the onions and toss until evenly coated.

2. Preheat a dehydrator to the temperature you prefer (see above). Arrange the onions in a single, loose layer on the drying trays. Overlapping slightly is okay. About halfway through the drying time at either temperature or when the onions are firm, turn over to finish drying. Dry until crisp; timing is dependent on the drying temperature (see above).

STORAGE: Up to 1 week at room temperature or 1 month refrigerated in an airtight container.

SPICY CAULIFLOWER CRISPS

Prep Time: 15 minutes | **Drying Temp & Time: 105° to 115°F for 16 to 24 hours or 125° to 135°F for 8 to 12 hours** | **Yield: 2 to 4 servings**

Cauliflower dries into a crispy, crunchy snack and takes well to any type of seasoning. Here a hot pepper blend is suggested, but feel free to substitute mild flavors such as Ranch Dressing Seasoning Mix (page 51), dried herbs, or spices such as cumin and turmeric. You can't go wrong if it's a seasoning you enjoy. Like all dried vegetables, cauliflower shrinks quite a bit.

A serving of fresh cauliflower is typically 1 cup, but you may find yourself with just a cup or so of dried crisps when preparing this recipe. Technically, it's still four servings. But if you share them with only yourself, I'll never tell.

1 medium head cauliflower
   (1¼ to 1½ pounds)

2 tablespoons fresh lemon or
   lime juice, vinegar, soy
   sauce, or liquid aminos

1 tablespoon olive or
   vegetable oil

1 to 2 tablespoons Taco and
   Chili Seasoning Blend,
   Berbere Ethiopian Spice
   Blend, or Madras Curry
   Spice Mix (pages 50–51)

1 teaspoon kosher or sea salt

1. Separate the cauliflower head into florets, wash, drain, and pat dry. Cut the florets into thin, ½- to ¾-inch pieces; it doesn't matter how long the pieces are if the width is kept thin. You should have about 4 cups of slices. Place in a large bowl and toss with the lemon juice and oil until evenly coated. Sprinkle with the seasoning blend to taste and salt, then toss until evenly coated.

2. Preheat a dehydrator to the temperature you prefer (see above). Arrange the slices in a single layer on the drying trays without overlapping. Dry until crisp; timing is dependent on the drying temperature (see above).

STORAGE: Up to 1 week at room temperature or 1 month frozen in an airtight container.

VEGAN BURGER PATTIES

Prep Time: 20 minutes | **Drying Temp & Time:** 105° to 115°F for 4 to 8 hours or 125° to 135°F for 3 to 5 hours | **Yield:** 6 patties

This vegan burger recipe uses vegetables along with mushrooms and seasonings to suggest a "meaty" flavor. It includes potatoes and tomato paste to help bind the ingredients together. If you want a very neat shape to your patties, use a burger press or egg ring. Don't make the patties too thick, or they won't dry properly. (For more tips on making vegan burger patties, see page 182.) Enjoy raw vegan burgers in the same way you would a hamburger. You can also use the mixture to replace ground meat in many recipes (soup, stew, casserole, etc.).

1 pound portobello mushrooms (stems discarded if woody), chopped (5 cups)

2 cups chopped raw vegetables, such as onion, carrot, celery, zucchini, beet, or eggplant, or 1⅓ cups vegetable pulp (leftover from juicing)

1 cup shredded cooked potato or sweet potato, or 1 cup cold cooked rice, quinoa, or drained beans (black beans, chickpeas, etc.)

½ cup chopped onion

1 tablespoon olive or vegetable oil

1 tablespoon soy sauce

2 teaspoons liquid smoke (optional)

1 teaspoon salt

1 teaspoon paprika

1 teaspoon onion powder

½ teaspoon garlic powder

½ teaspoon ground black pepper

1. In a food processor, pulse the mushrooms, vegetables, potato, and onion until finely chopped. Add the oil, soy sauce, liquid smoke (if using), salt, paprika, onion powder, garlic powder, and pepper. Pulse or blend until just well mixed but still having some texture, like ground meat. The mixture should hold together, but don't blend it into a uniform paste. If your mixture is too dry or too mushy, see Tips for Making Great Vegan Burger Patties (page 182).

2. Preheat a food dehydrator to the temperature you prefer (see above). Divide the mixture into 6 portions. Flatten each portion to ¼ to ⅓ inch thick. Arrange the patties on the drying tray so they don't touch. Dry until firm and moist but not wet; timing is dependent on the drying temperature (see above).

3. Unless you are following a raw diet, vegan burgers can be cooked in one of the following ways: baked in a 400°F oven, seared in a skillet with oil, or placed on a piece of foil and grilled. Cook the burgers until crisped and browned, about 20 minutes, turning once.

STORAGE: Up to 1 week in the refrigerator or 6 months frozen in an airtight container. Be sure to separate the patties with parchment or foil.

TIPS FOR MAKING GREAT VEGAN BURGER PATTIES

Pulse-chop ingredients in a food processor (or chop by hand) until the mixture resembles ground meat with small flecks throughout and holds together when pressed into a ball. Do not mix into a uniform smooth paste.

Use a burger press to help form firm patties. If the mixture is too dry, you won't be able to form patties that hold together. If it is too wet, it will be mushy and stick to your hands when you press it into a ball. Here are some solutions for these problems.

If your vegan burger mixture is too dry or the patties fall apart, try these tips:

- Add 1 tablespoon of ground flaxseed, flaxseed meal, or chia seeds soaked in 3 to 5 tablespoons of water until it gels.

- Combine 1 tablespoon of cornstarch, potato, or tapioca starch or 2 tablespoons of rice flour, potato powder, or all-purpose flour with an equal amount of water and stir into the chopped mixture.

- Add an "egg replacer" powder, which is a commercial product that will contain starchy ingredients such as soy flour, wheat gluten, potato starch, tapioca flour, arrowroot powder, agar, ground nuts or beans, or grains. A variety of vegetarian and vegan formulations are available, including gluten-free and soy-free.

If your vegan burger mixture is too wet or mushy, try these tips:

- Add dry ingredients such as cooked rice or quinoa, ground flaxseed or flaxseed meal, potato powder or cooked shredded potatoes, wheat germ, bread crumbs, or oats.

- Pulse the ingredients together in a food processor, but finish mixing by hand, so you don't overmix.

TRADITIONAL FALAFEL BITES

Prep Time: 30 to 45 minutes | **Drying Temp & Time:** 105° to 115°F for 4 to 8 hours or 125° to 135°F for 3 to 5 hours | **Yield:** 8 to 12 falafel bites, or 4 servings

Falafel is essentially a vegan "meatball" that is crisp on the outside and soft on the inside. Usually deep-fried, falafel are equally delicious when eaten raw or dried. Serve falafel as a snack or layered in a pita with vegetables, pickles, and yogurt sauce. You can also use the falafel mixture to replace ground meat in soups, stews, or casseroles.

1 (15-ounce) can beans (any variety), drained and rinsed

1 cup cooked rice, bulgur, quinoa, or polenta

½ cup minced onion, bell pepper, or celery

¼ cup shredded carrot, chopped parsley, or diced tomato

1 tablespoon chickpea or all-purpose flour

1 to 2 teaspoons Egyptian Dukkah Nut and Spice Seasoning or Berbere Ethiopian Spice Blend (page 52 or 50)

½ teaspoon salt

½ teaspoon red pepper flakes

1½ teaspoons garlic powder, divided

½ teaspoon ground coriander

¼ teaspoon ground cumin

1 cup plain 2 percent yogurt

1 tablespoon crushed dried parsley leaves

1 tablespoon Lemon-Pepper Seasoning or Ranch Dressing Seasoning Mix (pages 50 or 51)

1 teaspoon garlic powder

1. In a food processor, pulse the beans, rice, onion, carrot, flour, spice mixture, salt, red pepper, ½ teaspoon of the garlic powder, the coriander, and cumin, until the mixture is well blended and holds together when squeezed. If the mixture is too dry, add a dash of water (or liquid from the beans). If the mixture is too soft, add more flour, 1 tablespoon at a time. Taste and season with salt or pepper.

2. Preheat a food dehydrator to the temperature you prefer (see above). Divide the mixture into 8 to 12 portions, roll each portion into a ball, and place on the drying trays. Rotate every few hours. Dry until chewy and soft or crisp as desired; timing is dependent on the drying temperature (see above). While the falafel is drying, in a small bowl, stir together the yogurt, parsley, seasoning blend of your choice, and remaining 1 teaspoon garlic powder. Refrigerate until ready to serve.

3. Unless you are following a raw diet, falafel can be cooked in one of the following ways: baked in a 400°F oven or sautéed in a skillet with oil until crisped and browned, 6 to 8 minutes, turning once.

STORAGE: Up to 1 week refrigerated or 6 months frozen in an airtight container.

TIP: Use any variety of beans or legumes, including fava beans, chickpeas, black beans, black-eyed peas, lentils, and red or white beans.

SAVORY VEGETABLE WRAPS

Prep Time: 15 minutes | **Drying Temp & Time:** 105° to 115°F for 6 to 10 hours or 125° to 135°F for 2 to 6 hours | **Yield:** 3 to 4 wraps

Theoretically, you can make any of the cracker recipes in this cookbook into a wrap by drying until pliable instead of crisp, although ones containing a lot of flaxseed meal are more likely to split when you try to use them as a wrap. So it usually works better to spread flax batters or doughs thicker and use like a slice of bread rather than a wrap. However, this recipe contains more vegetables, plus creamy avocado and just enough flaxseed to bind the mixture, giving this wrap a supple texture that is flexible for wrapping.

2½ cups chopped vegetables, such as zucchini, carrot, spinach leaves, bell pepper, or tomatoes

½ avocado, seeded and peeled

3 tablespoons ground flaxseed, flaxseed meal or chia seeds

1 to 2 teaspoons crushed dried Italian Herb Seasoning Blend or Berbere Ethiopian Spice Blend (page 50), or other herbs or spices of your choice

½ teaspoon onion or garlic powder

½ teaspoon kosher or sea salt

¼ teaspoon ground black or red pepper flakes

1 to 2 tablespoons fresh lemon juice or water, as needed

1. In a blender or food processor, combine the vegetables, avocado, flaxseed, seasoning blend, onion powder, and salt and pepper to taste. Blend to your desired consistency (see Tips for Successful Raw Breads, Wraps, Tortillas, and Crackers, page 185), adding the lemon juice as needed. Taste and correct the seasoning with salt or pepper.

2. Preheat a food dehydrator to the temperature you prefer (see above). Spread the mixture evenly ⅛ to 3/16 inch thick on lined drying trays. Alternatively, place a mound of batter on the liner and flatten into a round; space the wraps apart without touching. About halfway through the drying time at either temperature, when the wraps are firm, peel carefully from the drying trays and turn over to finish drying. Dry until evenly colored and flexible with no sticky spots; timing is dependent on the drying temperature (see above).

3. Carefully peel the wraps from the liners while still warm. Cut large sheets into wrap-size portions.

STORAGE: 3 days in the refrigerator or 1 month frozen in an airtight container. Separate the wraps with parchment paper. If they dry out during storage, spritz or brush sparingly with water and let stand until flexible, about 30 minutes.

TIPS FOR SUCCESSFUL RAW BREADS, WRAPS, TORTILLAS, AND CRACKERS

- The consistency of cracker or bread mixtures can vary from a thick batter (like a pudding) to a spreadable dough (like cookies or bread). Pourable batters containing more liquid will take longer to dry. Stiff doughs can be spread with a rolling pin.

- Most hand or countertop blenders may be used to mix batters. To mix stiff doughs, use a food processor or high-speed blender. Alternatively, you can finely chop or grate the ingredients and mix batters or doughs by hand.

- Turn the batter or dough over, when firm (about halfway through the drying time) to speed up complete drying.

- Score the batters after flipping over or simply cut or break apart the breads and crackers after drying. Score the doughs into serving pieces immediately after spreading on drying trays, or cut with scissors after drying.

- Ground flaxseed or flaxseed meal goes rancid quickly. For the freshest flavor, grind the seeds just before making crackers, or purchase refrigerated flaxseed meal and keep frozen until ready to use.

- The texture of the mixture can vary from smooth to coarse or chunky depending on the desired result.

- Substitute chia seeds in bread and cracker recipes 1:1 for ground flaxseed or flaxseed meal.

- Chia seeds are bland compared to the nuttiness of flaxseeds, so they are best used in recipes with other flavors such as nuts, vegetables or fruits, and seasonings.

- The quickest, simplest dehydrator bread or cracker can be made by stirring together ground flaxseed or flaxseed meal with water and seasoning. Combine the flaxseed meal with water in a ratio of 2:1 for dough or 1:1 for batter, or to desired consistency. Let the mixture stand for 30 minutes, spread on lined drying trays, and dry until firm or crisp.

- Batter or dough must have enough structure to hold together. Besides flaxseed meal or chia seeds, other ingredients that can help provide structure in varying degrees include ground psyllium husks, ground nuts or seeds, mashed avocado, banana, and vegetable or fruit pulp from juicing.

- If not stored in an airtight container, breads can dry out and crack, while crackers can lose crispness and soften after a few days. If desired, re-moisten breads by brushing lightly with water, or re-dry crackers until crisp.

SWEET SNACK WRAPS

Prep Time: 15 minutes | **Drying Temp & Time:** 105° to 115°F for 6 to 10 hours or 125° to 135°F for 2 to 6 hours | **Yield:** 3 to 4 wraps

This recipe uses carrots or coconut plus a creamy element for a flexible wrap especially suitable for breakfast ingredients, fruity snacks, and desserts. Fill the wraps with soft cheese and fruit, rice and vegetables, tofu and peanut sauce, scrambled eggs, peanut butter and jelly, or any other snack or meal combination that appeals to you and your family. These wraps tend to lose their flexibility after a couple days, so freeze them if you don't plan to use them soon.

2½ cups grated carrots, carrot pulp, or unsweetened coconut flakes

½ cup ground flaxseed, flaxseed meal, or chia seeds

½ cup mashed banana, ripe mango, or sweet potato, or unsweetened applesauce or nut butter

1 tablespoon sweetener, such as maple syrup, honey, or raw or coconut sugar

1 teaspoon seasoning, such as Coconut Curry Spices, Egyptian Dukkah Nut and Spice Seasoning, Japanese Hot Pepper Blend (pages 51–52), pumpkin-pie spice, or ground cinnamon

1 to 4 tablespoons coconut or almond milk or water, as needed

1. In a blender or food processor, combine the carrots, flaxseed, fruit, sweetener, and seasoning to taste. Blend to your desired consistency (see Tips for Successful Raw Breads, Wraps, Tortillas, and Crackers, page 185), adding the milk to taste as needed. Taste and correct the seasoning.

2. Preheat a food dehydrator to the temperature you prefer (see above). Spread the mixture evenly ⅛ to ³⁄₁₆ inch thick on lined drying trays. Alternatively, place a mound of batter on the liner and flatten into a round; space the wraps apart without touching. About halfway through the drying time at either temperature, when the wraps are firm, peel carefully from the liners and turn over to finish drying. Dry until evenly colored and flexible with no sticky spots; timing is dependent on the drying temperature (see above).

3. Carefully peel the wraps from the liners while still warm. Cut large sheets into wrap-size portions.

STORAGE: 3 days in the refrigerator or 1 month frozen in an airtight container. Separate the wraps with parchment paper. If they dry out during storage, spritz or brush sparingly with water and let stand until flexible, about 30 minutes.

MIXED VEGETABLE BREAD (OR CRACKERS)

Prep Time: 20 minutes | Drying Temp & Time: 105° to 115°F for 8 to 12 hours for bread and 16 to 24 hours for crackers or 125° to 135°F for 4 to 8 hours for bread and 10 to 12 hours for crackers | Yield: 6 bread slices or wraps, or 18 to 24 crackers

This is an easy-to-make bread well known among raw foodists. It uses simple ingredients, comes together quickly, and makes bread that holds together and tastes great with all kinds of filling. The recipe is very adaptable. Feel free to substitute other chopped vegetables. Aim for 4½ to 5 cups of chopped vegetables.

2 medium zucchinis, roughly chopped

2 medium carrots, roughly chopped

2 medium onions, roughly chopped

¼ cup olive or sunflower oil

1 to 2 tablespoons soy sauce or liquid aminos, divided

½ to 1 teaspoon kosher or sea salt

1 cup shelled sunflower seeds

1 cup ground flaxseed, flaxseed meal, or chia seeds

1 to 2 tablespoons water, as needed

1. In a food processor, pulse the zucchini, carrots, onions, oil, 1 tablespoon of soy sauce, and salt to taste, 10 to 20 times, until the mixture is finely chopped. Add the sunflower seeds and flaxseed. Process into a coarse mixture (see Tips for Successful Raw Breads, Wraps, Tortillas, and Crackers, page 185), adding water and soy sauce, 1 tablespoon at a time, as needed.

2. Preheat a food dehydrator to the temperature you prefer (see above). Spread the mixture evenly on lined drying trays, ¼ inch thick for bread or ⅛ inch thick for wraps or crackers. Score into bread slices or crackers; if the mixture is very soft, score after it has dried for 2 hours or becomes firm enough to score. Alternatively, wraps can be formed by flattening a mound of batter or dough into a round, spaced apart without touching. About halfway through the drying time at either temperature, when the mixture is firm, turn over to finish drying. Dry breads or wraps until they feel light or crackers until they are crisp; timing is dependent on the drying temperature (see above).

3. Cut or break apart at scored sections or into pieces.

STORAGE: For bread, up to 7 days refrigerated, or 1 month frozen in an airtight container; for crackers, up to 1 month at room temperature or 6 months frozen.

ONION-SEED BREAD (OR CRACKERS)

Prep Time: 20 minutes | **Drying Temp & Time:** 105° to 115°F for 8 to 12 hours for bread and 16 to 24 hours for crackers or 125° to 135°F for 4 to 8 hours for bread and 10 to 12 hours for crackers | **Yield:** 6 bread slices or wraps, or 18 to 24 crackers

This recipe smells heavenly while drying, and the thin crackers are very light and airy when dried. Using just five ingredients (plus water), it is quick to put together. You can vary the flavor using different types of onions, nuts, seeds, oil, and optional seasonings as suggested in the ingredient list.

1 cup shelled raw or roasted sunflower seeds, pumpkin seeds, almonds, cashews, or walnuts

1 cup ground flaxseed, flaxseed meal, or chia seeds

2 pounds (8 to 10 medium) onions, coarsely chopped (about 5 cups)

⅓ cup oil such as olive, walnut, almond, avocado, or coconut

¼ cup soy sauce or liquid aminos

1 to 2 tablespoons water, as needed

1. In a food processor, combine the sunflower seeds and flaxseed, and pulse 10 to 20 times, until finely chopped; transfer to a large bowl. Place the onions in the food processor and pulse until finely chopped. Return the seeds to the food processor, add the oil and soy sauce, and process to a coarse mixture, adding 1 tablespoon of water at a time if needed, for consistency. Taste and correct the seasoning.

2. Preheat a food dehydrator to the temperature you prefer (see above). Spread the mixture evenly on lined drying trays, ¼ inch thick for bread or ⅛ inch thick for wraps or crackers. Score into the bread slices or crackers; if the mixture is very soft, score after it has dried for 2 hours or becomes firm enough to score. Alternatively, wraps can be formed by flattening a mound of batter or dough into a round, spaced apart without touching. About halfway through the drying time at either temperature, when the mixture is firm, turn over to finish drying. Dry breads or wraps until they feel light or crackers until they are crisp; timing is dependent on the drying temperature (see above).

3. Cut or break apart at scored sections or into pieces.

STORAGE: For bread or wraps, up to 7 days refrigerated, or 1 month frozen in an airtight container; separate the wraps with parchment paper. For crackers, up to 3 months at room temperature or 1 year frozen.

VARIATION: Other coarsely chopped nuts or seeds may be substituted, roasted if desired, such as pumpkin seeds, almonds, cashews, or walnuts

AVOCADO FLAXSEED CRACKERS

Prep Time: 2½ to 8½ hours | Drying Temp & Time: 105° to 115°F for 16 to 24 hours or 125° to 135°F for 10 to 12 hours | Yield: 24 to 36 crackers

This simple recipe livens up plain flaxseed crackers with avocado, greens, and seasonings from your dehydrator pantry. They're great eaten alone for a crunchy snack or as a tasty dipper for guacamole, salsa, hummus, yogurt dip, nut butter, or other spreads. You can customize your crackers and replace some of the greens with shredded carrots or zucchini or dried tomato, as well as seeds or nuts such as sunflower or pumpkin seeds, almonds, or pecans.

1 cup whole flaxseed

1 cup plus 1 to 2 tablespoons water, divided

1 avocado, seeded and flesh scooped out with a spoon

2 to 3 cups chopped fresh parsley, spinach, or kale

¼ cup minced onion

1 tablespoon vinegar or fresh lemon or lime juice

3 tablespoons seasoning blend of your choice (see pages 50–52)

⅛ teaspoon kosher or sea salt

1 to 2 tablespoons water, as needed

1. Soak the flaxseed in 1 cup of water for up to 2 hours at room temperature or 8 hours in the refrigerator. In a food processor, combine the avocado, parsley to taste, onion, vinegar, seasoning blend, and salt to taste. Pulse 10 to 20 times, until mixed. Add the soaked flaxseed (and any residual water), which should be gelatinous, and process into a coarse mixture (see Tips for Successful Raw Breads, Wraps, Tortillas, and Crackers, page 185), adding 1 tablespoon of water at a time if needed. Taste and correct the seasoning.

2. Preheat a food dehydrator to the temperature you prefer (see above). Spread the mixture thinly to ⅛ inch thick on lined drying trays. Score into crackers; if the mixture is very soft, score after it has dried for 2 hours or becomes firm enough to score. About halfway through the drying time at either temperature, when the mixture is firm, turn over to finish drying. Dry until crisp; timing is dependent on the drying temperature (see above).

3. Cut apart at scored sections or break sheets into serving pieces.

STORAGE: Up to 1 week at room temperature or 1 month frozen in an airtight container.

SEEDED VEGETABLE CRACKERS

Prep Time: 20 minutes | Drying Temp & Time: 125° to 135°F for 10 to 12 hours or 105° to 115°F for 16 to 24 hours | Yield: 24 to 36 crackers

Use any vegetables you wish for these crackers, including carrot, onion, celery, fresh or dried tomato, bell pepper, beet, cucumber, spinach, kale, or eggplant. If you are not using vegetable pulp left over from juicing, it is important to remove as much water as possible by wringing freshly grated vegetables in a towel. It's an easier task if you wring a small amount (½ cup) at a time. Nutritional yeast is inactive, so it can't be used for leavening bread. But it adds a cheesy, nutty flavor to many dishes and is especially enjoyed by vegans. You can find nutritional yeast in powdered or flaked form in natural-food stores and many supermarkets. It's an optional ingredient, and some people find the flavor to be an acquired taste.

1½ cups vegetable pulp left over from juicing, or grated fresh vegetables squeezed dry

½ cup ground flaxseed, flaxseed meal, or chia seeds, or a combination

4 tablespoons nutritional yeast, divided (optional)

1 tablespoon crushed dried herb blend of your choice

⅛ teaspoon garlic powder

⅛ teaspoon kosher or sea salt

¼ cup water, divided, or as needed for blending

½ cup sesame seeds, toasted if desired (page 30)

½ cup shelled sunflower seeds, toasted if desired (page 30)

1. In a food processor, combine the vegetable pulp, flaxseed, 2 tablespoons of nutritional yeast (if using), herb blend, garlic powder, and salt. Pulse 10 to 20 times, until well mixed, then process into a smooth mixture (see Tips for Successful Raw Breads, Wraps, Tortillas, and Crackers, page 185), adding 1 tablespoon of water at a time if needed. Transfer the mixture to a bowl and stir in the sesame seeds, sunflower seeds, and the remaining 2 tablespoons of nutritional yeast (if using) until well blended. Taste and correct the seasoning.

2. Preheat a food dehydrator to the temperature you prefer (see above). Spread the mixture ⅛ inch thick on lined drying trays. Score into crackers; if the mixture is very soft, score after it has dried for 2 hours or becomes firm enough to score. About halfway through the drying time at either temperature, when the mixture is firm, turn over to finish drying. Dry until crisp; timing is dependent on the drying temperature (see above).

3. Cut apart at scored sections or break sheets into serving pieces.

STORAGE: Up to 1 week at room temperature or 1 month frozen in an airtight container.

NUT, SEED, AND HERB CRACKERS

Prep Time: 4½ to 8½ hours | **Drying Temp & Time:** 105° to 115°F for 16 to 24 hours or 125° to 135°F for 10 to 12 hours | **Yield:** 24 to 36 crackers

Enjoy this basic cracker recipe that you can adapt with different types of nuts or seeds and herbs. Here cashews, sunflower seeds, and an Italian herb blend are suggested, but you could also use walnuts, pumpkin seeds, and lemon-pepper seasoning, or almonds, sesame seeds, and chile powder, or any other nut, seed, and seasoning combination you prefer. The ground flaxseed or chia seeds help hold the crackers together—technically you can leave them, out, but some nuts and seeds will perform better with them. The nutritional yeast is optional but enhances the nutty flavors and gives the crackers a "cheesy" taste.

1 cup cashews

1 cup shelled
   sunflower seeds

¼ cup ground flaxseed,
   flaxseed meal, or
   chia seeds

¼ cup nutritional yeast
   (optional)

1 tablespoon crushed Italian
   Herb Seasoning Blend
   (page 50)

½ teaspoon kosher or
   sea salt

½ teaspoon red pepper
   flakes or ground
   black pepper

1. In a medium bowl, combine the cashews and sunflower seeds, and add water to cover by at least 1 inch. Cover and refrigerate for 4 to 8 hours. Drain the soaking water, reserving 1 cup.

2. In a food processor, place the soaked cashews and sunflower seeds, flaxseed, nutritional yeast (if using), seasoning blend, salt, and pepper. Pulse 10 to 20 times, until combined and finely chopped, then process into a coarse mixture (see Tips for Successful Raw Breads, Wraps, Tortillas, and Crackers, page 185), adding 1 tablespoon of reserved soaking liquid or water at a time, as needed. Taste and correct seasoning.

3. Preheat a food dehydrator to the temperature you prefer (see above). Spread the mixture ⅛ inch thick on lined drying trays. Score into crackers; if the mixture is very soft, score after it has dried for 2 hours or becomes firm enough to score. About halfway through the drying time at either temperature, when the mixture is firm, turn over to finish drying. Dry until crisp; timing is dependent on the drying temperature (see above).

4. Cut apart at scored sections or break sheets into serving pieces.

STORAGE: Up to 1 week at room temperature or 1 month frozen in an airtight container.

CARROT AND WALNUT CRACKERS

Prep Time: 15 minutes | **Drying Temp & Time:** 105° to 115°F for 16 to 24 hours or 125° to 135°F for 10 to 12 hours | **Yield:** 24 to 36 crackers

Make sure the carrots and walnuts are ground or very finely chopped, or these crackers won't hold together. You can chop by hand, pulse in a food processor, or throw the whole mixture into a high-speed blender. The amount of water needed depends in part on how moist the carrots are. So, if you are chopping fresh carrots, wring them by handfuls in a towel or adjust the amount of water in the recipe.

1½ cups finely grated carrots or pulp after juicing

1½ cups ground walnuts

½ cup ground flaxseed or flaxseed meal

1 tablespoon tomato powder

1 teaspoon kosher or sea salt

¼ teaspoon red pepper flakes or ground black pepper (optional)

1 tablespoon fresh lemon juice (optional)

½ to 1 cup water, divided, or as needed

1. In a large bowl, combine the carrots, walnuts, flaxseed, tomato powder, salt, and pepper (if using). Add the lemon juice (if using) and ½ cup of water and stir to form a coarse mixture (see Tips for Successful Raw Breads, Wraps, Tortillas, and Crackers, page 185), adding 1 more tablespoon of water at a time as needed. Taste and correct the seasoning.

2. Preheat a food dehydrator to the temperature you prefer (see above). Spread the mixture ⅛ inch thick on lined drying trays. Score into crackers; if the mixture is very soft, score after it has dried for 2 hours or becomes firm enough to score. About halfway through the drying time at either temperature, when the mixture is firm, turn over to finish drying. Dry until crisp; timing is dependent on the drying temperature (see above).

3. Cut apart at scored sections or break sheets into serving pieces.

STORAGE: Up to 1 week at room temperature or 1 month frozen in an airtight container.

ROSEMARY POTATO CRACKERS

Prep Time: 15 minutes | **Drying Temp & Time:** 105° to 115°F for 16 to 24 hours or 125° to 135°F for 10 to 12 hours | **Yield:** 24 to 36 crackers

When you have leftover baked or mashed potatoes, make good use of them by whipping up a batch of these delicious crackers. You can also use dried potato flakes or powder from your pantry, but decrease the amount to ¾ to 1 cup to be sure the crackers will hold together. Instead of sweet onion, you can use any other type of onion, but strong onions sometimes give a bitter taste to dehydrator crackers dried at a low temperature.

1½ cups chia seeds, ground flaxseed, or flaxseed meal

1½ cups mashed potatoes

½ cup minced sweet onion (Walla Walla, Maui, Vidalia, Bermuda, Texas, etc.)

1 teaspoon chopped dried rosemary leaves

½ teaspoon garlic powder

½ teaspoon kosher or sea salt

¼ teaspoon red, white, or black pepper

½ to 1 cup water, divided, or as needed

1. In a large bowl, combine the chia seeds, potatoes, onion, rosemary, garlic powder, salt, and pepper until combined. Add ½ cup of water and stir to form a smooth mixture (see Tips for Successful Raw Breads, Wraps, Tortillas, and Crackers, page 185), adding 1 more tablespoon of water at a time as needed. Taste and correct the seasoning,

2. Preheat a food dehydrator to the temperature you prefer (see above). Spread the mixture ⅛ inch thick on lined drying trays. Score into crackers; if the mixture is very soft, score after it has dried for 2 hours or becomes firm enough to score. About halfway through the drying time at either temperature, when the mixture is firm, turn over to finish drying. Dry until crisp; timing is dependent on the drying temperature (see above).

3. Cut apart at scored sections or break sheets into serving pieces.

STORAGE: Up to 1 week at room temperature or 1 month frozen in an airtight container.

SWEET POTATO AND CRANBERRY CRACKERS

Prep Time: 15 minutes | Drying Temp & Time: 105° to 115°F for 16 to 24 hours or 125° to 135°F for 10 to 12 hours | Yield: 24 to 36 crackers

These crackers have a sweet side, which you can enhance with maple syrup or honey. They are also beautifully flecked with cranberries and pumpkin seeds. Season them any way you wish, with pumpkin-pie spice or cinnamon or a homemade seasoning blend from your pantry. Finely chop the add-ins—the cranberries and seeds—or your crackers may not hold together, especially if they are very thin. In fact, that's a good rule of thumb: Spread the dough only as thin as the thickest add-in. The more they poke out from the dough, the more fragile the crackers can be.

1 cup ground pumpkin seeds

1 cup mashed sweet potatoes

½ cup tapioca, rice, almond, potato, or chickpea flour or flaxseed meal, or ¼ cup cornstarch, arrowroot, or tapioca or potato starch

¼ cup maple syrup or honey (optional)

1 to 3 teaspoons Madras Curry Spice Mix, Coconut Curry Spices, Taco and Chili Seasoning Blend, or Berbere Ethiopian Spice Blend (pages 50–51), pumpkin-pie spice, or ground cinnamon

1 teaspoon kosher or sea salt

¼ to ½ cup water, divided, or as needed

½ cup dried cranberries, finely chopped

½ cup pumpkin or sunflower seeds, finely chopped

1. In a large bowl, combine the ground pumpkin seeds, sweet potatoes, flour, maple syrup (if using), seasoning blend, salt, and ¼ cup of water to form a smooth mixture (see Tips for Successful Raw Breads, Wraps, Tortillas, and Crackers, page 185), adding 1 more tablespoon of water at a time as needed. Taste and adjust the seasoning, then mix in the cranberries and chopped pumpkin seeds.

2. Preheat a food dehydrator to the temperature you prefer (see above). Spread the mixture ⅛ inch thick on lined drying trays. Score into crackers; if the mixture is very soft, score after it has dried for 2 hours or becomes firm enough to score. About halfway through the drying time at either temperature, when the mixture is firm, turn over to finish drying. Dry until crisp; timing is dependent on the drying temperature (see above).

3. Cut apart at scored sections or break sheets into serving pieces.

STORAGE: Up to 1 week at room temperature or 1 month frozen in an airtight container.

NO-BAKE GRANOLA CEREAL OR BARS

Prep Time: 2¼ hours | Drying Temp & Time: 105° to 115°F for 10 to 20 hours or 125° to 135°F for 6 to 12 hours | Yield: 12 snack-size bars, or 6 to 8 cereal servings

If you follow a raw diet, you can use Scottish oats, or substitute Irish oats or whole oat groats, but the texture of the bars will be different, as neither of these substitutes will soften as much as Scottish oats. If you aren't following a raw diet, you can use rolled oats and do not need to soak them, as they have already been steamed and softened. Old-fashioned rolled oats will give the firmest texture, instant oats will be softer, and quick-cooking oats will fall somewhere in between these two. The recipe gives instructions for granola bars. Alternatively, you may dry the granola in a single layer to crumble and serve as hot or cold breakfast cereal with milk.

2 cups stone-ground (Scottish) oats

1 cup mixed dried fruit, such as apricots, cranberries, pineapple, figs, pitted dates, or raisins

½ cup nuts (cashews, almonds, peanuts, pistachios, etc.), toasted (page 30)

¼ cup pumpkin or sunflower seeds, toasted (page 30)

¼ cup dried shredded coconut

1 tablespoon ground cinnamon

½ cup unsweetened applesauce

¼ cup honey or maple syrup

2 tablespoons nut butter of your choice

1 tablespoon vanilla extract

1. Put the oats in a medium bowl and cover with water. Soak for 2 hours at room temperature, then drain. Using a food processor or grinder, coarsely chop the dried fruit, nuts, and seeds. In a large bowl, combine the drained oats, fruit, nuts, seeds, coconut, and cinnamon. In another bowl, whisk together the applesauce, honey, nut butter, and vanilla. Pour over the oat mixture and stir until well combined.

2. Preheat a food dehydrator to the temperature you prefer (see above). *For bars:* Spread the mixture evenly on lined drying trays. Press firmly into a compact mixture ½ inch thick and score into 12 rectangles. About halfway through the drying time at either temperature, when the mixture is firm, turn over to finish drying. Dry the bars until chewy, firm, or crisp. Cut apart at scored sections. *For granola:* Arrange the mixture on lined drying trays in a loose, even layer. Every 2 hours, rub the mixture between your fingers to break up the pieces. Dry the granola until crisp. For both, drying time is dependent on the drying temperature (see above).

STORAGE: Store bars or granola in an airtight container. If bars are chewy, layer with parchment paper. Crisp bars and granola will keep for up to 1 month at room temperature, 6 months refrigerated, or 1 year frozen. Chewy bars will keep for 1 to 2 weeks at room temperature, 3 months refrigerated, or 6 months frozen.

FRUIT, NUT, AND SEED ENERGY BARS

Prep Time: 30 minutes | **Drying Temp & Time:** 105° to 115°F for 12 to 20 hours or 125° to 135°F for 6 to 10 hours | **Yield:** 12 snack-size bars

Here is a simple chewy energy bar packed with fruits, nuts, and seeds. Use two or three types of nuts and seeds to create a more interesting snack. However, if you love just one kind of nut, say peanuts, then use all peanuts. Any favorite nuts or seeds will do. Many recipes for dehydrator energy bars use dried fruit and nuts, which can be difficult to mix, and drying is optional, since the ingredients are already dried. Instead, this recipe uses fresh fruit that is easier to blend with dried dates or figs, and then stirs in chopped nuts. Drying is also optional but will extend the storage life from weeks to months.

1 cup chopped dried figs or Medjool dates, pitted (12 to 14 figs)

1 cup chopped fresh fruit or berries (strawberries, blueberries, pineapple, mango, etc.)

1 cup coarsely chopped, unsalted, raw or roasted nuts or seeds, such as peanuts, cashews, almonds, pecans, pumpkin, sesame, or hemp

2 tablespoons dried shredded coconut

2 teaspoons chopped dried orange zest

½ teaspoon ginger powder or ground cinnamon

½ teaspoon kosher or sea salt

1. In a food processor, combine the figs and fruit and process until it is mostly pureed but still chunky. Transfer the mixture to a large bowl and stir in the nuts, coconut, orange zest, ginger powder, and salt to taste.

2. Preheat a food dehydrator to the temperature you prefer (see above). Spread the mixture evenly on lined drying trays ⅛ to ¼ inch thick. Score into 12 rectangles. About halfway through the drying time at either temperature, when the top is no longer sticky, turn over to finish drying. Dry until pliable with no sticky spots when pressed lightly; timing is dependent on the drying temperature (see above).

3. Remove from the dehydrator while still warm and cut into bar-size portions. Wrap each bar in a piece of parchment paper for storage.

STORAGE: Well-dried bars will keep for up to 1 month at room temperature, 6 months refrigerated, or 1 year frozen in an airtight container.

DOUBLE-CHOCOLATE BISCOTTI

Prep Time: 15 minutes | **Drying Temp & Time:** 105° to 115°F for 8 to 12 hours or 125° to 135°F for 6 to 10 hours | **Yield:** 8 to 12 biscotti

Biscotti means "twice baked." Traditionally, the dough is baked once in a loaf or log, then sliced and baked again until hard. This dehydrator "biscotti" recipe is "twice dried" and uses almonds, chocolate, and flavorings to create a dried cookie, very similar to the baked version. It is a wonderfully rich treat, using two kinds of chocolate—melted into the dough and chips flecked throughout the cookies. Dry the cookies until chewy, firm, or crisp as desired. Serve them with tea or dip them into red wine after dinner.

1 cup almond flour

½ cup slivered almonds, toasted if desired (see page 30)

½ cup white or semi-sweet chocolate chips, vegan if desired

2 ounces semi-sweet chocolate, melted and still warm

2 tablespoons honey or brown rice syrup

1 teaspoon vanilla extract

1 to 2 tablespoons almond or dairy milk, orange juice, or water, as needed

1. In a food processor, combine the almond flour, almonds, chocolate chips, melted chocolate, honey, and vanilla, and pulse until the mixture comes together. If too dry, add the milk, 1 tablespoon at a time, as needed to form a stiff dough that holds together when a handful is pressed into a ball.

2. Preheat a food dehydrator to the temperature you prefer (see above). Place the dough on a drying tray, form into a log shape about 6 inches long, and flatten to ¾ inch high. Dry until firm, 2 to 4 hours.

3. Remove from the dehydrator and cut into ½-inch-thick slices. Return the slices to the drying trays, spacing slightly apart, and dry until chewy, firm, or crisp; timing is dependent on the drying temperature (see above).

STORAGE: If the biscotti are chewy, layer with parchment paper. Firm or crisp bars will keep at room temperature for up to 1 month at room temperature, 6 months refrigerated, or 1 year frozen in an airtight container. Chewy bars will keep for 1 week at room temperature, 1 month refrigerated, or 1 year frozen.

RAW APPLE-ZUCCHINI-CARROT BREAD

Prep Time: 15 minutes | **Drying Temp & Time: 105° to 115°F for 8 to 12 hours or 125° to 135°F for 6 to 10 hours** | **Yield: 18 slices, or 36 to 54 cookies**

Raw breads are incredibly easy to make and a great alternative to yeasted or quick breads. There are many savory and sweet recipes. This fruit and vegetable bread tastes great with a schmear of nut butter and a drizzle of honey. Enjoy it for breakfast or an afternoon pick-me-up. You can also portion the dough into equal mounds and flatten into cookies. If you make the cookies thin—about ⅛ inch—you can dry until crisp.

3 medium apples, grated down to the core (about 2¼ cups)

1 medium zucchini, grated (about ⅔ cup)

1 medium carrot, grated (about ⅓ cup)

¾ cup ground almonds or walnuts

¾ cup ground flaxseed or flaxseed meal

⅓ cup oil, such as olive, walnut, or pumpkin

1 teaspoon vanilla extract

¼ teaspoon ground cinnamon

Pinch kosher or sea salt

1. In a large bowl, combine the apples, zucchini, carrot, almonds, flaxseed, oil, vanilla, cinnamon, and salt, and toss until well mixed.

2. Preheat a food dehydrator to the temperature you prefer (see above). Spread the mixture evenly on lined drying trays, ¼ inch thick. About halfway through the drying time at either temperature, when the mixture is firm, turn over to finish drying. Score to make 18 slices. Dry until the bread feels light; timing is dependent on the drying temperature (see above).

3. Cut apart at scored sections.

STORAGE: Well wrapped, up to 1 week refrigerated, or 1 month frozen.

BISHOP'S BANANA BREAD

Prep Time (including refrigeration): 1 to 3 hours | Drying Temp & Time: 105° to 115°F for 8 to 12 hours or 125° to 135°F for 6 to 10 hours | Yield: 16 to 20 slices

You can keep this banana bread simple without adding chopped nuts and dried fruit to the final dough. With these add-ins, it becomes "bishop's bread," a festive quick bread most often made at Christmastime. The history of the bread is murky, but it seems to have evolved in America in the first part of the 20th century, descending from northern and central European fruitcake recipes. What's curious is that no bishops seem to have been involved, either as baker or as recipient. An early version of the recipe published in the *Chicago Tribune* in 1916 called for walnuts and dates. Other variations call for candied fruits. Chocolate was added to later recipes. Here are some possible combinations for you to consider: pecans and peaches with dark chocolate, peanuts and strawberries with milk chocolate, or macadamias and pineapple with white chocolate.

3 cups rolled oats

1 cup nuts (almonds, cashews, macadamias, peanuts, etc.)

½ cup ground flaxseed or flaxseed meal

1 teaspoon chopped dried orange or lemon zest

½ teaspoon kosher or sea salt

4 ripe bananas, peeled and cut into 1-inch pieces

½ cup quartered or coarsely chopped pitted dates or prunes

½ cup water

1 teaspoon vanilla extract

½ cup finely chopped nuts (optional)

¼ cup finely chopped dried fruit (optional)

¼ cup grated chocolate or chocolate chips (optional)

1. In a food processor, combine the oats, nuts, flaxseed, zest, and salt. Pulse 10 to 20 times, until coarsely chopped and evenly mixed. Process on high until the mixture forms a dry, uniform crumb. Don't overprocess and allow the dough to form a ball, as it will be harder to mix. Transfer the oat mixture to a large bowl. In the food processor, combine the bananas, dates, water, and vanilla. Process until the mixture is a smooth, uniform puree. Pour over the oat mixture and stir until well combined. Stir in the chopped nuts, dried fruit, and/or chocolate (if using).

2. Place the dough on a parchment- or silicone-mat-lined baking sheet and form into a loaf shape about 9 inches long. Place in the freezer for 30 minutes to 2 hours to firm for slicing.

3. Preheat a food dehydrator to the temperature you prefer (see above). Cut the loaf into ½-inch-thick slices and arrange on the drying trays ½ inch apart. About halfway through the drying time at either temperature, when the dough is firm, turn over to finish drying. Dry until firm and not doughy in the center of each slice; timing is dependent on the drying temperature (see above).

STORAGE: 3 days refrigerated, or 1 month frozen in an airtight container.

LEMON-CASHEW COCONUT MACAROONS

Prep Time: 15 minutes | Drying Temp & Time: 105° to 115°F for 16 to 24 hours or 125° to 135°F for 8 to 12 hours | Yield: 16 to 20 macaroons

Coconut macaroons can be quite addictive, and this nutty version spiked with lemon is no exception. They are extremely simple to make, requiring a quick blending of ingredients before they go into the dehydrator. Don't be tempted to make them bigger, as they can take a long time to dry, although you can enjoy them when they are still quite chewy. In fact, many people report that half the batch never makes it out of the dehydrator to storage and is consumed along the way. Be sure to mix the nuts and sugar thoroughly so the sugar dissolves completely.

1 cup raw, dried, or roasted cashews (almonds may be substituted)

¼ cup raw cane or coconut sugar

3 tablespoons fresh lemon juice

2 to 4 tablespoons coconut or almond milk, divided, or as needed

1 tablespoon fresh lemon zest or 1 teaspoon chopped dried lemon zest

½ teaspoon salt

2 cups unsweetened shredded coconut, or as needed

1. In a food processor, combine the cashews, sugar, lemon juice, 2 tablespoons of nut milk, zest, and salt. Pulse 10 to 20 times, until the nuts are finely chopped, then process until the mixture is smooth. Scrape down the sides of the bowl. Add the coconut and pulse 10 to 20 times, until well combined and the mixture forms a firm but not wet dough. Add more milk, as needed. If the dough is too wet, add more shredded coconut.

2. Preheat a food dehydrator to the temperature you prefer (see above). Drop the dough by rounded spoonfuls onto the drying trays, spacing 1 inch apart. Dry until chewy or crisp as desired on the outside and soft on the inside; timing is dependent on the drying temperature (see above).

STORAGE: 3 to 4 days at room temperature, 2 weeks refrigerated, or 2 months frozen in an airtight container.

OATMEAL COOKIES WITH NUTS AND RAISINS

Prep Time: 15 minutes | **Drying Temp & Time:** 105° to 115°F for 8 to 12 hours or 125° to 135°F for 6 to 10 hours | **Yield:** 24 to 30 cookies

This is a familiar recipe for old-fashioned oatmeal cookies with raisins, held together with peanut butter and rolled in crushed nuts. Feel free to substitute almond butter and sliced almonds, walnut butter and chopped walnuts, pumpkin seed butter and sunflower seeds, or any favorite nut butter and nut. The cookies can take some time to dry unless you want them chewy. If you do prefer a crisp cookie, flatten them to less than ¼ inch.

2 cups stone-ground
    Scottish oats,
    steel-cut Irish oats, or
    quick-cooking rolled oats

½ cup unsweetened
    applesauce

½ cup raisins or chopped
    dates or figs

¼ cup peanut butter or other
    nut butter

1 teaspoon vanilla extract

1 teaspoon ground
    cinnamon

½ teaspoon kosher or
    sea salt

1 cup finely chopped
    peanuts or another nut

1. In a food processor, combine the oats, applesauce, raisins, peanut butter, vanilla, cinnamon, and salt, and process until the ingredients are well combined and form a dough.

2. Preheat a food dehydrator to the temperature you prefer (see above). Divide the dough into 24 to 30 portions, form each into a ball, roll in the chopped nuts, use a glass to flatten to ¼ to ½ inch thick, and arrange on the drying trays 1 inch apart. Dry until the cookies are chewy, crumbly, or crunchy as desired; timing is dependent on the drying temperature (see above).

STORAGE: 3 to 4 days at room temperature, 2 weeks refrigerated, or 2 months frozen in an airtight container.

CHOCOLATE CHIP COOKIES

Prep Time: 15 to 30 minutes | **Drying Temp & Time:** 105° to 115°F for 8 to 12 hours or 125° to 135°F for 6 to 10 hours | **Yield:** 20 to 24 cookies

Chocolate chip cookies are as much a part of American culture as hamburgers and apple pie. This dehydrator recipe comes together in a flash and produces a wonderfully chewy cookie flecked with chocolate that is very reminiscent of the familiar baked version.

6 pitted dried dates (preferably Medjool)

1 cup unsalted cashews or almonds

½ cup stone-ground Scottish oats, steel-cut Irish oats, or quick-cooking rolled oats

½ cup unsweetened shredded coconut

1 teaspoon vanilla extract

½ teaspoon sea salt

¼ to ½ cup cacao nibs or grated chocolate

1. In a small bowl, cover the dates with hot water and soak until soft, 10 to 20 minutes. Drain and cut into small pieces. In a food processor, combine the cashews, oats, and coconut, and pulse 10 to 20 times, until finely chopped. Add the dates, vanilla, and salt, and process until the mixture begins to form a dough but is still crumbly. Transfer to a bowl and mix in the cacao nibs to taste.

2. Preheat a food dehydrator to the temperature you prefer (see above). Divide the dough into 20 to 24 portions, form each into a ball, use a glass to flatten to ½ inch thick, and arrange on the drying trays 1 inch apart. Dry until the cookies are chewy or crumbly as desired; timing is dependent on the drying temperature (see above).

STORAGE: 3 to 4 days at room temperature, 2 weeks refrigerated, or 2 months frozen in an airtight container.

MEASUREMENT CONVERSIONS

Volume Equivalents (Liquid)

US STANDARD	US STANDARD (OUNCES)	METRIC (APPROXIMATE)
2 tablespoons	1 fl. oz.	30 mL
¼ cup	2 fl. oz.	60 mL
½ cup	4 fl. oz.	120 mL
1 cup	8 fl. oz.	240 mL
1½ cups	12 fl. oz.	355 mL
2 cups or 1 pint	16 fl. oz.	475 mL
4 cups or 1 quart	32 fl. oz.	1 L
1 gallon or 4 quarts	128 fl. oz.	4 L

Oven Temperatures

FAHRENHEIT	CELSIUS (APPROXIMATE)
250°F	120°C
300°F	150°C
325°F	165°C
350°F	180°C
375°F	190°C
400°F	200°C
425°F	220°C
450°F	230°C

Volume Equivalents (Dry)

US STANDARD	METRIC (APPROXIMATE)
⅛ teaspoon	0.5 mL
¼ teaspoon	1 mL
½ teaspoon	2 mL
¾ teaspoon	4 mL
1 teaspoon	5 mL
1 tablespoon	15 mL
¼ cup	59 mL
⅓ cup	79 mL
½ cup	118 mL
⅔ cup	156 mL
¾ cup	177 mL
1 cup	235 mL
2 cups or 1 pint	475 mL
3 cups	700 mL
4 cups or 1 quart	1 L

Weight Equivalents

US STANDARD	METRIC (APPROXIMATE)
½ ounce	15 g
1 ounce	30 g
2 ounces	60 g
4 ounces	115 g
8 ounces	225 g
12 ounces	340 g
16 ounces or 1 pound	455 g

INDEX

ACKNOWLEDGMENTS

To the many friends, family members, and colleagues who are excited to hear about my projects, encourage and congratulate me about my work, buy my books, and tell their friends to do the same. Thanks for being my village.

To my young niece Dominique, who reminds me through her dedication to purpose that I only need to do me. And that's enough. Love you back.

Not all writers love editors, but I sincerely do. They have my back and make my writing better. It has been a pleasure to work with the editors at Callisto Media, Salmon Taymuree, Pam Kingsley, and Anne Egan. Friendly and professional are they all. Thank you so much.

It may seem odd to salute *all* the people who, over a period of decades, worked to develop the Internet and the World Wide Web, but as one who first tapped out papers on a manual typewriter and did research in the dusty bowels of Suzzallo Library on the University of Washington campus, I can say that it's simply an amazing resource. The ability to exhume vast amounts of information is a marvelous thing. I am grateful to have lived in this era to research and write this book.

And to Lynne Olver, food historian, librarian, and editor of FoodTimeline.org until her death in 2015. She created an astonishing resource. We should all try to be more like her: passionate and generous. The world is a better place because of people like Lynne. And so is this book.

ABOUT THE AUTHOR

Carole Cancler has enjoyed a lifelong love affair with cooking. Her Midwestern mother and Slovenian grandmother instilled in her a love of wholesome food at an early age. She has decades of practice in food preservation.

Carole especially loves studying the anthropology of food—how indigenous foods and methods of preparation have been integrated throughout the world. She has journeyed by jet, train, and ship to over 20 countries. Her travels often feature visits to local food markets and cooking schools, including Le Cordon Bleu in Paris. Some of her most memorable culinary stops were in Belgium, Bulgaria, France, Italy, Japan, Mexico, Portugal, Singapore, Thailand, and Vietnam.

Her first cookbook, *The Home Preserving Bible*, is a comprehensive guide to food preservation methods, covering salting, drying, fermenting, curing, pickling, cellaring, freezing, and canning and including over 300 recipes.

A Seattle, Washington, native, Carole holds degrees in food science and nutrition and computer programming. Her corporate career crisscrossed the food and technology industries. Her culinary experience includes restaurant management, catering, and food product development. She transferred her business and management skills to entrepreneurial roles that include food product manufacturer, website developer, and business development consultant.

Carole currently resides in Hawaii. She's developing a Food Preservation Expo and writes about food for *Mother Earth News*.